MEDIA MARKETS AND COMPETITION LAW:
Multinational Perspectives

Editors
Antonio Bavasso
David S. Evans
Douglas H. Ginsburg

CPI COMPETITION POLICY
INTERNATIONAL

AUTORITÀ GARANTE
DELLA CONCORRENZA
AGCM E DEL MERCATO

Antitrust
&
Public Policies

Copyright © 2019 by Competition Policy International
111 Devonshire Street · Boston, MA 02108, USA
www.competitionpolicyinternational.com
contact@competitionpolicyinternational.com

Printed in the United States of America

First Printing, 2019
Publisher's Cataloging-in-Publication Data
provided by Five Rainbows Cataloging Services

Names: Bavasso, Antonio, editor. | Evans, David S. (David Sparks), 1954- editor. | Ginsburg, Douglas H., 1946- editor.
Title: Media markets and competition law : multinational perspectives / Antonio Bavasso, David S. Evans [and] Douglas H. Ginsburg, editors.
Description: Boston: Competition Policy International, 2019.
Identifiers: LCCN 2019944603 | ISBN 978-1-950769-50-6 (paperback) | ISBN 978-1-950769-51-3 (hardcover) | ISBN 978-1-950769-52-0 (ebook)
Subjects: LCSH: Competition, Unfair. | Commercial law. | Antitrust law. | International law. | Mass media--Law and legislation. | BISAC: LAW / Antitrust. | LAW / International. | LAW / Media & the Law.
Classification:
LCC KF1649 .M43 2019 (print) | LCC KF1649 (ebook) | DDC 343.072/1--dc23.

Cover and book design by Inesfera. www.inesfera.com

Editors' Note

Antonio Bavasso
David S. Evans
Douglas H. Ginsburg

This book by Competition Policy International, in partnership with the *Antitrust & Public Policy Review (formerly Italian Antitrust Review)*, builds on the contributions made for the Jevons Institute Colloquium on *Future Perspectives on Media Markets*, held in Rome on May 22, 2018, and widens the horizon to a number of related themes. Over the years, media markets have attracted a wide range of enforcement initiatives across the world. The theory of two-sided markets that has emerged over the last 20 years has had a profound impact on the analytical foundation of competition enforcement in this area and is now established as the leading paradigm.

A brief piece by Bruno Julien – of the Toulouse School of Economics – gives an overview of a set of analytical issues that are affected by this paradigm. Yet the implications of two-sidedness on competition enforcement are still being debated. In 2018 the U.S. Supreme Court issued an important opinion (*American Express*) in relation to the analytical framework to be applied to competition issues affecting a two-sided platform under U.S. law. That opinion applies to transaction platforms (in that specific case, credit cards). A piece by Wright & Yun in this volume argues that the economic principles detailed in *American Express* should also apply to non-transaction platforms such as newspapers. Evans compares the *American Express* opinion with Times-Picayune, another Supreme Court opinion dating back to 1953, arguing that the tension between the two cases is overstated given that in the earlier case the Court mainly considered tying under a per se analysis and to the extent it analyzed the case under the rule of reason considered the platform overall.

Newspapers are often subject to specific competition rules and regulatory regimes, such as the Newspaper Preservation Act in the U.S. Horton highlights their ongoing importance to society. In some jurisdictions, mergers affecting newspapers attract public interest considerations relating to media plurality or accuracy in presentation of the news. Pouncey & Roberts illustrate the UK regime. Fels gives an overview of the status of Australian's media industry. But the economics of newspapers and other forms of traditional media are being disrupted by new technologies and business models. Yoo explores the economics of advertising support v. direct payment in the media industry. Owen looks at some of the challenges faced by players in a variety of markets from transmission to content.

A number of contributions in this volume give an overview of enforcement activities and issues faced by enforcers. Laitenberger gives such on overview on the activities of the European Commission in this area, ranging from tackling misinformation to antitrust and merger control enforcement. Steenbergen describes the rich menu of cases analysed by the Belgian competition authority, from sports competition to online subscriptions for newspapers and magazines. Kuik & Monte analyse European regulatory interventions (either through enforcement or legislative measures) in licensing of sports media rights. Ohlhausen looks at the FTC decision in *1-800 Contacts* in relation to a restriction on key word searches and other advertising restrictions. Muscolo & Pitruzzella analyse the legal challenges of blockchain under both competition law and IP law.

The volume collects a series of eclectic and heterogeneous contributions of lawyers and economists which provides an overview of the interesting topics and new challenges faced by competition authorities worldwide. The debate over the role of antitrust law in the digital sector and the possibility of reforms is very lively, particularly in Europe. Geradin looks at some possible reform themes in light of the work being conducted for expert reports on digital competition commissioned by DG Competition of the European Commission and the UK Treasury.

This debate will no doubt continue in the months and years to come. We hope the contributions contained in this book published by Competition Policy International will provide useful reference points as jurisdictions worldwide seek to resolve these cutting-edge issues.

Finally, we would like to sincerely thank Elisa Ramundo, Sam Sadden, and Mitchell Khader for their tireless organizational and editorial work in getting this book published.

Contributors

David S. Evans (Global Economics Group)

Allan Fels AO (Melbourne Law School)

Damien Geradin (Euclid Law)

Thomas J. Horton (University of South Dakota School of Law)

Bruno Jullien (Centre National de la Recherche Scientifique - CNRS)

Krzysztof Kuik (Directorate-General for Competition, European Commission)

Johannes Laitenberger (Directorate-General for Competition, European Commission)

Gianluca Monte (Directorate-General for Trade, European Commission)

Gabriella Muscolo (Italian Competition Authority)

Maureen K. Ohlhausen (Baker Botts)

Bruce M. Owen (Stanford University)

Giovanni Pitruzzella (Court of Justice of the European Union)

Craig Pouncey (Formerly, Herbert Smith Freehills)

Veronica Roberts (Herbert Smith Freehills)

Jacques Steenbergen (Belgian Competition Authority)

Joshua D. Wright (Antonin Scalia Law School, George Mason University)

Christopher S. Yoo (University of Pennsylvania)

John M. Yun (Antonin Scalia Law School, George Mason University)

Table of Contents

COOL PLATFORMS: MEDIA, MARKETS, AND COMPETITION

By Bruce M. Owen[1]

ABSTRACT

Media markets are complex and multisided. They are buffeted by technological and regulatory changes and constrained by the detritus of ancient political disputes. Technological change in media is largely derivative, reflecting advances in the semiconductor industry. Competition law intersects U.S. communications media chiefly in the context of monopolization and merger transactions. Several federal agencies and congressional committees have overlapping media jurisdiction; politics always plays a role in merger reviews. In addition, there is tension between the supremacy of the federal government in matters of interstate commerce and the roles of di-verse local policymakers. The first step in antitrust analysis and regulatory policymaking is definition of the "relevant" market, a task nearly always problematic. Markets may involve media content or services for consumers, the production of audiences for sale to advertisers, and the purchase or sale of local or national transmission capacity. Vertical mergers may involve any of these relationships. Mass media play an increasingly perfidious role in the current populist atmosphere of the republic because it is now possible for people to consume only content that reinforces their prior beliefs and permits them to avoid dissonant views. For all these reasons the boundaries between media firms and their input and output markets are changing. When boundary changes are transactional rather than organic, antitrust law is subject to un-usual political stresses. Predicting the future of antitrust policy applied to media markets is fraught. Un-necessary neologisms such as "platform" do nothing to aid understanding.

I. MEDIA AND THEIR MARKETS

Media markets in the United States were once limited primarily to newspapers, magazines, and perhaps billboards. Over the last century radio and then broadcast television, cable television, satellite television, and of late the Internet joined this list. In addition to advertising, most of these media also sell "content" (entertainment and information) and other services to consumers. The major exceptions were broadcast radio and television,

---

1 Doyle Professor in Public Policy, Emeritus, School of Humanities and Sciences, Stanford University. BruceOwen@stanford.edu. I am indebted to Scott Wallsten and Gregory Rosston for helpful comments and suggestions.

offered for free. Today, however, few consumers rely on over-the-air broadcasts, using wired and wireless Internet access instead. Broadcasters still use portions of the electromagnet spectrum which likely would be more valuable in other uses. This combination of content and transmission complicates market definition. This section discusses some of the difficulties in defining markets generally, and then specifically as applied to media.

The world of law and regulation is political, always sensitive to interest groups and public opinion. The media industry is active in shaping policy, generally by engaging in intramural lobbying conflicts between incumbent firms and new entrants and between content providers and transmission providers. As a rule, consumer interests are not effectively represented in these battles. The laws and regulations that result are difficult to repeal even when they have become obsolete, because they have created or maintained permanent interest groups.

The first step in antitrust analysis and regulatory policymaking is definition of the "relevant" market, a task nearly always problematic. Markets may involve media content or services for consumers, the production of audiences for sale to advertisers, and the purchase or sale of local or national transmission capacity. Vertical mergers may involve any or many of these relationships. Because of the endogenous and exogenous environmental changes affecting the industry, the boundaries between media firms and their input and output markets are also changing. When boundary changes are transactional rather than organic, antitrust law and regulatory policy are subject to unusual political stresses. Predicting the future of antitrust policy applied to media markets is fraught. Unnecessary neologisms such as "platform" do nothing to aid understanding.

Economic competition among media industry players is the subject of this paper, but media also compete or facilitate competition among content providers.

Competition in the marketplace of ideas has been intensified by the changes in media technology and the new abundance of access to specialized content. New online media provide every user with a cheap megaphone that can be heard around the world. But it is also now easier for people to consume only content that reinforces their prior beliefs and permits each more easily to avoid dissonant views on social and political matters. Many now believe that increased media competition has facilitated a surge in political and social unrest as well as a threat to those who value privacy.[2] On the other hand, consumers have long enjoyed access to a highly diverse and competitive magazine industry

---

[2] See, for example, Apple CEO Tim Cook's remarks in a keynote address to European officials on October 24, 2018, as reported by Jack Nicas in the New York Times online: "Mr. Cook criticized how companies like Facebook and Google — while taking care not to mention them by name — deliver personalized news feeds that lead to so-called filter bubbles and confirmation bias. 'Your profile is then run through algorithms that can serve up increasingly extreme content, pounding our harmless preferences into hardened convictions,' Mr. Cook said. 'If green is your favorite color, you may find yourself reading a lot of articles — or watching a lot of videos — about the insidious threat from people who like orange.'" https://www.nytimes.com/2018/10/26/technology/apple-time-cook-europe.html. (Cook's full speech is available at https://www.youtube.com/watch?v=kVhOLkIs20A).

whose structure closely resembles the online content industries. It is unclear whether or why the political and social impact of online services should differ from the impacts of printed media.

A. Market Definition is Almost Always Complicated

Market definition, especially in an antitrust setting, is intended to identify the customers whose welfare is potentially at risk because of a proposed merger or already impaired by an alleged monopolist. In either case, the issue is whether and how many alternatives exist to which customers can turn. Customers who can readily substitute many other products or services for those of merging firms or the alleged monopolist are not at risk of any economic injury. The same is true if entry into and exit from the industry is easy.

One general problem with market definition in cases regarding common consumer products is that decision makers — commissioners, prosecutors, judges, and jurors — have experience with such goods and services and therefore arrive on scene with strong *a priori* views on what substitutes are available. Such *a priori* views tend to generalize from limited personal experience and can be unreliable as a basis for decision-making. A proposed merger between two producers of industrial chemicals, in contrast, can be analyzed more objectively because decision makers are unlikely to have *a priori* beliefs about competition among industrial chemicals. Is cyclohexanol, for example, a reasonable substitute for sodium linear alkyl benzene sulfonate? If so, in which processes? But when it comes to media services people tend to know, or think they know, quite a lot. It is difficult to overcome these often-passionate beliefs with more accurate information in the short period available to evaluate the arguments, pro or con, concerning proposed mergers or monopolies. This tendency is difficult to overcome even when technical experts — usually economists — provide quantitative evidence.

Quantitative economic evidence and its statistical underpinnings are easily dismissed when decision makers lack expertise and the parties' experts themselves disagree, as they inevitably do. Contending parties for obvious reasons seek out experts whose views are consistent with the parties' interests. In the end, decision makers rely largely on their own intuitions and experience, if any, and use the arguments provided by the prevailing party's briefs to justify their findings.

A second general problem in market definition is the tendency of non-experts to believe, implicitly, that inclusion in the relevant market requires that *all* customers who use Product A would switch to Products B or C if the price of A were to increase. But that is not the relevant issue. Price competition takes place at the margin. Some customers for A receive a surplus — they would stick with A even if price were increased substantially. Other customers receive little or no surplus from A and would stop purchasing it if prices increased even slightly. The pertinent question is what percent of customers for Product

A would be lost if the price of A were increased. Such customers are marginal. Is that number sufficiently large that it would be unprofitable for the seller of Product A to raise price above *competitive* levels (if A is thought to be a monopoly).

Markets generally contain differentiated products or services, including markets for what are commonly thought of as commodities. For example, wheat is often characterized as a homogeneous commodity, but several types of wheat are available at different times of year in a variety of locations. For this reason, in recent years it has become customary to substitute "unilateral effects" analysis for traditional market definition in merger cases. The focus is on whether the proposed combination will give the acquiring firm an incentive to increase its prices. In the case of a merger, the question is whether the seller of A could profitably raise price above *prevailing* levels if it also owned the producer of Product B or C (proposed merger partners). A higher price for A may drive some customers to buy product B or C instead, and thus benefit the seller of A, once it is merged with B or C. Any firm will stop increasing its prices if the result is to divert "too many" of its customers to rival suppliers. Acquisition of one or more of the rivals may serve to recapture enough of these lost customers to permit a profitable price increase.

But unilateral effects analysis requires a good deal of data regarding demand elasticities and production costs, econometric analysis, and models of firm behavior and competitive strategies. Both the econometric analysis and the underlying abstract models require admittedly unrealistic simplifying assumptions and subjective judgement calls, such as econometric specification and functional forms associated with strategic behavior. These are issues upon which experts can reasonably disagree and laymen have little basis to apprehend. For example, most models predicting the price effects of a proposed merger assume that the rival firms are in a "Nash equilibrium."[3] In the real world there is no reason to believe that firms are in any sort of equilibrium.

The real world is one of constant change in which firms must adapt to survive; there is never a moment when a firm can be content with its product positioning, price, or production and distribution choices. Indeed, a spate of mergers is consistent with a competitive race to achieve increased efficiency, reflecting an exogenous or endogenous change in the most profitable boundaries of firms. Econometric methodology, for this and other reasons, has been subjected to strong criticism by experts inside and outside the profession.[4] Further, the chief emphasis of antitrust analysis is on price competition even though for many media products content competition and production efficiency may be more important determinants of consumer welfare.

---

3 A Nash equilibrium is one in which no firm would change its pricing strategy even if it knew the strategies of each competitor.

4 John P. A. Ioannidis, T. D. Stanley & Hristos Doucouliagos, The Power of Bias in Economics Research, 127 The Econ. Jour. F236-F265 (2017) https://doi.org/10.1111/ecoj.12461; Garret Christiansen & Edward Miguel, Transparency, Reproducibility, and the Credibility of Economics Research, 2018 Jour. Econ. Lit. 920-980, https://doi.org/10.1257/jel.20171350.

B. Regulators Tend to Categorize Media by the Transmission Technologies They Use

Curiously, media are classified chiefly not by the content with which consumers' choices are concerned or the audiences that advertisers seek, but by media technologies — how they transmit content and audiences. Each technology is regarded by regulators as if it were an isolated market. Media customers include both advertisers and consumers of content as well as those seeking transmission services, such as content creators. In general, content producers, consumers and advertisers are numerous and unconcentrated, while transmission facilities are often concentrated, at least within each category of technology. Also, media transmission technologies are usually regulated, sometimes along with their vertically integrated inputs and outputs. The implication of classifying media this way, as discussed below, is that "relevant" markets are defined too narrowly — without regard to the competition that takes place at the margins among the technologies.

C. Data Transmission Markets are Generally Competitive

Regulated telephone service was once a distributor of radio and, later, television network content to broadcast stations. The first radio networks were owned by AT&T, using long distance telephone lines to connect studios in New York to radio stations around the country. Later, AT&T microwave towers connected TV stations. AT&T was forced by the FCC late in the Depression to divest its radio networks, which became NBC and ABC. CBS competed with AT&T using AT&T's long-distance lines. The long-distance lines were initiated to support point-to-point "switched" analog telephone service, local and long distance, now largely defunct. The successor to analog switched telephony is digital telephony — voice-over-internet-protocol ("VOIP") — a minor user of broadband facilities that competes with otherwise similar mobile radio frequency services. Increasingly, "telephone companies" provide the same broadband digital services as other interconnected broadband providers comprising the Internet.

Long haul transmission of content and services is provided today chiefly by fiber optic cables, which have enormous capacity, much of which is not yet used, and have replaced microwave towers and satellite facilities, except on sparse routes. There are many providers of such services, and even fiber optic undersea cables typically have multiple owners, each in command of its own share of capacity. Thus, after nearly a century of effective monopoly on long distance and local transmission, we now can enjoy the fruits of competition among transmission providers.

D. *Vertical Integration Complicates Regulatory and Antitrust Oversight*

The recent spate of mergers among media firms has highlighted the role of federal antitrust policy in the media industry.[5] Complicating matters, competition issues are often regulated not only by the long-established antitrust agencies (the U.S. Department of Justice Antitrust Division and, to a lesser extent, the Federal Trade Commission) but also by a regulatory agency — the Federal Communications Commission ("FCC").[6] The FCC has joint jurisdiction with the antitrust agencies whenever the merger involves use of the electromagnetic spectrum, which is licensed by the FCC. The involvement of the FCC carries with it the barnacles of historical regulatory policy, often reflecting past outcomes of industry-financed political struggles and technology-based distinctions among media that are mistaken for market boundaries when, in fact, they are used to compete for the same customers. These factors affect the first and most subjective issue in any competition analysis: market definition.

II. MARKETS FOR "CONTENT" AND SERVICES

Traditional mass media sold audiences to advertisers. Advertisers search for the medium that delivers the highest concentration of likely customers. Traditional mass media such as network broadcasting typically reached many individuals, only a subset of whom had any interest in each product, or more specifically, were likely to be effectively influenced by a given ad. Paying to reach such consumers is wasteful if they are a small part of the medium's reach. Innovation by Google and other online services customized delivered audiences to include only those consumers most likely to be influenced by a specific ad. This makes online advertising far more efficient, for many products, than traditional mass media. It also makes advertising more useful for some consumers, who value advertising information related to products and services they plan to purchase. The result is that

---

6 The FCC jealously protects its supremacy over the states in matters of policy affecting interstate commerce, most recently in preempting local site regulation of 5G mobile broadband antennas. FCC, ACCELERATING WIRELESS BROAD-BAND DEPLOYMENT BY REMOVING BARRIERS TO INFRASTRUCTURE INVESTMENT, WT Docket No 17-79; ACCELERATING WIRELESS BROADBAND DEPLOYMENT BY REMOVING BARRIERS TO INFRASTRUCTURE INVESTMENT, WC Docket No. 17-84, Declaratory Ruling and Third Report and Order (released September 27, 2018).

5 Media concentration may have an indirect effect on political outcomes, although the effect, if any, is much less dangerous to welfare than the specialization of content that discourages cognitive dissonance. Leon Festinger, A THEORY OF COGNITIVE DISSONANCE, (1957). See Cook, *supra* note 2. However, competition in the "marketplace of ideas" is different from and generally much broader than competition in antitrust relevant markets. For one attempt to define and measure media power in the marketplace of (political) ideas, see Andrea Prat, *Media Power*, 126 JOUR. POL. ECON. 1747-1783 (August 2018), https://doi.org/10.1086/698107. Competition in the marketplace of ideas has long been thought desirable (see *Marketplace of Ideas*, Wikipedia, https://en.wikipedia.org/wiki/Marketplace_of_ideas) except when it produces "fake news." Compare Max Fisher & Amanda Taub, *The Interpreter: How Facebook Wields Its Vast Global Power*, NEW YORK TIMES Online, November 15, 2018, with Learned Hand's famous affirmation of diversity, "The First Amendment ... presupposes that right conclusions are more likely to be gathered out of a multitude of tongues, than through any kind of authoritative selection. To many this is, and will always be, folly; but we have staked upon it our all." *United States v. Associated Press*, 52 F. Supp. 362 S.D.N.Y. (1943), aff'd, 326 U.S. 1 (1945). All of this, albeit important, is not directly concerned with economic competition.

online advertising is a collection of highly differentiated products, each tailored to the target audiences of specific advertisers. Only a subset of these markets contains enough target customers to make mass advertising a possible substitute. Inevitably, the result has been a steep downward ad revenue share for local print media and broadcast networks and stations.

To produce audiences, traditional mass media offered content — news, entertainment, sports, politics, and opinion, for example. The supply sides of markets for content included writers, reporters, movie studios, sports teams and leagues, wire services, editors, and many other sources of material intended to attract audiences. Online media attract audiences using similar or the same inputs as traditional media. The basis for the recent increased supply of content, and its specialization, is not limited to the expansion of transmission capacity. Consumers, users, or viewers have a much higher willingness to pay for desired content than advertisers have for consumer eyeballs. The effective economic demand for content expanded considerably as new media allowed consumers to pay for content.

In addition to traditional categories of content, online sellers offer consumer *services*. Major examples are Google, Facebook, and Amazon, offering search, online retail sales, email, Internet access, "social media," and other services that generate information about user characteristics and thus tailor audiences to advertisers. As with broadcast media, some online services are offered to consumers without charge or at below-cost prices, because potential audience reach is important to advertisers. Also, of course, the cost of producing entertainment or information content is independent of how many people consume it, corresponding to high fixed cost and low or zero marginal cost per sale. For some services, such as email or "social media," network effects are important: the value of the service to any individual increases with the number of other persons accessible through the service or interconnected services.

Many online and traditional media content providers do not rely on advertising revenue, either because they produce small audiences with no associated demand from advertisers or because the absence of advertising is a source of value to consumers. Online video entertainment, such as movies, is one example. In any case, online content and service providers appear to engage in Schumpeterian competition "for the market." The advantages of size in distributing content are considerable and rapid growth at the expense of actual or potential rivals is essential to success. This strategy requires substantial upfront capital investment to finance sustained losses. Success may be rewarded by a monopoly of the service provided, if not of an antitrust market. Such competition benefits consumers at least during the period of negative profits; whether subsequent monopoly power fully offsets these early consumer gains depends in part on how long the monopoly can be sustained and on consumers' time preferences.

Market definition is often difficult when it comes to media content and services, at least from the demand side, chiefly because of product differentiation but also due to the interactive roles of consumer and advertiser demand and the economies of scale in distribution of high fixed cost-low marginal cost services. Monopoly and merger analysis are best approached from the supply side: How easy is it for a new supplier to enter production and sale of a category of content or service, or for an existing supplier of one service to add a new service? Leaving aside issues of intellectual property, the key entry issue is access to providers of transmission capacity.

III. MARKETS FOR TRANSMISSION CAPACITY

Traditional media used the printing press and physical delivery or the electromagnetic spectrum for radio and TV broadcasting. Before World War II, newspaper content was highly differentiated by political or ethnic readers and content, and this tended to support multiple competitors in urban areas despite economies of scale. Political and ethnic differentiation declined after the war, and by the end of the twentieth century most cities that had any daily newspaper had only one. Some called for an advertiser right of access to local monopoly daily newspapers, but the Supreme Court rejected this idea on First Amendment grounds in the *Tornillo* case.[7]

Similar access issues arose for broadcasters, especially local TV broadcasters, because the FCC limited the number of competitors in most cities to three. In contrast to *Tornillo*, FCC forays into content regulation of radio and TV broadcasts were upheld by the Court.[8] The Court reasoned that broadcasters were dependent on use of a public resource, the radio spectrum, which distinguished them from print media in a First Amendment context. That distinction ignores the lack of any convincing *necessity* for the radio spectrum to belong to the public, as evidenced by the fact that much of it has been auctioned off and is bought and sold in private transactions routinely approved by the FCC.

Broadcasters steadfastly promoted their vaporous "public interest" obligations under FCC policies because the obligations rationalized other FCC policies limiting entry into broadcasting and restricting competition from rival suppliers such as cable television.[9]

---

7 Tornillo sought a court order to force the Miami Herald to accept paid editorial as well as advertising content. The Supreme Court upheld the denial of Tornillo's request, even though the Miami Herald was a monopoly newspaper. *Miami Herald Publishing Co. v. Tornillo*, 418 US 241, 1974.

8 *Red Lion Broadcasting Co. v. FCC*, 395 US 367, 1969. Cases in which the Court must balance disparate provisions of the Constitution present obvious challenges, but it is strange indeed to find the Court upholding a discretionary administrative policy in the face of an unambiguous contrary constitutional provision. Economists have long advocated the creation of private property rights and markets in the spectrum. Thomas W. Hazlett, THE POLITICAL SPECTRUM: THE TUMULTUOUS LIBERATION OF WIRELESS TECHNOLOGY, FROM HERBERT HOOVER TO THE SMARTPHONE, 2017.

9 Barry R. Litman, *Public Interest Programming and the Carroll Doctrine: A Re-examination*, 23 JOUR. OF BROADCASTING 51-60 (2009) https://doi.org/10.1080/08838157909363917.

The public interest obligations of broadcast licensees thus deprived viewers and listeners of additional sources of content for nearly half a century. These anti-competitive FCC policies were terminated, at least in theory, by the Communications Act of 1996.[10] The Act promoted competitive market solutions to policy issues, a trail the FCC has since hiked only fitfully.

New electronic ("online") media, whether wired or wireless, because they are not wholly dependent on mass advertising, have already eclipsed a large portion of the print media, and this trend is likely to continue as the quality and capacity of electronic media increase. Wired and wireless transmission media are increasingly substitutable. Both use Internet protocol ("IP") digital transmission standards. The principal factor limiting this convergence is the failure of the FCC to make enough spectrum available for wireless transmission to non-mobile, i.e. fixed, destinations. This has forced technology to substitute for spectrum. Each new generation of wireless technology is more capacious than the last. The current fourth generation ("4G") is nearing the end of its life, while the industry debates the specifications of 5G, expected to be introduced in the next few years. Already, a large fraction of mobile and fixed transmission capacity is devoted to broadband video services.[11] The FCC has encouraged 5G development with the promise of robust mobile broadband capacity and possibly fixed services which would compete with local wireline suppliers.

Media transmission remains heavily influenced by the history of FCC and antitrust regulation. Broadly speaking, the right to be regulated by the government has substantial commercial value because typically it has been accompanied by entry barriers and other restraints on competition. The FCC has long acted as a largely political entity, controlled by congressional committees in thrall to interest groups, or, more recently, the executive. Given the extensive susceptibility of U.S. government policymaking to corporate and other well-funded interests, the current state of media markets has been determined chiefly by a series of political accommodations rather than market forces.[12]

---

10 Michael I. Meyerson, *Ideas of the Marketplace: A Guide to the 1996 Telecommunications Act,* 49 FED. COMM. L.J. 251 (1996-1997).

11 *Reply Comments* of The Free State Foundation in the FCC's *Inquiry Concerning the Development of Advanced Telecommunications Capability to All Americans in a Reasonable and Timely Fashion,* (GN Dockets Nos. 18-231 and 238, http://www.freestatefoundation.org/images/FSF_Comments_-_Deployment_of_Advanced_Telecommunications_Capability_to_All_Americans_in_a_Reasonable_and_Timely_Fashion_091718.pdf (2018)), provides convenient evidence from the FCC's own data supporting the view that mobile services already play a significant role in broadband video local distribution.

12 Political corruption is often seen as an unavoidable consequence of the mere existence of a state, even a libertarian's hypothetical "minimum protective state." See, for example, Michael Munger & Mario Villarreal-Diaz, *The Road to Crony Capitalism,* THE INDEPENDENT REVIEW (forthcoming 2019) and Christopher J. Coyne & Abigail R Hall, *Cronyism: Necessary for the Minimal, Protective State,* (Working Paper 18-26, Dept. of Econ., Geo. Mason Univ.(2018) https://papers.ssrn.com/sol3/Delivery.cfm/SSRN_ID3250892_code1368948.pdf?abstractid=3223013&mirid=1. But for a discussion of methods to reduce or eliminate corrupt public policy see Bruce M. Owen, *Addressing Political Corruption in America,* 5 BRIT. J. AMER. LEG. STUD. 3, (2016), DOI: https://doi.org/10.1515/bjals-2016-0001.

Regulated media do not produce the same welfare outcomes as competitive media. The rate and direction of technological change, the structure of markets, and the available corporate tactics and strategies to a substantial degree have been the product of competition, but a perverted form of competition in which the interests of consumers play at best a supporting role. Further, political outcomes are not guided by a consistent set of policy objectives, such as economic welfare. It is characteristic that the heated debate over "net neutrality" — FCC regulation of Internet content and pricing — is funded by opposing industry interests, with no serious role for interests promoting consumer welfare. The short run contest is between content providers and transmission providers. The longer run contest is between those who hope to see competitive markets rather than politics determine outcomes and those, such as power brokers, who prefer to preserve the advantages of being able to influence outcomes through the political process rather than the market.[13]

The long-run contest brings us back to market definition and market structure in the antitrust context. Recent controversial mergers or merger proposals have included both horizonal and vertical combinations. Content providers such as Amazon and Netflix acquire smaller content producers or rights and now produce their own content. Transmission competitors such as Sprint and T-Mobile merge in pursuit of increased market share. But it is the vertical mergers, such as AT&T's (primarily transmission) acquisition of Time Warner (primarily content) that have been most controversial, chiefly because they raise concerns like those involved in the net neutrality debate. Specifically, some fear that monopoly transmission suppliers that also supply content will discriminate against or even exclude rival content providers, acting just as the old Bell System did before it was dismantled in 1983.[14] The fear is likely unjustified because most local broadband transmission suppliers lack monopoly power, competing with other wireline and mobile broadband suppliers. In addition, a key factor in explaining the Bell System's pre-dissolution behavior was the presence of rate regulation, absent in the present case. Rate regulation limits prices and therefore profits. Excluding competitors also reduces profits. But the reduction of profits from exclusionary behavior can be erased by increasing monopoly prices back up to the level of the regulatory constraint.

---

13 Courts too play what amounts to a political role in the policy debates. See for example the filings in *Mozilla Corporation, et al. v. Federal Communications Commission and United States of America*, On Petition for Review of an Order of the Federal Communications Commission, DC Cir. Case #18-1051 (2018), in which the FCC's recent attempt to repeal the Commission's prior net neutrality policy is challenged.

14 The Bell System excluded competing long-distance companies and equipment suppliers. The exclusion was implemented by the local telephone monopolies, who resisted interconnection with competing long-distance carriers and refused to buy equipment from competing manufacturers. This benefitted Bell's Long Lines division and its Western Electric subsidiary. Roger G. Noll & Bruce M. Owen, *United States v. AT&T: The Economic Issues*, in THE ANTITRUST REVOLUTION, Kwoka & White, eds., 2nd ed. 1994.

IV. WHAT IS A PLATFORM?

The term *platform*, often modified by *two-sided*, has come into general use to describe what one would formerly have described as a "market" or a "multi-product firm"— a place where people exchange or trade things, to mutual benefit. All markets have a least two "sides" (buyers and sellers) and often more, as when a firm produces multiple products linked in demand, production cost, or both. Such neologisms often arise in the business community or in business schools and spread as evidence that the user is cool.[15] The *place* of a market is sometimes a geographic location, like the ancient Athenian Agora or Christie's auction house. More generally it is an abstract location where buyers and sellers of goods connect, as happens in any retail store or on eBay or in the classified ad section of a newspaper or magazine.

Each of the examples above involves buyers and sellers along with a means of communication and often a standard for describing the things being exchanged and a record of recent prices, to facilitate the flow of information. A stock exchange is a market either at a physical place or in cyberspace. A (mass) medium of communication is often such a market, generally with more than one "side," such as the newspaper that sells both to readers and to advertisers and buys both paper and content. Often, as with newspapers, advertiser demand depends in part on the number and type of readers and the number and type of readers depends in part on the nature of the medium's information, entertainment, and, yes, advertising. Therefore, prices on all the sides of the market may be interdependent. Indeed, most prices in the economy are interdependent with other prices. Two conclusions are important here: First, the "markets" attending to newspaper publishing (and other technology-defined media) are not, in general, relevant antitrust markets. Second, it accomplishes nothing new to characterize a newspaper as a "platform" or to use "multisided" in place of the traditional "multiproduct."

A steel mill, to illustrate the point with a different example, is also a "multisided platform" in the sense that it produces many physically different products whose customers vary considerably, but the prices paid by different customers for the different products are interdependent. (Production processes and costs are affected by the prices paid for the various products and therefore the quantity sold of each. There are similar interdependencies between inputs and outputs.) It would be strange to speak of a steel mill as a multisided

---

15 The word "cool" in this sense was first published in Abraham Lincoln's famous Cooper Union speech in 1860 https://en.wikipedia.org/wiki/Cooper_Union_speech.

16 See Bruce M Owen, *Antitrust and Vertical Integration in 'New Economy' Industries with Application to Broadband Access*, REV. IND. ORG. 38:363-386 (2011) DOI 10.2007/s11151-011-9291-y, and more generally, Laura Alfaro et al., *Come Together: Firm Boundaries and Delegation*, (NBER Working Paper 24603, 2018) http://www.nber.org/papers/w24603; and Simon Loertscher & Michael H. Riordan, *Make or Buy: Outsourcing, Vertical Integration, and Cost Reduction*, Amer. Econ. Rev.: Microeconomics 2019, 11(1):105-123 https://doi.org/10.1257/mic.20160347.

platform, or at least doing so would add nothing to our previous understanding of the economics of a multiproduct firm. In this sense it is pointless, perhaps even obscurantist, to characterize Amazon, Google, eBay, Yahoo, and so on as "platforms."

V. VERTICAL TRANSACTIONS

In general, media firms face make-or-buy decisions that must be continuously revisited. Vertical integration and vertical divestiture generally result from the dynamic process in which the boundaries of firms are in flux, reacting to changes in the firm's external environment through internal reorganization.[16] Managers inside a firm directly control the allocation of resources to produce outputs. The distribution of outputs to buyers may be accomplished by the firm itself (via vertical integration) or by contract with independent intermediaries such as wholesalers or retailers or sold as inputs to other producers. Decisions about the boundaries of a firm are made either by its managers or by capital markets, and those decisions are under continuous review, reflecting changes in prices, technologies, corporate and contract law, taxation and trade regulation, and the competitive strategies of rivals. Vertical integration or disintegration[17] are, in general, benign[18] strategic initiatives motivated by a desire to improve customer satisfaction and to gain a competitive advantage.

Nevertheless, there are circumstances in which vertical integration, like its horizontal counterpart, can harm consumers, as was the case with the old Bell System.[19] Abstract models of vertical integration nearly always can be made to predict bad (welfare-reducing) outcomes given certain parameter assumptions. The likelihood of harm to consumers is remote if the stages of production to be combined are each reasonably competitive. Interdictions of vertical integration in that context are "prophylactic" and risk foregoing the likelihood of benefits to consumers. Even integrations that include a monopoly stage can benefit consumers, especially if production costs are thereby reduced. Also, interventions, through their effects on expectations, may deter boundary changes that would improve consumer welfare, including even organic changes that may attract private litigation. It is likely that most of the welfare impact of antitrust interventions (or failures to intervene) is felt through changes in expectations and their effects on risk assessments of proposed boundary changes.

---

17 Vertical disintegration apparently has become more common, a change attributed to the rise of outsourcing of production to Chinese factories. See Fariha Kamal, *A Portrait of U.S. Factoryless Goods Producers*, (NBER Working Paper 25193, 2018) http://www.nber.org/papers/w25193.

18 Francine Lafontaine & Margaret Slade, *Vertical Integration and Firm Boundaries: The Evidence*, 45 JOURNAL OF ECONOMIC LITERATURE, 629 25193 –685, 2007; *Inter-Firm Contracts: Evidence*. in Gibbons & Roberts (eds.) HANDBOOK OF ORGANIZATIONAL ECONOMICS, 2012; *Exclusive Contracts and Vertical Restraints: Empirical Evidence and Public Policy*, in B. Paolo (eds.), HANDBOOK OF ANTITRUST ECONOMICS 391–414, 2008. For a summary of economic literature affirming the benign nature of vertical integration of Internet transmission entities with content providers, see *Brief of The Technology Policy Institute as Amicus Curiae in Support of Respondents*, (2018) in *Mozilla*, supra note 13.

19 See *supra* note 14.

The tendency to equate individual technologies of communication with markets, despite the existence of competition at the margin between technologies, has led to wrongheaded policies and unwise litigation. Recent such errors include the repeated failure to include radio frequency broadband carriers as competitors with wired media.

A focus on preventing harm to consumers as the principal objective of competition policy has held center stage in U.S. antitrust law for about half a century. But there have always been dissenting voices. Populists often argue that bigness is bad per se because it allegedly concentrates political power and supports greater income inequality. There has been a recent resurgence of interest in populist criticism of consumer welfare as the sole objective of antitrust.[20] As Judge Learned Hand pointed out long ago in his famously ambivalent Alcoa opinion: "Throughout the history of these [antitrust] statutes it has been constantly assumed that one of their purposes was to perpetuate and preserve, for its own sake and in spite of possible cost, an organization of industry in small units which can effectively compete with each other."[21] As applied to media transactions, such thinking is especially potent because of the political impacts of mass media in a world increasingly influenced by populist sentiments.

VI. CONCLUSIONS

Media markets are complex and multisided. It accomplishes nothing useful to call them "platforms." They are buffeted by rapid technological and regulatory changes. The addition of the new online media plays a potentially perilous role in the recent populist political atmosphere of the American republic, which appears to have echoes in Europe. The boundaries between media firms and their input and output markets are therefore changing. When boundary changes are transactional rather than organic, antitrust law is subject to unusual political stresses. Predicting the future of antitrust policy applied to media markets requires careful attention to the election returns.

---

20 See, for example, the widely publicized paper by Lina M. Kahn, *Amazon's Antitrust Paradox*, 126 The Yale Law J. 710 (2017) https://www.yalelawjournal.org/note/amazons-antitrust-paradox; *Sources of Tech Platform Power*, 2 Geo. L. Tech. Rev. 325 (2018) https://www.georgetownlawtechreview.org/wp-content/uploads/2018/07/2.2-Khan-pp-225-34.pdf; and Lina Khan & Sandeep Vaheesan, *Market Power and Inequality: The Antitrust Counterrevolution and Its Discontents*, 11 Harv. Law & Policy Rev. 235 (2017) https://papers.ssrn.com/sol3/papers.cfm?abstract_id=2769132. For push back, see Joshua D. Wright, et al., *Requiem for a Paradox: The Dubious Rise and Inevitable Fall of Hipster Antitrust*, (draft working paper) GLOBAL ANTITRUST INST., SCALIA LAW SCH., GEO. MASON UNIV. September 14, 2018, https://papers.ssrn.com/sol3/papers.cfm?abstract_id=3249524.

21 *United States v. Aluminum Co. of America*, 148 F.2d 416 (2nd Cir. 1945) at 429. Emphasis added.

ARE KEY WORD SEARCHES KEY TO COMPETITION? AN ANALYSIS OF *FTC v. 1-800 CONTACTS*

By Maureen K. Ohlhausen[1]

ABSTRACT

As consumers having increasingly turned to the Internet to find sellers, compare products and prices, and purchase items, the attention of antitrust agencies to online advertising and marketing markets has necessarily followed. This shift has required antitrust doctrine to try to sort out how various players may legally join forces, accommodate rivals, and settle disputes involving online advertising and marketing.

The latest example of these dynamics at play is the FTC's decision in 1-800 Contacts, Inc. In 2016, the FTC brought an administrative complaint against 1-800 Contacts, the largest seller of contact lenses over the Internet, challenging settlements it entered with 13 other online lens sellers to refrain from a certain type of online advertising (keyword searches) involving each others' trademarked terms. The FTC administrative law judge upheld the complaint and, upon appeal, a majority of the Commission found that the agreements not to bid on each other's trademarked terms in keyword searches and to implement "negative keywords" that stopped ads from being placed in response to searches that included trademarked terms unreasonably restrained trade and harmed competition for the online sales of contact lenses and in bidding for search engine keywords.

What makes this case important is how the FTC applied precedent about advertising restrictions to the new world of online advertising and marketing, in particular key word advertising. The role of online advertising also lies at the heart of the disagreement between the majority and dissenting Commissioner Noah Joshua Phillips about how much the agreements affected competition, given the availability of other forms of advertising. In the majority's view, key word search is not just one advertising channel among many, but a uniquely effective way to reach potential buyers. The fact that the agreements affected a "particularly significant type of advertising for online sales at the crucial moment when sales are about to be made" was sufficient to show a substantial competitive effect.

---

1   Partner, Baker Botts L.L.P. I was a member of the FTC when it issued the complaint and sat as a Commissioner during the oral argument for 1-800 Contacts' appeal of the ALJ liability decision. I retired from the Commission before it ruled on the appeal and issued the decision discussed in this article. This article is based solely on publicly available information.

I. INTRODUCTION

As consumers having increasingly turned to the Internet to find sellers, compare products and prices, and purchase items, the attention of antitrust agencies to online advertising and marketing markets has necessarily followed. Notable cases include the DOJ's challenge to Bazaarvoice's purchase of PowerReviews,[2] the FTC and DOJ's online real estate listing cases,[3] and the EU case against Google's behavior in its display of shopping ads in connection with online searches.[4] These cases, and others, are indicators of how much of the competitive battlefield has shifted to the online sphere. It is no exaggeration to say that the Internet, with its abundance of ad-supported free services and content, has reshaped advertising and marketing as thoroughly as did the advent of radio and television in their day. In turn, this shift has required antitrust doctrine to try to sort out how various players may legally join forces, accommodate rivals, and settle disputes involving online advertising and marketing.

The latest example of these dynamics at play is the FTC's decision in 1-800 Contacts, Inc.[5] The FTC majority characterizes the case as grappling with "issues of enormous import" involving "consumer marketplaces that embody the very basic institutions of 21st century commerce."[6] What does the FTC deem an enormously important issue and a basic institution of modern commerce? The answer is online advertising and marketing in general, and keyword search advertising in particular.

In 2016, the FTC brought an administrative complaint against 1-800 Contacts, the largest seller of contact lenses over the Internet, challenging settlements it entered with 13 other online lens sellers to refrain from a certain type of online advertising (keyword searches) involving each others' trademarked terms. 1-800 Contacts had sued these competitors alleging that their use of the term "1-800 Contacts" to trigger ads that appeared on search engine results pages violated the company's trademark, as well as the Lanham Act.

After an administrative trial, the FTC administrative law judge ("ALJ") upheld the complaint and the company appealed to the full Commission. In November 2018, a majority of the Commission found that the agreements not to bid on each other's trademarked

---

2 *United States v. Bazaarvoice, Inc.*, 2014 U.S. Dist. LEXIS 3284 (N.D. Cal. 2014) (challenging consummated acquisition of rival online review and rating platform).

3 See, e.g. *Realcomp II Ltd.*, 2009 F.T.C. LEXIS 250 (2009) (charging unlawful restriction of distribution of information about discount real estate broker listings on MLS and the Internet in violation of Section 5 of the FTC Act); *Realcomp II v. FTC*, 635 F.3d 815 (6th Circ. 2001) (upholding FTC decision); *cert. denied*, 132 S. Ct. 400 (2011); and *United States v. Nat'l Assoc. of Realtors*, 73 Fed. Reg. 36,104 (DOJ June 25, 2008) (settling claims that association suppressed competition from Internet-based real estate agents by restricting access to listings).

4 Case AT.39740 - *Google Search (Shopping)*, Comm'n Decision (June 27, 017) (summary at 2018 O.J. (C 9) 11), available at http://ec.europa.eu/competition/antitrust/cases/dec_docs/39740/39740_14996_3.pdf.

5 *In the Matter of 1-800 Contacts, Inc.*, Majority Opinion, FTC DOCKET NO. 9372 (Nov. 14, 2018) [hereinafter Maj. Op.], available at https://www.ftc.gov/system/files/documents/cases/docket_no_9372_opinion_of_the_commission_redacted_public_version.pdf.

6 *Id.* at 1.

terms in keyword searches and to implement "negative keywords" that stopped ads from being placed in response to searches that included trademarked terms, such as "1-800 Contacts," unreasonably restrained trade and harmed competition for the online sales of contact lenses and in bidding for search engine keywords.

Of course, the issue of the competitive impact of competitor agreements about advertising is hardly new for antitrust.[7] What makes this case important, however, is how the FTC applies that precedent to the new world of online advertising and marketing, in particular key word advertising.[8] The role of online advertising also lies at the heart of the disagreement between the majority and dissenting Commissioner Noah Joshua Phillips about how much the agreements affected competition, given the availability of other forms of advertising. Their dispute revolves around the import of a 1997 case dealing with a single agreement between two competitors not to advertise a name found confusingly similar to a trademarked name. That case predated the advent of the consumer Internet, however, and its continued vitality given the revolutionary change to advertising and marketing brought about by the Internet is debatable.

The remainder of this article will discuss the basics of online advertising and key word searches, the competitive importance of advertising, the likely anticompetitive impact of advertising restrictions, and the different views of the FTC majority and dissenting positions regarding whether such concerns are, or should be, heightened in the online environment. Finally, it offers some thoughts about how antitrust may look at behavior implicating online advertising and marketing going forward.

II. PRIMER ON SEARCH ADVERTISING AND KEY WORDS

Before delving into the 1-800 Contact decision's analysis of the competitive importance of online advertising and marketing, this section will provide a brief overview of search term advertising. Search engines, such as Google and Bing, offer what is called "organic search" on their search engine results page (or SERP), which are the links that the search engine's algorithm generates in response to a user's query. Search engines' organic results represent the search engine's assessment of the best answer to a user's query, based on a variety of factors such as the popularity of websites. For example, a search for "contact lenses" may generate links to websites for lens manufacturers, eye care professionals, and a variety of lens sellers, both online and offline. The search engines do not sell ad placement in the organic results on the SERP or charge users for conducting the search.

---

7   E.g. *California Dental Ass'n v.* FTC, 121 F.T.C 190 (1996), *aff'd*, 128 F.3d 720 (9th Cir. 1997), *rev'd*, 526 U.S. 756 (1999), *remanded*, 224 F.3d 942 (9th Cir. 2000) and *PolyGram Holding v.* FTC, 136 F.T.C. 310 (2003), *aff'd*, 416 F.3d 29 (D.C. Cir. 2005).

8   Although the proper antitrust treatment of intellectual property in settlements between competitors is a prominent part of the FTC decision, that topic is beyond the scope of this article.

Search engines instead sell ads, designated as such, that appear (either alongside or above) the organic results. If the user clicks on an ad on the SERP and goes to the advertiser's website, the advertiser then pays a fee to the search engine. The ads are placed in response to the user's search query through computerized auctions, in which advertisers submit bids to the search engines that specify their maximum price for placement on the SERP. Search engines do not simply place ads on their SERPs based on the highest bid by an advertiser, however. Instead, they employ sophisticated algorithms that consider the quality of the ad, as measured by whether it is relevant and useful to the user.

Search engines can charge a premium for advertising on SERPs because such ads are widely viewed as more effective than other advertising channels, given that they present ads to a person when he or she is more likely looking to buy a particular product. In contrast, it is hit or miss whether consumers are interested in a particular purchase when they see ads in other media — such as print, TV, or on news or entertainment websites.[9] As a result, other advertising channels have lost revenue as online search advertising has grown, and many online retailers spend most of their advertising budget on search advertising.

Advertisers may rely on the search engine to identify pertinent auctions for them through algorithms or they may specify auctions they wish to enter by bidding on particular words or terms, called "keywords," that appear in the user's search query. Keywords can be any word or term that the advertiser believes will best target possible customers and, as the FTC majority in the *1-800 Contacts* decision noted, "it is common for companies to pay search engines to present their ads in response to a user's search query of another company's brand name."[10] For example, a person searching for Toyota sedans may theoretically see ads for Kia and Honda cars on the SERP.

Some keywords may sweep too broadly. For example, a search for "glasses" might trigger ads for both an eyewear retailer and a kitchenware store. To overcome this effect, advertisers can also employ "negative" keywords that prevent their ads from being placed if the user's search also includes that term. Continuing the example, a keyword search for "glasses" with a negative keyword for "wine" would stop an ad for wine glasses from being placed in response to a query about eye glasses.

In the 1-800 Contacts case, the defendant entered into a series of agreements with most of its online rivals prohibiting each side from causing or allowing ads to appear in response to a search for the other rival's trademarks. These agreements not only prohibited a rival from using "1-800 Contacts" as a keyword, they also required that "1-800 Contacts" be a negative key word. The agreements did not prohibit parties from bidding on generic keywords such as "contacts" or "contacts lens," as long as they used negative keywords.

---

9 As retailer John Wannamaker reportedly observed, "Half of my advertising is wasted. The problem is, I don't know which half."

10 Maj. Op., *supra* note 5, at 6.

Pursuant to these agreements, a rival's ad would not appear in response to a user search for "1-800 Contacts," a search for "cheaper than 1-800 Contacts," or when the rival did not bid on the other party's trademark as a keyword but the ad would have appeared because the search engine algorithm determined that the ad was relevant and useful to the consumer. Before these agreements, search engines displayed ads for many of 1-800 Contacts' retail competitors when those retailers bid on searches with "1-800 Contacts" as a keyword or because of the search engine's algorithm.

This article will next explore the competitive importance of advertising. Finally, it will examine the disagreement between the majority and the dissent in the FTC's 1-800 Contacts decision about the extent to which agreements limiting keyword searches impacted competition, given that they do not prevent advertising through other channels.

III. THE COMPETITIVE IMPORTANCE OF ONLINE ADVERTISING AND MARKETING

The link between advertising and competition has long been recognized. As the Supreme Court explained over 40 years ago, advertising "serves to inform the public of the availability, nature, and prices of products and services, and thus performs an indispensable role in the allocation of resources in a free enterprise system."[11] The FTC has long been a defender of advertising and has submitted many amicus briefs and advocacy filings urging states and other actors to avoid restrictions on advertising beyond what is necessary to prevent deception.[12] The Commission has also brought antitrust enforcement actions challenging a variety of restrictions on advertising, including in cases such as those against the American Medical Association,[13] Massachusetts Board of Registration in Optometry,[14] California Dental Association,[15] and PolyGram Holding.[16] The FTC majority followed this traditional approach in the 1-800 Contacts decision. Highlighting the relationship between advertising and competition, the majority opinion pointed to

---

11 *Bates v. State Bar of Ariz.*, 433 U.S. 350, 364 (1977).

12 See, e.g. Federal Trade Comm'n Staff, Comments to the Dep't of Health and Human Servs. Food and Drug Administration In the Matter of Request for Comment on First Amendment Issues, Docket No. 02N-0209 (Sept. 13, 2002), available at https://www.ftc.gov/sites/default/files/documents/advocacy_documents/ftc-staff-comment-food-and-drug-administration-concerning-first-amendment-issues/fdatextversion.pdf and Brief of the Federal Trade Comm'n as Amicus Curie Supporting Arguments to Vacate Opinion 39 of the Comm. on Att'y Advertising Appointed by the S. Ct. of N.J. (No. 60,003) (May 9, 2007).

13 F.T.C. 701, 1010 (1979) (condemning an agreement among physicians not to advertise), *aff'd*, 638 F.2d 443 (2d Cir. 1980), *aff'd by an equally divided Court*, 455 U.S. 676 (1982) (per curiam).

14 110 F.T.C. at 598 (condemning a licensing board's ban on advertising).

15 121 F.T.C. 190 (1996) (prohibiting professional organization from restricting, regulating, impeding, declaring unethical, or interfering with the advertising and publishing of the prices, terms or conditions of sale of dentists' services and the solicitation of patients, patronage or contracts to supply dentists' services).

16 136 F.T.C. 310 (2003) (condemning agreement between two record distributors to restrict discounts applying to products produced outside the joint venture).

economic theory that "indicates that restrictions on this type of advertising are likely to harm competition" by interfering with the "flow of information between buyers and sellers [that] is an essential part of the market system."[17]

Specifically, the complaint in the 1-800 Contacts case alleged that the agreements prevented competitors from disseminating certain types of online ads that would have informed consumers that lenses were available at different prices, which reduced price competition among online contact lens retailers and made it costlier for consumers to search prices offered by the retailers. As a result, at least some consumers paid higher prices for contact lenses.

In considering the competitive effect of the advertising restriction, the FTC majority not only harkened back to the Commission's own case against *PolyGram*,[18] it looked to the influential D.C. Circuit *PolyGram*[19] decision for guidance. Consistent with the traditional FTC approach, the D.C. Circuit opinion views advertising as serving a vital competitive function in a free market system. It is therefore not surprising that the majority opinion relied heavily on *PolyGram* in its analysis, ultimately holding that the agreements 1-800 entered with its competitors were "[i]nherently suspect" with a likely tendency to suppress competition.[20] Using the *PolyGram* framework, the FTC majority found, "the Challenged Agreements are, in essence, agreements between horizontal competitors to restrict the information provided by advertising to consumers [that] consumers could have used . . . to compare and evaluate the prices and other features of competing online sellers . . . [making] consumer comparisons more difficult and costly to obtain."[21]

IV. ARE CONCERNS ABOUT ADVERTISING AND MARKETING RESTRICTIONS HEIGHTENED IN THE ONLINE ENVIRONMENT?

The *1-800* Contacts decision updates and extends the *PolyGram* precedent into the world of online advertising and marketing, particularly search and keyword advertising. In the decision, the FTC highlighted that consumers use online search as a vital way to "discover vendors and compare products and services." Describing paid search advertising as "an

---

17 Maj. Op., *supra* note 5, at 20.

18 *Id.* at 21 ("Among the more recent cases, in PolyGram, we concluded that an agreement between music companies not to advertise two recordings for a short time period was inherently suspect. See PolyGram, 136 F.T.C. at 353-58.").

19 *PolyGram Holding, Inc. v. FTC*, 416 F.3d 29 (D.C. Cir. 2005). It is worth noting that challenged agreement in PolyGram involved restrictions on advertising and discounting.

20 Maj. Op., *supra* note 5, at 19 (citing *PolyGram*).

21 *Id.* at 20.

important method for marketing contact lenses online to obtain new customers and increase brand awareness," the FTC majority deemed advertising that appears in response to particular search terms "especially effective" because the user sees the ad when he or she is very likely looking to purchase a product. They noted that this distinguishes it from traditional advertising channels, which may not have been able to target consumers with such precision at this crucial point in their purchase decision making.

In addition to laying out the inherently suspect mode of analysis, *PolyGram* also teaches that "as economic learning and market experience evolve," so too will the competitive analysis of such restraints. The 1-800 Contacts majority took up this invitation by looking not simply to whether there is an advertising restriction but in grappling with the fact that this restriction affected online search marketing and advertising. The majority found that the agreements restricted a particularly effective advertising channel, which presented competitive options to consumers at the crucial time when they were looking to make a purchase. They observed that the "settlement agreements effectively shut off an entire — and very important — channel of advertising triggered by an alleged use of the trademark in the generation of search advertising . . . effectively eliminating an entire channel of competitive advertising at the key moment when the consumer is considering a purchase."[22]

By contrast, Commissioner Phillips' dissent strongly disagreed that the settlement agreements shut off a crucial advertising channel. Relying on a case that predated the explosion of online advertising, Commissioner Phillips emphasized that the settlements "did not prevent 1-800 Contacts or other online contact lens retailers from engaging in any form of non-infringing advertising," such traditional offline channels like print, TV, radio ads, or "other forms of electronic/online advertising," such as "internet display advertising, affiliate marketing, social media advertising, and search engine optimization."[23] In his view, the settlements merely "reduce one avenue for discovering products" and "the cost of additional discovery is minimal: another search, a scroll down the results page, a moment's hesitation."[24] He concluded that because the agreements did not restrict rivals from producing and selling competing products, "so long as they do not advertise in response to searches for 1-800 Contacts' Trademarks" the link between the advertising restrictions and an effect on contact lens prices was "attenuated."[25]

---

22 Maj. Op., *supra* note 5, at 14.

23 *In the Matter of 1-800 Contacts, Inc.*, Dissenting Statement of Commissioner Noah Joshua Phillips, FTC DOCKET NO. 9372 (Nov 14, 2018), at 9 [hereinafter Dissent], available at https://www.ftc.gov/system/files/documents/public_statements/1421309/docket_no_9372_dissenting_statement_of_commissioner_phillips_redacted_public_version.pdf Commissioner Phillips also dissented on the ground that the "novel setting and questions this case raised precluded the proper application of an abbreviated ["quick look"] analysis." Prepared Remarks of Commissioner Noah Joshua Phillips, *IP and Antitrust Laws: Promoting Innovation in a High-Tech Economy* (Mar. 20, 2019), available at https://www.ftc.gov/system/files/documents/public_statements/1508165/app_association_keynote_final.pdf.

24 Dissent at 12.

25 *Id.*

V. A KEY DIFFERENCE IN VIEWS

At heart, the difference between the majority and the dissent in *1-800 Contacts* lies in whether the view expressed in the 1997 case, that having a variety of advertising channels renders an advertising restraint on a single channel too narrow to have an anticompetitive restraint, is still accurate today. Commissioner Phillips seemed to embrace this case as binding precedent and looked primarily at the number of other channels available.[26] The majority, by contrast, emphasized that "[o]nline search advertising is a key method for consumers to discover, compare, and reach online contact lens vendors and for lower-priced retailers to compete . . . It enables online sellers to increase brand awareness and to obtain new customers . . . It is displayed at the key moment when the consumer is more likely to be looking to buy."[27]

In the majority's view, key word search is not just one advertising channel among many, but a uniquely effective way to reach potential buyers. Record evidence also demonstrated that online lens sellers found it "much more effective in reaching potential buyers than other types of advertising," generating "the most new customer orders and the most revenue."[28] Thus, unlike Commissioner Phillips' view, the majority did not require the agreements to prohibit multiple avenues of advertising for online sales of contact lenses. The fact that they affected a "particularly significant type of advertising for online sales at the crucial moment when sales are about to be made" was sufficient to show a substantial competitive effect.[29]

VI. CONCLUSION

PolyGram's prediction that "as economic learning and market experience evolve," so too will the competitive analysis of such restraints, is borne out in the FTC's *1-800 Contacts* decision. The FTC majority found online search and key word advertising were key to competition because the person conducting the search had already signaled an interest in the product, and, for many users, an actual intent to buy. Thus, restricting this particular form of advertising had a strong impact on competition, despite the availability of other advertising channels.

Online search advertising, including key word advertising, has changed the advertising landscape, enriching search engines and reducing the value of traditional advertising channels such as TV and newspaper advertising. Antitrust analysis of advertising restraints is necessarily adapting to these seismic changes, as this case demonstrates.

---

26 "1-800 Contacts' approach to promoting itself is ... through 'a multichannel integrated marketing' strategy." *Id.* at 3.

27 Maj. Op., *supra* note 5, at 30.

28 *Id.* at 31.

29 *Id.* at 34.

WHAT *TIMES-PICAYUNE* TELLS US ABOUT THE ANTITRUST ANALYSIS OF ATTENTION PLATFORMS

By David S. Evans[1]

ABSTRACT

Times-Picayune, a 1953 Supreme Court decision involving newspapers, has gained notoriety from the Court's American Express decision concerning credit-card networks. The Amex dissent argued that the Court had already decided how to apply the rule-of-reason analysis to two-sided platforms in Times-Picayune, and got it right then, but got it wrong in Amex. Times-Picayune is a shaky foundation for that proposition. In that case, the Government had alleged per se tying involving advertising and monopolization of the dissemination of news and advertising. By the time the case reached the Supreme Court it was mainly about per se tying, and didn't pose the particular two-sided issues that concerned the Court in Amex. After dismissing the per se tying claim, the Court provided a short rule-of-reason analysis which is consistent with considering the newspaper platform overall, and not just one side. In particular, the lower court had analyzed the Government's predation claims for the newspaper by considering the platform in its entirety, and the Court relied on its conclusion.

I. INTRODUCTION

New Orleans is famous for Mardi Gras, Creole cuisine, Dixieland Jazz, and, of course, *Times-Picayune*.[2] That is a 1953 Supreme Court decision involving the only morning newspaper in the city at the time. It has gained recent fame in the debate over the proper antitrust analysis of two-sided platforms leading up to the *American Express* decision. *Times-Picayune* was featured in the dissent and the majority opinion distinguished it briefly.[3]

---

1 Chairman, Global Economics Group, Boston, MA.; Executive Director, Jevons Institute for Competition Law and Economics and Visiting Professor, University College London. I have benefitted from very helpful comments by Richard Schmalensee and Howard Chang. This article was first published in the April 2019 CPI Antitrust Chronicle.

2 *Times-Picayune Publishing Co. v. United States*, 345 U.S. 594 (1953).

3 *Ohio v. Am. Express Co.*, 138 S. Ct. 2274, 2286, 2295 (2018).

The dissent said the Court had already decided the central market definition issue before it — the other way. *Times-Picayune* concluded, it argued, that antitrust analysis of two-sided platforms, like newspapers, should focus narrowly on the service provided by the side of the platform subject to the challenged conduct.[4] The relevant antitrust market pertained to that side, and not the platform overall. There was no need to consider the other side. The majority decision distinguished *Times-Picayune* on the grounds that it was appropriate to analyze newspaper advertising as single-sided because the indirect network effects that connect the groups served by platforms were minor, given that readers did not care about advertising.

This article takes a closer look at the journey of *Times-Picayune* from a complaint filed by the U.S. Department of Justice, to the District Court, and then to the Supreme Court. The majority decision in *Times-Picayune*, and the lower court decision the Court relied on in part, don't provide much support for the notion that an antitrust analysis under the rule-of-reason should consider just one side of a two-sided platform. Even in the case of newspapers.

Times-Picayune is a useful case study of platform competition. The Government's complaint described a plausible strategy for destroying a platform competitor which could be relevant to other cases involving ad-supported platforms. The case provides insights for determining conditions when that strategy could work, and when it is implausible. This old newspaper case remains relevant for the antitrust analysis of other ad-supported media including digital platforms.

II. THE GOVERNMENT'S CASE AGAINST THE PUBLISHER OF THE TIMES-PICAYUNE

The U.S. Department of Justice filed a complaint against the Times-Picayune Publishing Company ("Company") on June 14, 1950.[5] At that time, the Company published the Times-Picayune, the only morning newspaper in New Orleans, the New Orleans States ("States"), an evening newspaper which the Company had purchased in 1933, and a Sunday newspaper ("Times-Picayune & States"). The other significant newspaper in New Orleans, the Item, had evening and Sunday editions. These newspapers earned money from paid circulation and advertising. There were three categories of advertising: local display, general national, and classified.

---

4 *Ohio v. Am. Express Co.*, 138 S. Ct. 2274, 2295 (2018) (Breyer dissenting opinion). The Justice Department and various *amici* in support upholding the District Court decision, based on a merchant-specific market, also cited *Times-Picayune* prominently as having already decided the issue. See "Brief for the United States in Opposition" *State of Ohio, et. al., v. American Express Company, et. al*, (2017) No. 16-1454 (SCOTUS) at pp. 11, 13; "Brief of 28 Professors of Antitrust Law as Amici Curiae Supporting Petitioners" *State of Ohio, et. al., v. American Express Company, et. al*, (2017) No. 16-1454 (SCOTUS) at p. 22; "Brief for Amici Curiae John M. Connor, Martin Gaynor, Daniel McFadden, Roger Noll, Jeffrey M. Perloff, Joseph A. Stiglitz, Lawrence J. White, and Ralph A. Winter in Support of Petitioners" *State of Ohio, et. al., v. American Express Company*, et. al, (2017) No. 16-1454 (SCOTUS) at p. 3.

5 *United States of America v. The Times-Picayune Publishing Company, et al.*, Complaint, No. 2797 (Eastern District of Louisiana, June 14, 1950).

The Government claimed that the Company engaged in an unlawful tie by offering advertising only as a unit at combined rates in both morning and evening newspapers. The "unit rule," as it was called, applied to classified and general advertising but not to local display advertising.

The Government also alleged that the Company "[u]sed the dominant advantage ... of the Times-Picayune to injure and destroy competition" for its evening and Sunday newspapers by (a) engaging in the tie; (b) using profits from the morning paper to subsidize arbitrarily low rates for advertising in the evening paper; and (c) "increasing the number of pages in the evening paper without a corresponding increase in revenue for the purpose of inducing and forcing circulation and advertising from the Item to the States."[6] (There were also a few other claims that are peripheral to the main story and were rejected by the District Court.)

These practices, according to the Justice Department, restrained competition in the "dissemination of news and advertising" and were an attempt "[t]o monopolize ... the dissemination of news and advertising."[7] Indeed, the Justice Department had described a strategy for ruining competing ad-supported media platforms that could be plausible with the right set of facts.

III. TWO-SIDED PLATFORMS AND AD-SUPPORTED MEDIA

Two-sided platforms serve two distinct groups of customers who could benefit from interaction. The platform helps them get together through a common meeting place and facilitates interactions between members of the two groups in a way that creates value for the parties to this interaction. Members on one side can typically expect more value when they can interact with more relevant members on the other side; these are what economists call positive indirect network effects.[8]

Platforms set prices recognizing that there is a feedback loop connecting the two sides. That results in their balancing prices between the two sides in a way that ensures that they have enough participants on each side to create value for those on the other side. Commonly, platforms set prices below cost on one side, because they can charge the other side more to get access to those on the subsidized side.

Platforms require a critical mass of customers on both sides to offer a valuable proposition to either side. A ride-sharing platform with few passengers would have trouble attracting drivers, since they would get few pickups, and a platform with few drivers would have

---

6 *Id.* at pp. 8-9.

7 *Id.* at p. 6.

8 Evans, David S. & Richard Schmalensee (2008), "Markets with Two-Sided Platforms," *Issues in Competition Law and Policy*, Vol. 1, American Bar Association

trouble attracting passengers, since they would have trouble getting rides. Platforms that can't reach critical mass therefore fail. There's a heap of defunct platform startups for that reason. Platforms that lose enough participants to fall below critical mass fail as well. The dead and dying malls across America are visible demonstrations.

Economists have considered ad-supported media businesses two-sided since the start of the economic literature on platform businesses.[9] An ad-supported media business serves both advertisers and readers. There's a twist compared to other platforms, though. Advertisers appreciate having access to more readers, but readers may not appreciate being exposed to more advertising. In this case, there are positive indirect network effects on one side but not on the other. It turns out, though, that having positive indirect network effects on one side is enough for the economic theories of two-sided platforms to apply, even if the other side has negative indirect network effects.

Indirect network effects aren't the whole story, though.[10] Even if consumers don't like ads, they do like content. And they can't get content, or as much of it, if the media business can't sell advertising, which funds production of that content and is the raison d'être for this content. Unfortunately, while they might like to get the content at subsidized prices, without the advertising, they are unlikely to find a willing media business for this proposition. These ad-supported media businesses are also known as attention platforms since they are in the business of trading consumer mindshare.

The basic business model for attention platforms has some similarities to the credit card networks considered in *American Express*. Ad-supported media provide readers with content to get them to come to the platform. They generally charge readers prices that don't nearly cover the cost of producing and distributing content. The content is the reward for coming to the platform and being exposed to advertising. The "content reward" plays a much more important role than "reward points" for payment cards, but they both result in a payment to one side to use the platform. Ad-supported media then sell advertisers access to those readers through ads that are interspersed throughout the content. The details of this vary by medium, but the principles are common.

For ad-supported media and for credit-card networks there are separate prices to two distinct groups of customers; those prices are interdependent and effectively negative to one side, and the businesses must compete for both types of customers. Of course, there are

---

9 Rochet, Jean-Charles & Jean Tirole (2003), "Platform Competition in Two-Sided Markets," *Journal of the European Economic Association* 1(4), pp. 990-1029 at p. 990; Anderson, Simon & Jean Gabszewicz (2006), "The Media and Advertising: A Tale of Two-Sided Markets," in *Handbook of the Economics of Art and Culture*, V. Ginsburgh & D. Throsby, eds., (Elsevier).

10 See Evans, David S. (2019), "Attention Platforms, the Value of Content, and Public Policy," *Review of Industrial Organization* (Feb. 2019).

11 See Whinston, Michael D. (1990), "Tying, Foreclosure and Exclusion," *The American Economic Review* 80(4), pp. 837-859 for the classic discussion of using tying to foreclose competition by preventing traditional scale economies. The two-sided strategy is similar but exploits demand-side scale economies resulting from indirect network effects. In both cases, since the tie imposes a cost on buyers, the strategy is profitable only if it eliminates the competitor. It is not possible to address that issue for a two-sided platform without considering both sides and the interdependencies.

differences as well, most notably that readers may not like being connected to advertisers, unlike cardholders who do value being connected to merchants.

So long as there are sufficient entry barriers the Justice Department described a clever and coherent strategy for destroying a competitor and monopolizing a market in its *Times-Picayune* complaint. The morning-evening advertising tie could have deprived the Item from earning enough advertising revenue to fund its content, and with less content it would attract less circulation, which in turn would make it even less attractive to advertisers. Meanwhile, the low advertising prices and an unprofitable expansion of content on the part of the States could have forced the Item to lose advertisers and readers and incur unsustainable loses. The combination of these strategies could have pushed the Item below critical mass and send it into a death spiral.[11]

The Company would have demolished its evening and Sunday competitor. Then it could have exercised anticompetitive market power by raising advertising prices, cutting content, or raising circulation prices. It could also have killed off a potential competitor for its morning newspaper. Since the reader and advertiser sides of the platform are intimately intertwined its strategies would have harmed both customer groups. Of course, the facts would have to support these claims.

IV. THE DISTRICT COURT DECISION ON PREDATION AND TYING

The U.S. District Court for the Eastern District of Louisiana issued a decision on May 27, 1952.

A. Market Definition, Dominance, and Separate Products

The District Court concluded that the three newspapers at issue "are the only significant media of news, advertising and other information disseminated regularly for residents of New Orleans through publication and circulation of newspapers." The Company claimed that its morning, evening, and Sunday newspapers were editions of a single newspaper. The judge rejected this on the ground that the papers had different appearances and content. As we will see, that finding was key.

The trial judge found that the Times-Picayune, the morning paper, was the dominant newspaper. "For at least twenty years," according to the court, "the Times-Picayune has been the largest newspaper in New Orleans in circulation, advertising lineage, and number of pages published." The Company's manager of general advertising had claimed, the judge noted, that the Times-Picayune is "the back-bone of any advertising effort" in New Orleans. "Enjoying as it does a monopoly position in the morning field, and an enormous advantage in circulation, advertising lineage, and number of printed pages," the judge continued, "newspaper advertisers who desire to cover the New Orleans market must, of necessity, use the Times-Picayune as a medium for the advertising." In effect, the trial court found that there was a separate market for morning newspapers since neither readers nor advertisers had substitutes.

The District Court's description of the business is silent on whether readers have any interest in seeing advertising.

B. The Unit Rule and Tying

The District Court examined the advertising contracts for classified and national advertising that had the unit rule. Put in terms of the modern language for analyzing tying, the judge found that the tying product was in a dominant position, that the defendant forced customers to take the tied product, and that the unit applied to a substantial portion of the market. He concluded that,

> The Times-Picayune, because of its monopoly position, has been able to force buyers of advertising space to purchase what they do not want, space in the States, in order to purchase what they require, space in the Times-Picayune. The very fact that the defendant corporation was able successfully to impose the unit rate on general and classified advertising tends to prove the monopoly position which the Times-Picayune enjoys....[12]

In addition to finding an unlawful tie, the trial judge found that the purpose of the unit rule, which was found to violate Section 1 of the Sherman Act, was to harm the Company's only evening rival.

> [I]is apparent from the record that it was also the intention of the [Company] to restrain general and classified advertisers from making untrammeled choice between the afternoon newspapers in purchasing advertising space, and also to substantially diminish the competitive vigor of the Item, the States' only competitor in the afternoon field.[13]

The same findings showed that the unit rule also violated Section 2 of the Act. The District Court found that the Company used the unit rule to attempt to monopolize "that segment of the afternoon newspaper general and classified advertising field which was represented by those advertisers who also required morning newspaper space."

The District Court was silent as to the impact of the unit rule on the dissemination of news and did not conclude that it had prevented the Item from operating a viable newspaper.

---

12 *United States v. the Times-Picayune Pub. Co.*, 105 F. Supp. 670, 678 (E.D. La. 1952)

13 *United States v. the Times-Picayune Pub. Co.*, 105 F. Supp. 670, 678 (E.D. La. 1952)

C. Tying, Predatory Pricing, and Content Expansion Under Section 2

As the District Court judge put it, "Considerable evidence was offered by the Government to establish that the defendants maintained a rate structure which, considered as a whole, resulted in the operation of the evening States at a loss." The Company's books showed that the States was operating at a profit, but the Government claimed that was the result of questionable allocations.

The judge found, however, "nothing in the evidence which would indicate, much less establish, that the States at any time was operated at a loss." He was persuaded by testimony from the Company's auditor that more careful allocations would not reveal that the States was operating at a loss.

The Justice Department and the District Court agreed on one thing though.

The relevant question was whether the States, which derived income from circulation and advertising, was operating at a loss. They both considered the platform as a whole. The Justice Department did not argue that the advertising rates were below cost for serving an advertising market. Rather, it argued that the combination of expenditures on content, which attracts readers, and advertising and circulation prices resulted in the States operating at loss. And the Item couldn't compete with that. Only a platform level analysis, that considered prices and costs overall, could address that monopolization claim.

Thus, the Government ended up victorious only on the claim that the unit rule was an unlawful tie that restricted competition for afternoon advertising. It was defeated on the claim that the States was operated at a loss to destroy competition.

V. THE SUPREME COURT DECISION ON THE UNIT RULE

The Times-Picayune Publishing Company appealed the decision that the advertising contracts with the unit rule violated Sections 1 and 2 of the Sherman Act. The Court, in a 5-4 decision issued on May 25, 1953, found that they did not.

A. The Newspaper Business

The Court situated the case in the newspaper business in the mid-20th century. "The daily newspaper, though essential to the effective functioning of our political system, has in recent years suffered drastic economic decline." It noted that the number of daily newspapers in 1951 was the lowest it had been since the turn of the 20th century. In fact, daily newspaper competition "has grown nearly extinct."[14]

---

14 *Times-Picayune Publishing Co. v. United States*, 345 U.S. 594, 602-603 (1953).

The Court recognized that "[a]dvertising is the economic mainstay of the newspaper business." After reporting that "more than two-thirds of a newspaper's total revenues flow from the sale of advertising space" it noted that, [o]bviously, newspapers must sell advertising to survive." Competition from other mass media — radio, television, and magazines — had reduced newspapers' share of total national advertising expenditures from 79 percent in 1929 to 35 percent in 1951.

B. The Tying Claim

Tying is a *per* se violation of Section 1 of the Sherman Act, according to the Court, when the seller has a monopoly position in the market for the tying product and when it forecloses competitors from "any substantial market."[15] In evaluating the per se claim the Court concluded that the key issue was whether the Times-Picayune occupied a dominant market position because it was the sole morning daily in New Orleans.

The Court described the two-sided features of the newspaper business. It noted that "every newspaper is a dual trader in separate though interdependent markets; it sells the paper's news and advertising content to its readers; in effect that readership is in turn sold to the buyers of advertising space."[16] It said that the case only concerned the advertising market which was the subject of the tie and that "dominance in the advertising market" was decisive in determining the legality of the unit rule.[17]

The Court stated it didn't think that the Times-Picayune was dominant in the advertising market. It noted that the morning paper's share of "both general and classified linage over the years hovered around 40%".[18] That conclusion assumed, however, that the relevant market consisted of general and classified advertising in all three papers.

Critical for that assumption, the Court rejected the trial judge's finding that these newspapers were separate products from the standpoint of the advertiser.[19] According to the Court, just because readers may distinguish between the papers, doesn't necessarily mean that advertisers do.[20]

---

15 *International Salt Co., Inc. v. United States*, 332 U.S. 392, 396 (1947). Of course, the antitrust law on tying has evolved considerably since then including the seminal decision in another case situated in New Orleans. See *Jefferson Parish Hosp. Dist. v. Hyde*, 466 U.S. 2 (1984).

16 *Times-Picayune Publishing Co. v. United States*, 345 U.S. 594, 610 (1953).

17 *Id.*

18 *Id.* at 612.

19 The Court noted that newspaper advertising might compete with other forms of advertising but lacked evidence on this. *Id.* at 611-612.

20 There doesn't appear to have been any evidence on the extent to which morning and evening readers were substitutes for classified and general advertisers. The morning and evening papers could have tried to differentiate themselves to attract readers with different characteristics that were relevant to advertisers. For example, the morning paper could have skewed towards women and the evening paper towards men.

But that readers consciously distinguished between two publications does not necessarily imply that advertisers bought separate and distinct products when insertions were placed in the Times-Picayune and States. So to conclude here would involve speculation that advertisers bought space motivated by considerations other than customer coverage; that their media selections, in effect, rested on generic qualities differentiating morning and evening readers in New Orleans.

That finding didn't just support the finding of lack of dominance. It defeated the tying claim since, from the standpoint of the advertiser, there was a single product and not two.

Here, however, two newspapers under single ownership at the same place, time, and terms sell indistinguishable products to advertisers; no dominant 'tying' product exists (in fact, since space in neither the Times-Picayune nor the States can be bought alone, one may be viewed as 'tying' as the other); no leverage in one market excludes sellers in the second, because for present purposes the products are identical and the markets the same.... In short, neither the rationale nor the doctrines evolved by the 'tying' cases can dispose of the Publishing Company's arrangements challenged here. [21]

There was no per se violation of Section 1, based on unlawful tying, because there was no separate tied product and there was no dominance once the two alleged tying and tied products were considered together.

C. *The Unreasonable Restraint of Trade Claim*

The Court then turned to whether the unit rule was an unreasonable restraint of trade under Section 1. It articulated the rule-of-reason analysis as requiring it to determine the amount of business controlled, the strength of the remaining competition, and "whether the action springs from business requirements or purpose to monopolize". It then eviscerated the District Court's finding that the unit rules were unreasonable restraints of trade.

Earlier the majority decision had reported that local display advertising accounted for 44 percent of total revenue (including circulation), classified 13 percent, and general display 14 percent. The District Court had rejected bundling claims related to local display, leaving only 27 percent for the Court to deal with.

The Court noted that the unit rule for classified ads was adopted in 1935 to compete with the Item. At that time the Item operated a morning and evening newspaper which together carried more classified ads than the Company's. The Item suspended its morning newspaper in 1940. It was also common practice among newspapers with morning and evening editions.

---

21 *Times-Picayune Publishing Co. v. United States*, 345 U.S. 594, 602-603 (1953).

Over the next decade, the Item's share of classified advertising linage declined by three percentage points overall (from 23 percent to 20 percent) and by five percentage points considering only the evening papers (from 37 percent to 32 percent). The unit rule was instituted for general advertising in 1950, by which time it was common in the industry. The Court found that there was no material change in 1951, the only later year for which there was data. It concluded that, taking the effects of classified and general together, the Item's revenue had declined by less than one percent.

Had this effect been larger, the unit rule could have harmed newspaper competition and, with it, the dissemination of news and advertising. However, as an exclamation mark on this analysis, the Court noted that, "The Item, the alleged victim of the Times-Picayune Company's challenged trade practices appeared, in short to be doing well."[22] It flourished in the decade before the trial in terms of expanding advertising, reaching record circulation, and in recent years had made a profit. The Court concluded there was no violation of Section 1.

The Court then turned to the Section 2 attempted monopolization claim. It noted that most of the attempted monopolization case had failed in the District Court, including the claim that "the Company deliberately operated the evening States at a financial loss to the detriment of the competing Item." Only the unit rates remained and, since the Court found that they advanced legitimate business aims, the Court rejected the Section 2 claim as well.

The Court never considered the Government's original claims that the Company had tried to monopolize dissemination of news, or newspapers overall, since they didn't survive the District Court decision. Readers didn't come up except whether they were the source of monopoly power for the morning newspaper over advertisers. And the record is silent on whether readers care about advertising, and therefore whether there's a feedback from advertisers to readers.[23]

VI. TIMES-PICAYUNE AND AMERICAN EXPRESS

By the time Times-Picayune made it to the Supreme Court it was mainly about whether certain advertising contracts were per se violations of Section 1. Consumers of news weren't the subject of the dispute. Caution signs thus abound for those seeking to place the weight of all subsequent rule-of-reason analysis for two-sided platform cases, or for ad-supported media, on this foundation.

---

22 *Times-Picayune Publishing Co. v. United States*, 345 U.S. 594, 610 (1953).

23 The Item was sold to the Times-Picayune Publishing Company five years after the Supreme Court's decision. It lived on another two decades as the Daily States-Item. The afternoon paper was closed in 1980. The Times-Picayune briefly stopped daily publication in October 2012 making New Orleans one of the few major cities without a daily newspaper. It resumed the next year and folded into a regional newspaper group in 2015.

However, upon a close read, there isn't actually much tension between American Express and *Times-Picayune*. To see why, we need to replay the movie, despite having seen its ending.

A. *Times-Picayune and the Rule-of-Reason*

Throughout the case, the courts, and the parties themselves, recognized that the newspaper business was about readers and advertisers. One couldn't be in the newspaper business without providing readers for advertisers, and without securing advertising which was essential for funding the paper. Those business realities, properly, colored everything.

The Government claimed that the Company had engaged in a series of practices, beginning with the purchase of the States in 1933, to establish monopoly control over the daily newspaper business, and the dissemination of news and advertising, in New Orleans. The alleged competitive harm wasn't limited to an advertising market. It was about destroying a competing two-sided platform and thus necessarily harming competition for both readers and advertisers.

The Government's predation case was premised on the newspapers providing a joint product for readers and advertisers. It didn't posit that the Company had lowed advertising prices to monopolize an advertising market. It claimed that the Company was operating the States at a financial loss to drive a competing platform out of business. That harmed newspaper competition and, with it, competition for the dissemination of news and advertising.

The Government, and the trial judge, examined the financials of the newspaper as a whole. That is essentially the two-sided analysis required by *American Express*. It aggregates the revenues received from both sides and costs incurred on both sides to determine whether the challenged conduct restrained competition at the platform level. If the Government could have shown that the States was operating at a financial loss overall, it would have had support for its claim that the Company was monopolizing the dissemination of news and advertising. The trial judge was firm that there no evidence to support these predation claims.

There was another opportunity for the trial judge to consider competitive harm to the dissemination of news. He examined whether the advertising contracts were an unreasonable restraint of trade under Section 1. He found that they were when it came to advertising, but was silent on the impact on the dissemination of news.

Since the Government didn't appeal the District Court's dismissal of their claims, when the case got to the Supreme Court there wasn't much of a rule-of-reason case. Furthermore, harm to newspaper competition overall, or for the dissemination of news, wasn't on the table.

The Court's rule-of-reason analysis of harm to competition in advertising sales, however, at least touches on the impact of the unit rule on newspapers overall. It noted that the Item was profitable and mentioned its circulation, as well as its advertising. It also gave a nod to the District Court's finding that the States was operating profitably overall as well. Most of its analysis concerns showing that the advertising contracts had a negligible effect on newspaper revenue. Since it recognized that advertising revenue was essential to the operation of newspapers these findings demonstrated, though the Court did not say, that the advertising contracts could not have harmed newspaper competition overall, or the dissemination of news. Since there were no claimed feedbacks between advertising and readers, and no meaningful jeopardy to funding content, that one-sided analysis of the importance of advertising revenue was dispositive.

On a different record the Court could have found that the Company had been running the States at a loss as a result of low advertising rates and that this practice would destroy the Company's only newspaper rival. There is nothing in the majority decision that suggests that the Court would have, if this were the case, limited its analysis to harm in the newspaper advertising market that was the subject of the challenged conduct. It had gone out of its way to emphasize that newspapers couldn't survive, and implicitly provide content to readers, without advertising. Nothing in the decision suggests that, just because the challenged conduct related to advertising, the Court would have rejected the Government's claim that the challenged conduct was harming competition in the dissemination of news. It understood well that, without advertising, there would be no newspaper and no dissemination of news for readers.

B. Times-Picayune and the Per Se Tying Analysis

The Court did say that the case "concerns solely one of the markets" and that "dominance in the advertising market, not in readership, must be decisive in gauging the legality of the Company's unit plan."[24] This language specifically referred to the analysis of whether the unit rule was an unlawful *per se* tie under *International Salt* and the related tying cases. It came between the Court's review of the tying cases and its lengthy analysis of tying in the matter at hand.

The issue was whether the morning newspaper had leverage over advertisers. It may be possible to conduct a sound economic analysis of that particular question without defining a single platform market or considering the interrelated pricing and feedback issues raised by *American Express*.[25] It is not possible, however, to conduct a sound economic analysis without considering how two-sided platform businesses operate.

---

24 *Times-Picayune Publishing Co. v. United States*, 345 U.S. 594, 610 (1953).

25 Generally, the courts would have to consider whether there were significant feedback effects between advertisers and readers, but none were claimed here.

Here the Court recognized that the analysis had to consider the relationship between the two sides to assess whether there was an unlawful tie. It found that advertisers wanted readers. But it didn't have any basis for finding that advertisers cared whether people saw their classified and general ads in the morning or evening papers. And where they might — as with local displays — there was no tie. That demolished the tying case.

The Court could have reached the same conclusion based upon a substantive examination of newspaper competition. Starting with the challenged conduct a court would have had to decide whether the morning and evening newspapers — the two-sided platforms at issue — were in one relevant antitrust market or two. Evidence that advertisers cared about whether readers were morning or evening would have led to separate newspaper markets while evidence that advertisers found readers fungible would have led to a single newspaper market.

As a general matter there are good economic reasons for considering competition among newspapers overall since advertisers may care about who readers are; readers may care about what the type of content that is attracting them as well as the amount and type of advertising. So long as economic analysis can fully account for inter-relationships, it can get to the right answers on substantive questions regardless of whether newspapers are analyzed in a single newspaper market or interdependent advertiser and reader ones.

C. American Express Discussion of Times-Picayune

The *American Express* dissent said that the *Times-Picayune* Court held that "an antitrust court should begin its definition of a relevant market by focusing narrowly on the good or service affected by a challenged restraint."[26] This claim is based on the Court's statement that "dominance in the advertising market, not in readership, must be decisive in gauging the legality of the Company's unit plan." The dissent goes on to say that the Government had claimed that the newspaper's advertising policy was unlawful under the rule-of-reason. But, as noted above, the Court's statement about focusing on dominance in the advertising market was made in the middle of its per se tying analysis.

The Court's rule-of-reason analysis at least touches on whether the Company had harmed newspaper competition through the unit rule and operating the evening newspaper at loss. The Court didn't need to go further because if newspaper advertiser competition was not harmed, it follows immediately that competition in the dissemination of news wasn't harmed. If the unit rule and low advertising rates had diminished the Item, it is hard to see why the Court would have stopped at the boundaries of an advertising market and not crossed over into newspapers and their readers; or why it should have taken such a restrictive view.

---

26 *Ohio v. Am. Express Co.*, 138 S. Ct. 2274, 2295 (2018) (Breyer dissenting opinion).

Faced with a different record the *Times-Picayune* Court would have had to grapple with similar issues raised in *American Express*. Suppose consumers value classified advertising. That's likely the case based on common experience and given that people patronize classified ad services such as Craigslist. If this is the case, then the Company could have provided more value to their readers by imposing the unit rule on advertisers. That could have increased the circulation of the Company's newspapers, which could have benefited its advertisers.

Depending on the facts, it is possible in this hypothetical case that the unit rule could have increased newspaper circulation and advertising in the market overall.[27] It is also possible that benefits to readers outweighed any costs to advertisers. It would therefore not have made economic sense to analyze harm solely in an advertising market for the reasons given in *Amex*.

Of course, we can't know what the *Times-Picayune* Court would have done with that hypothetical case. But its brief rule-of-reason discussion does not show, at least not clearly, that it would have focused on an advertising market rather than assessing the overall impact of the challenged practices on newspaper competition.

The *American Express* majority opinion gave newspaper advertising as an example of a platform in which indirect network effects were minor because readers do not value advertising. It said, citing *Times-Picayune*, that "the market for newspaper advertising behaves much like a one-sided market and should be analyzed as such."[28] The economic theory of two-sided platforms, which leads to the pricing and market power issues the *American Express* majority decision was concerned with, does not require positive indirect network effects in both directions. In fact, much of the theoretical and empirical literature concerns two-sided advertising platforms, for which there are possibly negative indirect effects of advertisers on readers. There may well be cases in which the feedback effects between the two-sides are immaterial, or in which they are not relevant to the question at hand. However, there is no economic basis for concluding that is commonly the situation for newspapers or other ad-supported media platforms.

VII. CONCLUSION

The Court's decisions in *American Express* and *Times-Picayune* share common ground. Both recognized the two-sided nature of the businesses under consideration and the interdependence of the two groups of customers. Each adhered to the two-sided business realities for the claims and facts before the Court.

---

27 If the Court was correct that the unit rule didn't materially reduce classified advertising in the Item, then it is plausible that the unit rule could have resulted in delivering more classified ads that readers valued. Nevertheless, there are certainly other circumstances in which the unit rule could have reduced newspaper competition to the detriment of readers and advertisers.

28 *Ohio v. Am. Express Co.*, 138 S. Ct. 2274, 2286 (2018).

WHAT *TIMES-PICAYUNE* TELLS US ABOUT THE ANTITRUST ANALYSIS OF ATTENTION PLATFORMS

The claimed tension between the two cases is overstated. The lengthy discussion of per se tying in *Times-Picayune* was based on the interaction between the two sides of the platform. The Court could then dispense with the per se tying claim by showing there was no separate tied product. In analyzing whether the challenged conduct restricted competition, it didn't need to go further than showing the negligible economic effect of the advertising contracts at issue.

The Court did not clearly limit the rule-of-reason analysis of competitive harm to a market restricted to the side of the platform on which the challenged conduct occurred. The very brief discussion in *Times-Picayune* is not inconsistent with looking at harm to platform competition overall.[29] Thus, it is quite a stretch to suggest that *Times-Picayune* established the general rule-of-reason framework for two-sided platforms and concluded that courts should limit their analysis to the side on which the challenged conduct applied.

---

29 Even if it had, the courts have, of course, repeatedly modified their approach to antitrust analysis of conduct under *per se* and rule-of-reason based on economic learning. There has been an explosive growth in the theoretical and empirical learning on two-sided platforms, including credit-card networks and newspapers, in the last 20 years. The Court relied on that learning in developing the fulsome approach towards applying the rule-of-reason to two-sided platforms with significant indirect network effects.

48   MEDIA MARKETS AND COMPETITION LAW: MULTINATIONAL PERSPECTIVES

OHIO v. AMERICAN EXPRESS: IMPLICATIONS FOR NON-TRANSACTION MULTISIDED PLATFORMS

By Joshua D. Wright & John M. Yun[1]

ABSTRACT

The Supreme Court's decision in Ohio v. American Express settled a number of critical issues concerning multisided platforms — including whether each side of a platform constitutes a separate relevant product market. The ruling also addressed whether a prima facie assessment of competitive harm must incorporate the impact to consumers on all sides of a platform. The Court, however, potentially narrowed the scope of its ruling by making an explicit distinction between "transaction" and "non-transaction" platforms. We examine whether this is a meaningful distinction and explain how the Court's logic applies to non-transaction platforms.

I. INTRODUCTION

The Supreme Court's recent decision in *Ohio v. American Express* has important implications for the antitrust analysis of multisided platforms.[2] The Court expressly addressed two fundamental issues: (1) defining the relevant product market(s) when there are two or more "sides" to a platform; and (2) specifying the "three-step" burden shifting paradigm under a rule-of-reason analysis.[3] The Court filled an immense void as practitioners had sought antitrust guidance on these central issues involving platforms.[4] The Court also left open a number of important issues. Perhaps most critically, *American Express*

---

1 Joshua D. Wright is University Professor and Executive Director of the Global Antitrust Institute, Antonin Scalia Law School, George Mason University. John M. Yun is Associate Professor of Law and Director of Economic Education, Global Antitrust Institute, Antonin Scalia Law School, George Mason University.

2 See *Ohio v. Am. Express Co., 138 S. Ct. 2274, 201 L. Ed. 2d 678 (2018)*, hereafter "*Am. Express Co.*".

3 Broadly, the court determines in Step One whether there is harm to competition; this is the *prima facie* burden. If harm to competition is established, the burden is shifted to the defendant in Step Two to produce evidence of procompetitive efficiencies that offset the competitive harm. If such efficiencies are identified, in Step Three, the decisionmaker weighs these two countervailing effects with the ultimate burden of persuasion remaining with the plaintiff.

4 For instance, see the dueling amicus briefs from attorneys and economists on each side of *American Express* representing vastly different positions on these questions (available at http://www.scotusblog.com/case-files/cases/ohio-v-american-express-co/).

limits the scope of its decision by introducing a distinction between "transaction" and "non-transaction" platforms.

The Court observes that transaction platforms, such as credit-cards, are different than non-transaction platforms, such as newspapers, since transaction platforms — as the name implies — "facilitate a single, simultaneous transaction between participants."[5] The Court further differentiates transactional and non-transactional platforms by explaining that, "[n]on-transaction platforms, by contrast, often do compete with companies that do not operate on both sides of their platform. A newspaper that sells advertising, for example, might have to compete with a television network, even though the two do not meaningfully compete for viewers."[6] Referencing newspapers, the Court further explains that "indirect network effects operate in only one direction; newspaper readers are largely indifferent to the amount of advertising that a newspaper contains."[7]

A critical question for antitrust practitioners, courts, and agencies is whether the underlying economic logic of the Court's analysis in *American Express* applies to non-transaction platforms as well. In Section 2, we detail the impact of the *American Express* decision on the antitrust analysis of multisided platforms. Section 3 details the similarities and differences between transaction and non-transaction platforms and argues why the economic principles detailed in *American Express* also apply to non-transaction platforms. Section 4 concludes.

II. *OHIO v. AMERICAN EXPRESS*

In *American Express* the Court was asked to address the proper methodology to address antitrust issues involving multisided platform. Evans & Schmalensee (2013) state that a multisided platform "has (a) two or more groups of customers; (b) who need each other in some way; (c) but who cannot capture the value from their mutual attraction on their own; and (d) rely on the catalyst to facilitate value creating interactions between them."[8] The appeal of this definition is that it can describe both transaction and non-transaction platforms — although there are important differences between the two types.[9] Examples of transactional platforms include payment card systems, ride sharing apps, and eBay. The common thread is that there is a direct, commercial transaction between the two sides, such as cardholders and merchants, that a platform, such as American Express, facilitates. In contrast, non-transaction platforms such as newspapers and search engines,

---

5   *Am. Express Co.* at 13.

6   *Am. Express Co.* at footnote 9.

7   *Am. Express Co.* at 12.

8   Evans & Schmalensee (2013), "The Antitrust Analysis of Multi-Sided Platform Businesses," NBER Working Paper No. 18783, pp. 1-72 at 7.

9   See Filistrucchi, Geradin, van Damme & Affeldt (2014), "Market Definition in Two-Sided Markets: Theory and Practice," *Journal of Competition Law & Economics* 10, pp. 293-339.

which bring together consumers and advertisers, facilitate an engagement, at some level, between the two groups that lacks a direct, commercial exchange. Importantly, as Schmalensee & Evans' definition highlights, a non-transaction platform is still a catalyst that brings together two groups and unlocks value for both.

The specific issue before the Court in *American Express* was whether the antisteering provisions in agreements between American Express and merchants violate Section 1 of the Sherman Act. When cardholders and merchants transact, there is a "swipe fee" that merchants must pay to the credit card company. American Express has a relatively high swipe fee compared to rivals such as Visa, MasterCard, and Discover; thus, merchants have an incentive to "steer" cardholders at the point-of-sale to use a rival credit card with a lower swipe fee. In order to protect against this, American Express — and others — included an antisteering provision in its contracts with merchants. The district court agreed with the U.S. Department of Justice ("DOJ") that the effect of the antisteering provision was to "restrain competition between networks."[10] The Second Circuit reversed, finding that petitioners failed to demonstrate market-wide anticompetitive harm — particularly given that there was no evidence of diminished output or quality.[11]

Importantly, a fundamental fact that the courts had to deal with is that American Express is a two-sided platform that must balance the interests of both groups due, in large part, to the presence of indirect network effects. Indirect network effects, also known as cross-group effects, occur when the size of one group, e.g. cardholders, increases the value of participating on the platform for the other group, e.g. merchants. The cross-group effect also goes from merchants to cardholders.

Within this context, the Supreme Court was asked to decide on the appropriate antitrust framework to apply to markets involving platforms including (1) whether each side of a platform constitutes a separate relevant product market for the purposes of antitrust analysis and (2) what evidence is required to satisfy a plaintiff's *prima facie* burden under the rule of reason in the context of platforms. Two primary schools of thought have developed around these questions. While each school appears to agree in principle upon the relevant economic considerations in evaluating the competitive effects of conduct in multisided platforms, there are critical differences between the two schools when it comes to how courts and agencies should structure and sequence their analysis.

The first school argues that platforms should be assessed in a manner similar to single-sided markets in that each side should, ultimately, be considered separately — which we

---

10 U.S Department of Justice, Complaint for Equitable Relief in United States v. American Express, ¶123. See also *United States v. Am. Express Co.*, 88 F. Supp. 3d 143 (E.D.N.Y. 2015).

11 See *United States v. Am. Express Co.*, 838 F.3d 179 (2d Cir. 2016).

can label as the "separate markets" approach.[12] Further, harm to a group of consumers on one side of a platform should be sufficient to dispel the plaintiff's *prima facie* burden and, without more, establish an antitrust violation regardless of the effects on other consumer groups. We can label this as the "separate effects" approach, as it finds that any effect that makes a group worse off somewhere on a platform — for example, a price increase to merchants — is generally sufficient to show antitrust harm.[13] Thus, countervailing welfare gains for consumers on the other side of a platform would only be considered a "defense," and defendants would bear the burden of proof to establish that resulting efficiencies outweigh harm to the first group.

In contrast, the second school of thought argues that platforms are inherently defined by the interrelationships between their various sides and thus, product market definitions should generally include all sides of a platform. Thus, courts and agencies must explicitly consider cross-group effects when defining markets.[14] We can label this as the "integrated market" approach. For instance, American Express would be considered a platform that operates in a single product market.[15] Given this integrated market definition, it follows that finding harm to one side of a platform is insufficient to meet the *prima facie* burden and a proper competitive effects analysis must jointly consider all sides of a platform — which we can label as the "integrated effects" approach. This approach does not simply treat the other side of a platform as a potential consideration for an "efficiencies defense," capable of rebutting a showing of harm, but rather as a fundamental part of determining whether there is competitive harm of the type proscribed by the antitrust laws — that is, the acquisition or exercise of monopoly power — in the first place.

The stakes between the two schools of thought, as it relates to competitive effects and the *prima facie* burden, cannot be understated. Central to the issue of liability in rule-of-reason cases is the idea of "harm to competition." It is well understood that harm to a specific group of consumers does not necessarily establish cognizable antitrust harm. For instance, price discrimination harms some groups of consumers but benefits others — yet,

---

12 See, e.g. Katz & Sallet (2018), "Multisided Platforms and Antitrust Enforcement," *Yale Law Journal* 127, pp. 2142-2175; Conner, Gaynor, McFadden, Noll, Perloff, Stiglitz, White & Winter (2017), "Brief for Amici Curiae un Support of Petitioners in *Ohio et al. v. American Express Company*," and Brief of 28 Professors (2017), "Brief of 28 Professors of Antitrust Law as Amici Curiae Supporting Petitioners in *Ohio et al. v. American Express Company*." There is a general recognition, however, that cross-group effects must still be considered, to some degree, even if separate markets are defined. See, e.g. Katz & Sallet (2018). For a detailed overview of the two schools of thought, see Wright & Yun (2018), "Burdens and Balancing in Multisided Markets: The First Principles Approach of *Ohio et al. v. American Express*," *Review of Industrial Organization*, forthcoming.

13 See Brief of 28 Law Professors (2018) at 14.

14 See, e.g. Ratliff & Rubinfeld (2014), "Is There a Market for Organic Search Engine Results and Can Their Manipulation Give Rise to Antitrust Liability?," *Journal of Competition Law & Economics* 10, pp. 517-541.; Ward (2017) "Testing for Multisided Platform Effects in Antitrust Market Definition" *The University of Chicago Law Review* 84, pp. 2059-2012; Evans & Schmalensee (2018), "Brief for Amici Curiae Prof. David S. Evans and Prof. Richard Schmalensee in Support of Respondents in *Ohio et al. v. American Express Company*," and Sidak & Willig (2018), "Brief for Amici Curiae J. Gregory Sidak and Robert D. Willig in Support of Respondents in *Ohio et al. v. American Express Company*."

15 See Sidak & Willig (2018).

it is generally not the type of conduct that results in a restriction of market output and increase in market price.[16] Another example would be an efficient merger that drives out a less-efficient rival. In this case, consumers who preferred the differentiated product of the rival would be worse-off — although consumers, as a whole, are better off.[17] Thus, it is not extraordinary that decisions in competitive markets harm some group of consumers but benefit others. Indeed, it is a fundamental feature of competition when products are differentiated. Consequently, the focus of antitrust laws is to condemn conduct that improperly creates or maintains monopoly power. It is, thus, critical to make a distinction between harm to a group of consumers and "competitive harm" or "anticompetitive effects" cognizable by the antitrust laws. This is particularly relevant for multisided markets where there are two or more distinct group of consumers.

Within this setting, the Supreme Court fully affirmed the Second Circuit and endorsed the integrated market and integrated effects approach — as it applies to transaction platforms such as American Express. Justice Clarence Thomas, writing for the majority, observes, "[C]redit-card networks are best understood as supplying only one product—the transaction—that is jointly consumed by a cardholder and a merchant. Accordingly, the two-sided market for credit-card transactions should be analyzed as a whole."[18] Thus, "[i]n two-sided transaction markets, only one market should be defined."[19] Moreover, "[e]vidence of a price increase on one side of a two-sided transaction platform cannot by itself demonstrate an anticompetitive exercise of market power."[20]

American Express filled a large void in the understanding how courts will analyze analytical claims of potential anticompetitive conduct involving platforms. One area, however, that the Court did not fully address is whether the principles underlying its analysis apply, and if so, to what extent, to what it describes as "non-transaction platforms." This gap in the Court's decision has not gone unnoticed — with commentators offering speculations and conjectures as to the impact of the case on non-transaction platforms, such as Google and Facebook, in the future.[21] In the following section, we explain why there are sound economic reasons the Court's decision should apply to non-transaction platforms as well.

---

16 See Klein (1996), "Market Power in Aftermarkets," *Managerial and Decision Economics* 17, pp. 143-164 ("[M]arket power is not necessary for a firm to successfully engage in discriminatory pricing. All that is necessary is that the firm face a negatively sloped demand for its products, as all firms selling unique products do. Although such a negatively sloped demand and ability to price discriminate would not exist under the assumptions of perfect competition, it must be distinguished from the negatively sloped demand and ability to price discriminate that is present because a firm possesses a large share of the market, p. 155").

17 See Heyer (2012), "Welfare Standards and Merger Analysis: Why Not the Best?," *Competition Policy International* 8, pp. 146-172 at 155.

18 *Am. Express Co.* at 2 (Syllabus).

19 *Am. Express Co.* at 14 (citing to Filistrucchi *et al.* (2014), p. 302).

20 *Am. Express Co.* at 15.

21 See, e.g. Forbes.com, "Will the Supreme Court's Amex Decision Shield Dominant Tech Platforms from Antitrust Scrutiny," July 18, 2018 (available at https://www.forbes.com/sites/washingtonbytes/2018/07/18/antitrust-enforcement-of-dominant-tech-platforms-in-the-post-american-express-world).

III. THE COMMON ECONOMIC LOGIC OF TRANSACTION & NON-TRANSACTION PLATFORMS

Early in the development of the economic literature on platforms, researchers recognized that not all platforms share the same features — particularly as it relates to the size, strength, and direction of cross-group effects and the presence of direct network effects.[22] Evans (2003) makes a distinction between three types of multisided platforms: (1) "market-makers," (e.g. eBay, shopping malls) (2) "audience-makers," (e.g. online search engines, newspapers) and (3) "demand-coordinators" (e.g. video game consoles, payment cards).[23] For market-makers, a platform such as eBay is the mediator in the direct transaction between buyers and sellers. Similarly, demand-coordinators such as video game consoles are enabling various groups, e.g. gamers, game developers, and manufacturers of peripheral devices, to interact. Evans places payment card platforms in the demand-coordinators category; although, there does not appear to be a great deal of substantive difference between market-makers and demand-coordinators other than perhaps where the direct transaction occurs. For market-makers, the transaction occurs "on" the platform itself, e.g. buyers and sellers on eBay's webpage, while for demand-coordinators the transaction does not necessarily have to physically occur "on" the platform, e.g. video game sales can occur at a third-party retailer. Finally, for audience-makers, platforms match advertisers with users, who are attracted to the platform primarily through the provision of compelling content. Examples are advertising-supported media such online search engines, newspapers, yellow pages, and some social media.

Likely recognizing the closeness in concept between Evan's market-makers and demand-coordinators, Filistrucchi et al. (2014) use a simpler classification system: (1) transaction and (2) non-transaction platforms.[24] As the name implies, transaction platforms enable a direct transaction between two or more groups — which encompasses both Evans' "market-makers" and "demand-coordinators." Whereas, non-transaction platforms map with Evans' "audience-makers." This simpler classification is what the majority decision in *American Express* relied upon when it stated: "The key feature of transaction platforms is that they cannot make a sale to one side of the platform without simultaneously making a sale to the other."[25]

The question then becomes: what are the meaningful economic differences between transaction and non-transaction platforms? And from this, does the logic that the Court

---

[22] Unlike cross-group effects, direct network effects stay *within* a group and either increase or decrease the value to existing members of the group as more members join.

[23] See Evans (2003), "The Antitrust Economics of Multi-Sided Platform Markets," *Yale Journal on Regulation* 20, pp. 325-381 at 334-336.

[24] Klein *et al.* (2006) also made this distinction; although, they did not use the explicit nomenclature suggested by Filistrucchi *et al.*

[25] *Am. Express Co.* at 1.

used in defining an integrated market for transaction platforms extend to non-transaction platforms? More importantly, even if the Court suggests that non-transaction markets should be assessed as separate, non-integrated, markets, did the Court's reasoning suggest that the competitive effects should be materially different between the two types of platforms? We address these questions below.

First, the Court identifies the following distinction, relying upon Klein et al. (2006): "'Because cardholders and merchants jointly consume a single product, payment card transactions, their consumption of payment card transactions must be directly proportional.'"[26] In other words, for a transaction platform such as credit cards, merchants and cardholders share the same "quantity" since both sides are necessary to execute a transaction. In contrast, a non-transaction platform involves advertisers engaging with some users but not others — or during certain times but not at all times. For instance, the number of newspapers sold does not match one-for-one with the number of advertising "engagements" with readers, i.e. the number of ads read by a reader. While this is an important distinction, it can be overstated. For a non-transaction platform, the level of user consumption will be highly correlated with the level of advertising engagement. For example, the number of advertising clicks on a search engine will be highly correlated with the number of search users/queries. Similarly, the number of ads viewed on a television station will be highly correlated with the number of viewers. Consequently, the larger point still holds — that in order to understand the participation level for one side of a platform, it is still necessary to understand the participation level for the other side. Profit maximization still depends on a joint assessment of the pricing and volume on both sides.[27] Whether the volume on each side is a precise one-to-one matching or something highly correlated does not change this fundamental fact.

The second critical distinction the Court highlights, using the example of a newspaper, is that "indirect network effects operate in only one direction; newspaper readers are largely indifferent to the amount of advertising that a newspaper contains."[28] In other words, for a non-transaction platform, the cross-group effects are strong from the perspective of advertisers, in that their participation depends heavily on the size of the user group, whereas the cross-group effects from the perspective of users are generally weaker, zero — or even negative, depending on user preference for ads. While this is generally true for newspapers, it does not necessarily hold for other non-transaction platforms such as yellow pages, where readers explicitly use yellow pages to find advertisers.[29] Thus, importantly, non-transaction platforms are not uniform in the strength and direction of

---

26 *Am. Express Co.* at 13.

27 See Rochet & Tirole (2003), "Platform Competition in Two-Sided Markets," *Journal of European Economic Association* 1, pp. 990-1029.

28 *Am. Express Co.* at 12.

29 Although, some readers can be interested in advertisements in certain sections of a newspaper, e.g. classifieds, or during certain times of the year, e.g. Memorial Day sales

the cross-group effects. While the Court certainly did not imply that all non-transaction platforms are the same, the sole use of newspapers to illustrate the point could create some confusion. Thus, the important economic take-away is to focus on the strength and direction of the cross-group effects rather than determining whether there is a direct transaction or not.

A third distinction that the Court identified is that "only other two-sided platforms can compete with a two-sided platform for transactions."[30] As a corollary, the Court states, "Non-transaction platforms, by contrast, often do compete with companies that do not operate on both sides of their platform."[31] As an example, the Court stated that "[a] newspaper that sells advertising, for example, might have to compete with a television network, even though the two do not meaningfully compete for viewers."[32] Is it correct that transaction platforms only compete with other transaction platforms? The Court appears to make an error in this distinction. For instance, Uber is a transaction platform that competes with non-platforms, to one degree or another, including taxis, subways, and buses — as well as with other platforms such as Lyft. The same holds for Airbnb, which compete with non-platforms such as hotels and owner-rentals. Even for American Express, alternative payment methods that arguably compete with payment cards include debit cards, checks, and cash, which are not multisided platforms. The Court's point regarding non-transaction platforms, however, is correct. Non-transaction platforms can involve advertisers who are relatively indifferent to the actual content of a platform — be it search results, news stories, social media feeds — as long as it has the intended effect of informing the consumer about their products. Consequently, from an advertiser's perspective, at some level search engines compete with social networks, other online sites, and even, potentially, offline advertising including newspapers, radio, and television. If this is the primary point that the Court was making, the implications could be profound for future antitrust cases involving non-transaction platforms and allegations of competitive harm to advertisers. Specifically, given this precedent, the relevant product market is credibly broader than just the specific type of media platform, e.g. a search engine-only market would be rejected as too narrow.

Given these distinctions, particularly as it relates to cross-group effects, the Court finds that "[a] market should be treated as one [or single] sided when the impacts of indirect network effects and relative pricing in that market are minor."[33] Thus, again using newspapers as an example, "the market for newspaper advertising behaves much like a one-sided market and should be analyzed as such."[34] While the Court used newspa-

---

30 *Am. Express Co.* at 14.

31 *Am. Express Co.* at footnote 9.

32 *Am. Express Co.* at footnote 9.

33 *Am. Express Co.* at 12.

34 *Am. Express Co.* at 12-13.

pers to illustrate this point, again, it is not a point that solely applies to non-transaction platforms.[35] Transaction platforms could also have weak cross-group effects. A potential example is Amazon Marketplace, which brings together third-party sellers with potential buyers. It is conceivable that the cross-group effect from third-party sellers to buyers, on Amazon, is relatively unimportant — rather what is more important to buyers is the fact that Amazon itself sells many of the items that they are looking for.[36] Again, it is the strength and direction of the cross-group effects that distinguish platforms from single-sided markets; consequently, that should be the primary focus in determining whether to define separate or integrated markets — given that both transaction and non-transaction platforms can have strong or weak cross-group effects. Wright & Yun (2018) discuss the strengths and weaknesses of the integrated or separate approach to market definition as it relates to non-transaction platforms. However, the critical implication of this distinction is not a matter of market definition, but competitive effects analysis.

Regardless of whether one or two relevant product markets are defined, an integrated approach to competitive effects analysis is the only approach that satisfies the requirements for a finding of anticompetitive harm as understood by the antitrust laws. The economic logic of the majority in *American Express* applies with as much force to non-transaction platforms, whether or not separate relevant markets are defined: "Evidence of a price increase on one side of a two-sided transaction platform cannot by itself demonstrate an anticompetitive exercise of market power."[37] The economic literature has clearly established the interrelationship between the two-sides of a platform in profit maximization.[38] Consequently, we cannot seek to assess market power when only half of the profit maximization equation is considered as relevant evidence to establish anticompetitive harm. The reason is that the very definition of the exercise of monopoly power — the reduction of market-wide output and increase in the market price — cannot be satisfied by evidence of a price effect on only one side of a given platform. Thus, the *prima facie* burden must necessarily involve an assessment of both sides of a platform. A price change on one-side of a platform can imply an increase, decrease, or neutral change in market-wide welfare. What matters is the structure of the interrelated relative prices — not the price levels themselves.[39] This interrelationship between the prices on both sides of a platform is one of the most fundamental findings in the now well-established economic literature on platforms.

---

35 *Am. Express Co.* at 12.

36 Of course, it is an empirical matter to determine this with certainty. The point is that there is nothing that *conceptually* prevents the possibility that a transaction platform has weak cross-group effects going in one direction.

37 *Am. Express Co.* at 15.

38 See, e.g. Rochet & Tirole (2003) and Klein, Lerner, Murphy & Plache (2006), "Competition in Two-Sided Markets: The Antitrust Economics of Payment Card Interchange Fees," *Antitrust Law Journal* 73, pp. 571-626.

39 See Rochet & Tirole (2006), "Two-Sided Markets: A Progress Report," *RAND Journal of Economics* 37, pp. 645-667 at 646.

Proponents of a separate market and separate effects approach suggest that potential, pro-competitive effects on a specific group can be assessed in a burden shifting step two of the rule-of-reason framework. We find that severing the two halves of a platform and then, subsequently, trying to piece them back to together in terms of an efficiencies defense is inadequate and likely to generate significant error. As discussed, competitive effects analysis under the antitrust laws requires the plaintiff to show that harm to a group of consumers is caused by conduct that creates or maintains monopoly power. An approach that artificially bifurcates sides of the market for the purpose of answering that funda-mental antitrust question is incapable of fulfilling this objective.

IV. CONCLUSION

The Court's guidance on multisided platforms settled a number of issues in regard to defining relevant product markets and assessing competitive effects. The Court, however, left open the potential that the ruling is narrowly aimed at specific types of platforms — namely, transaction platforms. We argue that the Court's distinctions between transac-tion and non-transaction platforms do not, nor should they, prohibit the application of the economic logic to the ruling on non-transaction platforms. Moreover, even if separate relevant product markets are defined for non-transaction platforms, an integrated effects analysis is the only proper approach in all platform settings, including the non-transac-tional platform analysis seemingly left unresolved by the Court.

FREE OR FEE?: THE ECONOMICS OF ADVERTISING SUPPORT v. DIRECT PAYMENTS FOR MEDIA CONTENT

By Christopher S. Yoo[1]

ABSTRACT

The print and video industries are taking widely divergent paths online. While the print industry typically offers its content for free and has faced serious obstacles in its attempts to augment advertising revenue with subscription fees, the video industry tends to rely heavily on direct payments from viewers. This Chapter explores the economic literature on the choice between advertising support and direct payments, beginning with the early economic literature that emphasizes that on the one hand, advertising support more closely approximates marginal cost pricing, while on the other hand, advertising support resembles a voting regime which is thus vulnerable to certain well-known potential market failures. It then reviews the modern theoretical and empirical analyses to identify the features that determine the choice between fee and free. It closes with some observations about competition policy issues surrounding advertising support, including the irrelevance of network effects and the competitiveness of the advertising industry.

I. INTRODUCTION

One of the most dramatic changes in media markets in the transition from offline to online distribution has been the radical shift from fee-based models to free, or more properly advertising-supported, models. This change is the most striking for the newspapers, which find the historical business model that relied on a mix of subscription and advertising revenue largely being supplanted by an online distribution model that relies exclusively on advertising, despite the efforts of many leading newspapers to reverse this trend. Online video, in contrast, seems to be following a different path. Although early video distribution was dominated by free services such as YouTube, pay television sys-

---

1 John H. Chestnut Professor of Law, Communication, and Computer & Information Science and the Founding Director of the Center for Technology, Innovation, and Competition University of Pennsylvania.

tems such as Netflix, Amazon Prime, and Hulu have become industry leaders. Although initially reluctant to do so, YouTube has responded by introducing advertising and later adding a pay system known as YouTube Red, later renamed YouTube Premium.

That two such parallel industries would take such different paths presents something of a puzzle. Fortunately, a largely overlooked economic literature exists exploring the relative merits of relying on direct payments and advertising support. Although it does not yet answer the question why video is characterized by direct payments, while the former print media is somewhat reluctantly being forced to rely almost exclusively on advertising support, this literature helps shed light on the factors determining when each regime is socially optimal. This chapter will explore this literature and offer a few observations to debunk some basic misunderstandings about the competition policy concerns raised by advertising support.

II. THE EARLY ECONOMIC LITERATURE

The choice for supporting the production of media content through advertising support versus and direct payments has drawn economists' attention for over half a century. The early literature focused largely on two opposing considerations. On the one hand, advertising support benefits consumers by providing a way to price content at marginal cost even when marginal cost is zero. On the other hand, advertising support is less effective at eliciting audiences' preferences for content.

A. *Advertising Support and Marginal Cost Pricing*

According to the early literature, advertising support's primary economic virtue is that it offers a solution to the marginal cost pricing problem that inevitably plagues media markets.[2] In the second of his seminal articles that laid the foundation for public good economics, Nobel Laureate Paul Samuelson mused that the emerging technology of descramblers, which enabled broadcasters to turn advertising-supported television into pay television, would violate the "well-known optimum principle that goods should be priced at their marginal costs," asking rhetorically "[f]or what, after all, are the true marginal costs of having one extra family tune in on the program? They are literally zero. Why then prevent any family which would receive positive pleasure from tuning in on the program from doing so?"[3]

Some scholars looked at this statement in isolation and concluded that Samuelson fa-

---

2   See generally Christopher S. Yoo, *Rethinking the Commitment to Free, Local Television*, 52 EMORY L.J. 1579, 1628–32, 1677–82 (2003) [hereinafter Yoo, *Free, Local Television*]; Christopher S. Yoo, *Architectural Censorship and the FCC*, 78 S. CAL. L. REV. 669, 676–83 (2005) [hereinafter Yoo, *Architectural Censorship*].

3   Paul A. Samuelson, *Aspects of Public Expenditure Theories*. 40 REV. ECON. & STAT. 332, 335 (1958).

vored advertising-supported television over pay television.[4] Indeed, Jora Minasian offered precisely this interpretation of Samuelson in his well-known colloquy with Samuelson.[5] As an initial matter, the fact that advertising imposes nuisance costs on audiences raises some doubts whether advertising support should be regarded as true marginal cost pricing. These nuisance costs may offset any benefits of being charged a lower (even a zero) price.[6] At the same time, advertising can also yield informational benefits.[7]

Even if one disregards the potential benefits and nuisance costs of advertising, Minasian's primary argument is that while pricing at marginal cost would allocate the existing goods so as to maximize static efficiency, it would provide no guidance as to how many resources should be allocated to producing the goods in the first place.[8] This in turn prompted a somewhat testy response from Samuelson arguing that he had never expressed a blanket opposition to pay television and that he recognized the marginal cost pricing's inability to answer questions of resource allocation when marginal cost is zero, which Minasian in turn acknowledged.[9]

A close inspection of Samuelson's writings reveals that he has the better of the argument.[10] Samuelson's prior writing explicitly noted that public goods, such as television programming, face difficulties that would remain even if the problems associated with nonmarginal cost pricing were somehow solved.[11] Specifically, Samuelson identified an additional necessary condition for efficient provision of public goods now known as the Samuelson condition: That the marginal rate of transformation (roughly the equivalent of the marginal cost of producing a public good of a particular size) should equal the sum of the marginal rates of substitution of all users (roughly equivalent to the sum of the marginal benefits to all users).[12] The essential problem is that each person's marginal benefit is private information and no mechanism has yet been devised that can induce people to reveal that information truthfully.[13] Although scholars have put forth a number

---

4 See, e.g., Michael Spence & Bruce Owen, *Television Programming, Monopolistic Competition, and Welfare*, 91 Q.J. Econ. 103, 104 (1977).

5 Jora R. Minasian, *Television Pricing and the Theory of Public Goods*, 7 J.L. & Econ. 71, 72 (1964). For commentary on this debate, see James M. Buchanan, *Public Goods in Theory and Practice: A Note on the Minasian-Samuelson Debate*, 10 J.L. & Econ. 193 (1967); Björn Frank, *Making Economics Exciting by Constructing a Quasi-Debate: The Samuelson-Minasian Controversy*, 29 J. Econ. Educ. 41 (1998).

6 Chris Doyle, *Programming in a Competitive Broadcasting Market: Entry, Welfare and Regulation*, 10 Info. Econ. & Pol'y 23, 33–34 (1998).

7 Yoo, *Free, Local Television, supra* note 2, at 1630.

8 Minasian, *supra* note 5, at 73–74.

9 Paul A. Samuelson, *Public Goods and Subscription TV: Correction of the Record*, 7 J.L. & Econ. 81, 82–83 (1964); Minasian, *supra* note 5, at 80.

10 See generally Christopher S. Yoo, *Copyright and Public Goods: A Misunderstood Relation*, 155 U. Pa. L. Rev. 635 (2007).

11 Samuelson, *supra* note 3, at 335–36.

12 *Id.* at 334.

13 *Id.* at 334, 336; *Paul A. Samuelson, The Pure Theory of Public Expenditure*, 36 Rev. Econ. & Stat. 387, 388 (1954).

of innovative mechanisms designed to induce consumers to reveal their true marginal valuations, all of these proposals have their limitations.[14]

B. Advertising as an Imperfect Signal of Users' Preferences

The foregoing discussion reveals that the choice between relying on adverting support and direct payments for media is inherently an exercise in comparative second best analysis.[15] The allocative efficiency benefits associated with advertising support must be traded off against the need to price above marginal cost in order to generate some revenue. Even if the marginal cost pricing problem were solved through Ramsey pricing, a prize system, or some other alternative institutional arrangement, the efficient provision of public goods like media content would still depend on identifying some mechanism for determining the optimal level of investment to create the content.

One of the problems with relying on advertising to support media is that advertising represents an imperfect signal of users' preferences for the media content in which the advertisement is placed.[16] Advertising support means that the total revenue that media receives is determined by viewers' and listeners' responsiveness to the advertising contained within programs, not by their preferences for the underlying programs themselves. There is no necessary relationship between audiences' responsiveness to advertising and their preferences for the underlying programs.[17]

The indirectness of the signal associated with advertising-support is exacerbated by the fact that advertising support in essence represents a voting mechanism.[18] As James Buchanan & Gordon Tullock noted in their landmark work, The Calculus of Consent, voting mechanisms limit people to indicating the direction of their preferences without providing them with any way to express the intensity of their preferences.[19] If those opposing a proposal have stronger preferences against it than those supporting it have in favor of it, a measure may be passed even when doing so is socially detrimental.[20] These problems disappear when voting is replaced by a price mechanism.[21] When direct payments are possible, audiences

---

14 See Yoo, *supra* note 10, at 639 & nn.12–13 (citing the relevant literature).

15 Spence & Owen, supra *note* 4, at 104–05.

16 Yoo, *Free, Local Television, supra* note 2, at 1678; Yoo, *Architectural Censorship, supra* note 2, at 679.

17 See Minasian, *supra* note 5, at 74–75 (finding no theory or empirical evidence indicating that advertising support would yield the same revenue as direct payments).

18 Yoo, *Free, Local Television, supra* note 2, at 1677–79; Yoo, *Architectural Censorship, supra* note 2, at 681.

19 JAMES M. BUCHANAN & GORDON TULLOCK, THE CALCULUS OF CONSENT: LOGICAL FOUNDATIONS OF CONSTITUTIONAL DEMOCRACY 152 (1962).

20 *Id.* at 126-27.

21 A voting regime can be turned into a de facto price mechanism by permitting side payments or related proxies such as vote trading and log rolling. *Id.* at 152–58; see also William H. Oakland, *Theory of Public Goods, in* 2 HANDBOOK OF PUBLIC ECONOMICS 486, 528 (Alan J. Auerbach & Martin Feldstein eds., 1987) (underscoring "the fundamental difficulty of the voting rule – people are unable to express the intensity of their preferences" and observing that "[i]ntensity of preference can be introduced into the voting mechanism by explicitly or implicit vote trading").

with intense preferences can still support the creation of content by signaling the strength of their desire for that content by paying higher prices. This allows products to be sustainable even when the number of customers who prefer them are small in number, in much the way that low-volume boutique goods survive by targeting the niche of customers with the strongest desires for a particular type of goods and charging them a premium for them.

The economic literature has long recognized the similarity between voting mechanisms and advertising support.[22] Revenue under advertising support is determined by audiences' responsiveness to the advertising, which makes revenue increase largely linearly with audience size.[23] A small audience will generate a fairly small amount of advertising revenue no matter how much they are willing to pay for particular content. The literature on voting confirms that advertising support is likely to reduce the amount of revenue that content is able to generate. This burden is likely to weigh especially heavily on diverse programming that appeals strongly to small audiences.[24]

There is one way in which advertising revenue is not purely a function of audience size. Some demographic groups are more desirable to advertisers and thus generate more revenue per capita, which implies that tailoring can increase the amount of revenue generated by advertising.[25] But these differences are a matter of status, not individual actions: Revenue is still determined by audience size, now metered by the size of particular subgroups of the audience rather than the entire audience as a whole.

The empirical literature has confirmed these theoretical predictions. Studies conducted during the primacy of broadcast television consistently found that advertisers place a significantly lower value on content than do viewers.[26] Other studies have confirmed that pay television generates more revenue than advertising support.[27] Alternatively, the ability to target

---

22 See, e.g., Minasian, *supra* note 5, at 75.

23 *Turner Broad. Sys. v. FCC*, 520 U.S. 180, 208–09 (1997) (collecting empirical research confirming the "direct correlation [between] size in audience and station [advertising] revenues" (alterations in original and internal quotation marks omitted)).

24 Minasian, *supra* note 5, at 75; Spence & Owen, *supra* note 4, at 113.

25 Franklin M. Fisher, John J. McGowan & David S. Evans, *The Audience-Revenue Relationship for Local Television Stations*, 11 BELL J. ECON. 694 (1980).

26 See ROGER G. NOLL, MERTON J. PECK & JOHN J. MCGOWAN, ECONOMIC ASPECTS OF TELEVISION REGULATION 23 (1973) (estimating that viewers were willing to pay seven times more for television programming than were advertisers); Harvey J. Levin, *Program Duplication, Diversity, and Effective Viewer Choices: Some Empirical Findings*, 61 AM. ECON. REV. 81, 82, 88 (1971) (concluding that entry by pay television supported more informational programming and other special interest programming than would advertising-supported television); Spence & Owen, *supra* note 4, at 118–19 (drawing on the Noll-Peck-McGowan data to show that reliance on advertising support was suppressing the emergence of a fourth television network). Although other economists have quibbled with the precise size of this disparity, they do not dispute the fundamental conclusion that consumers are willing to pay far more for television than advertisers. See Stanley M. Besen & Bridger M. Mitchell, *Noll, Peck, and McGowan's* Economic Aspects of Television Regulation, 5 BELL J. ECON. & MGMT. SCI. 301, 308–11 (1974) (book review); Bryan Ellickson, *Hedonic Theory and the Demand for Cable Television*, 69 AM. ECON. REV. 183, 188–89 (1979).

27 Claus Thustrup Hansen & Søren Kyhl, *Pay-Per-View Broadcasting of Outstanding Events: Consequences of a Ban*, 19 INT'L J. INDUS. ORG. 589, 590, 601, 604 (2001); Steinar Holden, *Network or Pay-Per-View?: A Welfare Analysis*, 43 ECON. LETTERS 59, 62–64 (1993).

advertising at preferred demographic groups that are the most responsive to certain types of advertising also enhances revenue, although the ability to do so is somewhat limited.[28]

III. THE MODERN ECONOMIC LITERATURE

In the wake of these early writings, a modern economic literature has emerged exploring the choice between direct payments and advertising support as the means for financing content. This research has only begun to scratch the surface of these issues, but still provides useful insights into the key drivers underlying the choice between advertising support and direct payments.

A. *Theoretical Models*

A number of theoretical models have attempted to identify the factors that determine whether advertising support or a direct payment model would provide greater benefits to society. For example, Prasad, Mahajan & Bronnenberg put forward a simple model in which the media providers set the level of two key variables: Subscription price and advertising level. They also expanded the available policy options: instead of framing the decision as an either-or choice between exclusive reliance on advertising support and exclusive reliance on direct payments, they also considered a range of intermediate options that combined subscription fees with advertising and allowed viewers to pay a higher price in return for having to watch fewer advertisements.[29] Although they identified cases in which relying exclusively on advertising support or direct payments would be optimal, they generally found that the optimal strategy is to present viewers with a range of options that combine direct payments and advertising.[30]

Anderson & Coate offered an influential model that focused on the impact of the nuisance cost of advertising and variations in preferences for different program types and used that model to compare economic welfare under advertising support and direct payments.[31] Under advertising support, the number of advertisements and variety of programming can fall above or below the social optimum depending on how much viewers regard advertising as a nuisance.[32] The key insight is that the nuisance cost of advertisements is an externality that broadcasters do not internalize unless and until they induce viewers to stop watching.[33] Direct pricing forces broadcasters to internalize that externality.[34] Although direct payments

---

[28] Ronald Goettler, *Advertising Rates, Audience Composition, and Competition in the Network Television Industry* (working paper, 2012), http://goettler.simon.rochester.edu/research/papers/adrates.pdf.

[29] Ashutosh Prasad, Vijay Mahajan & Bart Bronnenberg, *Advertising versus Pay-per-View in Electronic Media*, 20 INT'L J. RES. MKTG. 13 (2003).

[30] *Id.* at 24.

[31] Simon P. Anderson & Stephen Coate, *Market Provision of Broadcasting: A Welfare Analysis*, 72 REV. ECON. STUD. 947 (2005).

[32] *Id.* at 957–59.

[33] *Id.* at 950, 970.

[34] *Id.* at 953, 958, 962.

often facilitate an increase in welfare, there are circumstances in which they can have the opposite effect. Under Anderson & Coate's model, direct payments can reduce welfare if the number of programs does not increase, prices induce some viewers to switch off, or pricing induces a wasteful increase in programming.[35]

Peitz & Valletti extended Anderson & Coate's work, providing a model that similarly took as its main variables audiences' dislike for advertising and preferences for certain types of programming.[36] With respect to welfare, they found that the choice between advertising support and direct payments to be a complex question whose answer depended on both viewers' dislike for advertising and their dislike for viewing content that deviated from their preferences.[37] Thus, although early indications suggested that direct payments would consistently perform better than advertising support, closer inspection revealed that that was sometimes, but not always, the case.[38]

Finally, Halbheer et al. examine the intermediate case between pure direct payments and pure advertising support in which content providers allow users free access to a limited number of free samples without paying for them, in much the same way that the New York Times and the Washington Post are currently operating.[39] The optimal strategy depends on the effectiveness of advertising. If it is low, content providers should rely on direct payments. If it is high, content providers should rely on advertising support. If it falls somewhere in between, content providers should offer a mix of both by permitting sampling.[40]

These theoretical analyses help identify the factors that are driving the choice between advertising support and direct payments. They also indicate that the relationship among these factors is complex and will require more analysis before it can provide clear guidance as to which regime to adopt.

B. Empirical Studies

Like the theoretical literature, the empirical literature is somewhat ambiguous as to whether economic welfare would be better served under advertising support or direct payments. On the one hand, some studies favor direct payment models. For example, Pauwels & Weiss find that a firm found it profitable to shift from an advertising-based model to a

---

33 *Id.* at 950, 970.

34 *Id.* at 953, 958, 962.

35 *Id.* at 963–64.

36 Martin Peitz & Tomasso M. Valletti, *Content and Advertising in the Media: Pay-TV versus Free-to-Air*, 26 Int'l J. Indus. Org. 949 (2008).

37 *Id.* at 958–60.

38 *Id.* at 949–50.

39 David Halbheer et al., *Choose a Digital Content Strategy: How Much Should Be Free?*, 31 Int'l J. Res. Mktg. 192 (2014).

40 *Id.* at 193, 198–99.

fee-based model.[41] The direct payments more than offset the reduction in subscriptions caused by the price, the concomitant reduction in advertising revenue and the effectiveness of marketing communication caused by the reduction in audience size, and the diversion of recruitment efforts towards recruiting fee-paying customers.[42]

On the other hand, other studies suggest that advertising support yields special economic benefits. Some experiments have found that users seem to place a particularly high value on goods priced at zero.[43] In addition, Chiou & Tucker found that the introduction of paywalls by three local newspapers reduced visits by the overall population by 51 percent and reduced visits by 18–24-year olds by a stunning 99 percent.[44]

To the extent that advertising support understates audience preferences for content, allowing advertisers to target their advertisements to those customers most likely to be interested in their products would help close the gap. As Evans noted, online advertising allows for much more accurate targeting of the customers who are the most likely to purchase than was permitted by traditional media.[45] And the empirical evidence suggests that such targeting is quite effective. Goldfarb & Tucker's study of the 2002 implementation of the EU's Data Protection Directive found that preventing the targeting of online display advertising reduced purchase intent by two thirds.[46] Deng & Mela find that revenue increases still further when advertisements are targeted at individual devices rather than being targeted at viewers of particular content.[47] This implies that the targeting of advertisements can help bring the revenue generated by advertising closer to welfare maximizing levels.

IV. COMPETITIVE CONSIDERATIONS

In addition to questions regarding advertising support's institutional capability to promote economic welfare, some scholars have suggested that advertising support is prone to certain types of anticompetitive activity. A close examination of the basis of those claims raises serious doubts as to whether advertising support is susceptible to the network effects usually cited as the basis for the necessary market power. In addition, practices such as multi-homing and the substitutability of different types of advertising effectively dissipate any such concerns.

---

41 Koen Pauwels & Allen Weiss, *Moving from Free to Fee: How Online Firms Market to Change Their Business Model Successfully*, 72 J. MKTG. 14, 25 (2008).

42 *Id.* at 16.

43 Kristina Shampanier, Nina Mazar & Dan Ariely, *Zero as a Special Price: The True Value of Free Products*, 26 MKTG. SCI. 742 (2007); Eva Ascarza, Anja Lambrecht & Naufel Vilcassim, *When Talk Is "Free": The Effect of Tariff Structure on Usage Under Two- and Three-Part Tariffs*, 49 J. MKTG. RES. 882 (2012).

44 Lesley Chiou & Catherine Tucker, *Paywalls and the Demand for News*, 25 INFO. ECON. & POL'Y 61 (2013).

45 David S. Evans, *The Online Advertising Industry: Economics, Evolution and Privacy*, J. ECON. PERSP., SUMMER 2009, at 37, 43.

46 Avi Goldfarb & Catherine E. Tucker, *Privacy Regulation and Online Advertising*, 57 MGMT. SCI. 57, 65 (2011).

47 Yiting Deng & Carl F. Mela, *TV Viewing and Advertising Targeting*, 55 J. MKTG. RES. 99 (2018).

A. Network Effects as a Questionable Source of Market Power

Some scholars have asserted that advertising-driven businesses benefit from network effects that turn them into winner-take-all markets in which larger companies have an insuperable competitive advantage.[48] Such arguments suffer from two problems. First, the fact that the value of advertising support grows linearly with network size undercuts any claims that advertising support yields the unusual demand-side scale economies associated with network effects. The insight is best understood by looking at Metcalfe's Law, which is often identified as the theoretical foundation for network effects.[49] Metcalfe pointed out that the number of connections increases quadratically with the number of nodes, with the number of connections equaling (n2–n)/2, as depicted graphically in Figure 1 in which doubling the network size more than doubles the number of connections. If each connection adds equal value, Metcalfe's Law implies that the value of the network will increase quadratically with network size as well. This contrasts with a previously elucidated principle known as Sarnoff's Law, which predicted that network value would increase linearly with network size. If value increases quadratically with the number of nodes and the costs of adding more nodes increases linearly, large players would be given decisive advantages that would increase geometrically as the platform grows.

Figure 1: Metcalfe's Law

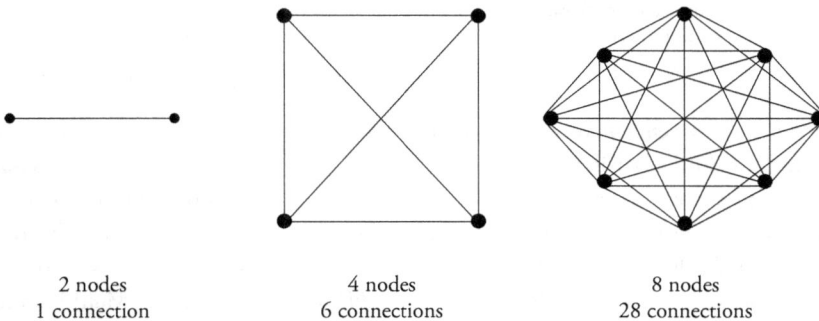

2 nodes	4 nodes	8 nodes
1 connection	6 connections	28 connections

Source: Yoo, *supra* note 49, at 92 fig.1.

---

48 For a recent example, see Jonathan M. Barnett, *The Costs of Free: Commoditization, Bundling and Concentration*, 14 J. INSTITUTIONAL ECON. 1097, 1109-10, 1111 (2018) (initially limiting network effects on platforms with social functions, but later extending the argument to include media distribution platforms such as YouTube).

49 Bob Metcalfe, *Metcalfe's Law After 40 Years of Ethernet*, COMPUTER, Dec. 2013, at 26. See generally Christopher S. Yoo, *Moore's Law, Metcalfe's Law, and Optimal Interoperability*, 14 COLO. TECH. L.J. 87, 91–94 (2015).

This reasoning is vulnerable to several critiques that I have stated in my earlier work.[50] For purposes of this Chapter, it bears emphasizing that the sources of increase in value associated with Metcalfe's Law do not apply to advertising. Specifically, the quadratic growth in the number of connections (and the purported accompanying quadratic increase in value) is the product of the increasing internal connections among different network participants. Advertisers care only about the total number of potential customers they can reach; the number of internal connections among viewers does not matter. Instead of the quadratic growth associated with Metcalfe's Law, advertising support are more associated with the linear growth in value associated with an alternative principle known as Sarnoff's Law.

Figure 2: The Inapplicability of Metcalfe's Law to Advertising

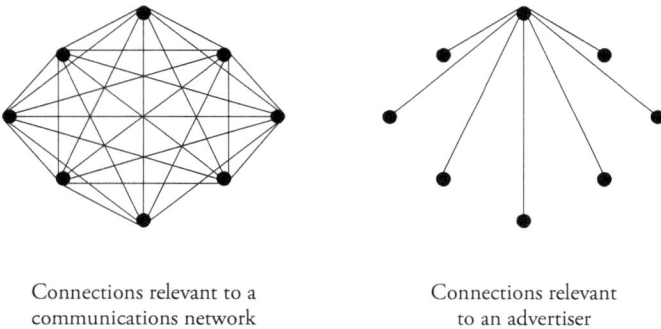

Connections relevant to a
communications network

Connections relevant
to an advertiser

There is an independent reason to question whether network effects inevitably cause markets based on advertising support to collapse into monopolies. The winner-take-all dynamic presumes that viewers will join one and only one network. Thus, in choosing one network, a viewer necessarily rejects all of the others. In many network industries, users join multiple networks, a practice known as multi-homing, as is the case with online video, in which the average user subscribes to 2.5 different video services.[51] Multi-homing eliminates the winner-take-all dynamic, as users' decisions to join one network do not preclude them from joining others as well.[52]

---

50 The primary critique is that not all connections are of equal value, and variations in valuations and diminishing marginal returns necessarily mean that at some point the addition of further links will not yield significant value. Yoo, *supra* note 49, at 96–100. In short, assuming that value will grow quadratically forever is the quintessence of a pyramid scheme.

51 Jeff Ewing, *Market Research Highlights Netflix's Continued Dominance of the SVOD Market*, FORBES (Dec. 10, 2018, 12:01 p.m.), https://www.forbes.com/sites/jeffewing/2018/12/10/netflix-continues-svod-market-dominance/#2464dc-5d2ea6.

52 Stanley M. Besen et al., *Advances in Routing Technologies and Internet Peering Agreements*, 91 AM. ECON. REV. (PAPERS & PROC.) 292, 294-95 (2001).

B. *The Substitutability of Different Types of Advertising*

Even if advertising support were to lead to a handful of dominant online firms, whether such dominance would harm consumers depends on the substitutability of different types of advertising. Although it is tempting to define different online functions, such as search engines and social networks, as distinct product markets, the fact that the services that these companies provide to end users are unpriced renders arguments that their actions would reduce consumer welfare highly implausible. The only customers who are paying positive prices to these companies are advertisers. So long as the different types of online and offline advertising serve as substitutes for one another, the market for advertising will remain fairly competitive, which in turn makes consumer harm is in this market unlikely as well.

Common sense suggests that advertisers are likely to regard different forms of advertising as substitutes. Advertisers' real interest is in generating sales. They typically do not care which advertising medium is used to generate those sales. The empirical record is very nascent and rather mixed, but on balance leans towards regarding online and offline advertising as substitutes. For example, Goldfarb & Tucker used two different methodologies to find that advertisers regard online and offline advertising as substitutes.[53] Zentner found a similar substitution effect between Internet advertising and print and television advertising, although he did not find a similar substitution effect for radio.[54] In contrast, He, Lopez & Liu found that online advertising was not a substitute for television and print advertising between 2005 and 2011, but that the data showed that online advertising was increasingly acting as a substitute for traditional media towards the end of their study.[55] If those trends continued, it is likely that the latter study would regard online and offline advertising as substitutes as of today.

If one regards the different types of advertising as substitutes, then the advertising market is likely to be quite competitive. Consider Table 1, which presents the most recent data on national advertising reported by the Federal Communications Commission ("FCC"). The entire sector of Internet advertising accounted for only 22 percent of national advertising. Even if the Internet advertising industry consisted of only two firms who divided that segment between them, it would not represent the level of concentration associated with market power.

---

53 Avi Goldfarb & Catherine Tucker, *Advertising Bans and the Substitutability of Online and Offline Advertising*, 48 J. Mktg. Res. 207 (2011); Avi Goldfarb & Catherine Tucker, *Search Engine Advertising: Substitution When Pricing Ads to Context*, 57 Mgmt. Sci. 458 (2011).

54 Alejandro Zentner, *Internet Adoption and Advertising Expenditures on Traditional Media: An Empirical Analysis Using a Panel of Countries*, 21 J. Econ. & Mgmt. Strategy 913 (2012).

55 Xi He, Rigoberto Lopez & Yizao Liu, *Are Online and Offline Advertising Substitutes or Complements? Evidence from U.S. Food Industries*, 15 J. Agric. & Food Indus. Org. (2017), https://doi.org/10.1515/jafio-2017-0031.

Table 2 reports the same data for local advertising. In this case, digital advertising represents 31 percent of all advertising. While larger, these are not the levels of concentration typically associated with market power.

If these different forms of advertising serve as substitutes for one another, as the empirical evidence appears to indicate, it is hard to see how online advertisers can harm consumers harm. It is true that the nature of certain types of advertisement may limit advertisers to a particular outlet. But the fact that a small subsegment of the advertiser community may be locked in is not a general reason to assume that every part of the online advertising ecosystem is doomed to market concentration and failure.

Table 1: 2015 National Advertising by Sector ($ millions)

Sector	Revenue	Percentage
Digital (Internet/Mobile)	$33,656	22%
Cable Networks & VOD	$28,190	18%
Broadcast Networks	$18,334	12%
Broadcast Television Stations	$6,749	4%
Barter Syndication	$3,089	2%
Radio	$2,675	2%
Daily Newspaper	$2,737	2%
DBS	$1,043	1%
Radio Network	$1,018	1%
Satellite Radio	$117	0%
Other	$55,617	36%
Total	**$153,224**	**100%**

Source: Annual Assessment of the Status of Competition in the Market for the Delivery of Video Programming, Eighteenth Report, 32 FCC Rcd. 568, 618 tbl.III.B.6 (2017).

Table 2: 2015 Local Advertising by Sector ($ millions)

Sector	Revenue	Percentage
Digital (Internet/Mobile)	$23,629	31%
Daily Newspaper	$12,700	17%
Broadcast Television Stations	$12,130	16%
Radio	$10,576	14%
Cable Television	$4,817	6%
Regional Sports Networks	$1,197	2%
Telco	$718	1%
Other	$9,563	13%
Total	**$74,970**	**100%**

Source: Annual Assessment of the Status of Competition in the Market for the Delivery of Video Programming, Eighteenth Report, 32 FCC Rcd. 568, 617 tbl.III.B.5 (2017).

V. CONCLUSION

What does the scholarship on the choice between advertising support and direct payments teach us about the current environment? The early literature appeared to suggest that advertising support is more efficiently priced, while pay television is better at reflecting the intensity of consumers' preferences for content. Neither approach provides a workable mechanism for determining how many resources to devote to content production. More recent analyses suggest that the choice between the two regimes should depend on factors such as the magnitude of the nuisance cost of advertising, audiences' taste for diverse content, and the effectiveness of the advertising. Whether these specific factors explain the current divergence of approaches in the print and video industries exceeds the scope of this Chapter except to observe that all three areas are likely to differ under advertising support and direct payments.

The foregoing analysis also shows the dangers of glibly assuming that reliance on advertising support will lead to market failure. As an initial matter, there is no reason to believe that advertising is characterized by the quadratic relationship between value and network size often regarded as the foundation for network effects. In addition, institutional realities such as the opportunity for multi-homing and the ability of other forms of advertising to serve as substitutes for online advertising effectively dissipate the likelihood that relying on advertising support will necessarily reduce economic welfare.

AUSTRALIA'S MEDIA INDUSTRY IN THE DIGITAL ERA

By Allan Fels AO[1]

ABSTRACT

Australia's media industry went into the digital age one of the world's most highly concentrated. Digitization has opened the doors for more voices at the cost of dramatic harm to the economic models that sustained the established providers. Technology giants such as Google and Facebook are increasingly taking the place of the established providers as the front door to the content they create, building a better relationship with their advertisers and consumers than they have themselves. Australia's competition regulator is wary about intervening, believing that while there is a case for regulating the power of the digital platforms, and that while journalism is a public good, it is not yet the case that there is not enough of it.

I. INTRODUCTION

By 2019 Australia had only three capital city newspaper publishers producing 12 papers; two in each of Sydney and Melbourne, one in each of the other six capitals, and two that serviced the nation, one of them specializing in business.

One single owner, the U.S.-headquartered News Corporation, produced seven of the 12. By circulation it accounted for 70 percent of the capital city papers sold. Another owner, Australian public company Fairfax Media, produced all but one of the others papers, accounting for 21 percent.

A hundred years earlier, when the population was not quite 4 million, Australia's capitals had 21 daily papers and 17 independent owners.[2] In short, Australia's media industry went into the digital age more concentrated than it had ever been.

II. A CONCENTRATED INDUSTRY

Across the entire nation, including regional towns, News Corporation's share of circulation was 58 percent.

---

1 Director-General for Competition, European Commission.

2 R. Finkelstein, *Report of the Independent Inquiry into the Media and Media Regulation*, Canberra, Australia. Commonwealth Government 2012, (p. 58), http://www.abc.net.au/mediawatch/transcripts/1339_fink.pdf accessed December 2018.

In 2009 an international research project on media concentration in 26 countries led by Professor Eli Noam of Columbia University identified Australia as the only one in which a single owner produced more than half of all newspapers sold, with the exception of China where the government produced 100 percent, and Egypt where the government produced 72 percent.[3] The share of Australia's top two private owners, 86 percent, was the highest by a considerable margin.[4]

Australia's television industry is also concentrated. Only three privately-owned networks service a population of 25 million, along with two government-owned networks. The government hasn't issued a new private capital city television license since 1964, when Australia was half the size, with a population of 11 million.

Although digital compression technologies in place since the turn of this century have made it possible to license many more networks, the existing networks have successfully lobbied to be gifted an extra four channels each rather than face competition.[5] Pay TV has had limited prenetration. The ownership of Australia's radio stations is much less concentrated, although each of Australia's four biggest cities have only one privately-owned news and talk station, all four owned by Macquarie Media, controlled by the number two newspaper publisher Fairfax Media, which in December 2018 was acquired by Nine Entertainment, one of the three private television networks.

The most successful television network, "Seven," is owned by Seven West Media, owner of, Perth's West Australian newspaper, and also a string of regional newspapers and Pacific Magazines, one of Australia's two big magazine publishers.

The third-placed network, Ten, went into voluntary administration in 2017 and was acquired by the US broadcaster CBS after a bidding war with News Corporation, the dominant newspapers owner.

The three networks receive competition from two government-owned but operationally-independent broadcasters, the Australian Broadcasting Corporation (ABC) which operates four TV channels and many radio stations, and SBS, which is licensed to provide multilingual and multicultural radio and television services.

III. CROSS-MEDIA RULES

So-called cross media rules in force between 1987 to 2006 meant no one person was able to control both a television and radio license in the same geographical area or to control a license of either kind and a newspaper in same area.[6] In addition, no one person was able to control more than one license in same geographical area, effectively outlawing mergers.

---

3 E. Noam and The International Media Concentration Collaboration, *Who Owns the World's Media?: Media Concentration and Ownership around the World*, Oxford, Oxford University Press, 2016.

4 Finkelstein, *Report of the Independent Inquiry into the Media and Media Regulation*, (pp. 59-60).

5 P. Martin, "Blinded in high definition," The Age, February 18, 2010, https://www.theage.com.au/business/blinded-in-high-definition-20100217-oe24.html (accessed December 18, 2018).

Foreign interests were limited to 20 percent. Explaining the legislation, Australia's then treasurer Paul Keating said proprietors had to choose. They could be "queens of the screen," or "princes of print," but not both.[7] The legislation ended three decades in which the dominant newspaper owners in each city had usually been the dominant television station owners, beginning with the introduction of television in 1956.

IV. AUSTRALIA'S COMPETITION LAWS DIDN'T PREVENT CONCENTRATION

The national Trade Practices Act, introduced in 1974, prohibits mergers that would result in a "substantial lessening of competition." For 15 years between 1977 and 1992 the prohibition was weakened to apply only where the merged entity would be in a position to "control or dominate a market."[8] But "substantial lessening of competition" has been taken to refer to competition within an economic market, such as the market for newspapers or for advertising, rather than competition within a non-economic market such as the market for ideas and viewpoints.

When the owner of Nine network joined a consortium that attempted to take over Fairfax Media in 1991, the Australian Competition & Consumer Commission framed the question as whether the acquisition would make it easier for Fairfax to increase its cover prices or advertising rates.

Its preliminary view was that it would not; that is, that it would not make it easier for Fairfax Media to lift newspaper prices just because its owner was a television station.[9] The Commission reached a similar decision in 2018 when it approved an actual takeover by Nine of Fairfax and its radio stations that was allowed to proceed after the repeal the previous year of a weaker version of the cross-media law that prohibited one person from owning outlets in all three mediums – television, radio, and newspapers – in the same market.[10]

Stymied in its own attempts to own a conventional television network by then-existing cross media rules, News Corporation went into business with the government-owned communications provider Testra in 1995, setting up a joint venture known as Foxtel, which was to transmit multi-channel television over cables that would be laid down by Telstra. A year later Foxtel sourced a 24-hour news channel from Sky News Australia; a

---

6 B. Bailey, Cross-media Rules-OK?, Parliamentary Library, June 3, 1997 Current Issues Brief 30 1996-97, https://www.aph.gov.au/About_Parliament/Parliamentary_Departments/Parliamentary_Library/Publications_Archive/CIB/CIB9697/97cib30 (accessed December 18, 2018).

7 P. Keating, Paul Keating On The Australian Media, text of a speech to the Sydney Institute, Australian Politics, June 14, 2000, http://australianpolitics.com/2000/06/14/keating-on-australian-media.html (accessed December 18, 2018).

8 Australian Competition Law, Competition and Consumer Act 2010, Section 50 Prohibition of acquisitions that would result in a substantial lessening of competition, https://www.australiancompetitionlaw.org/legislation/provisions/2010cca50.html (accessed December 18, 2018).

9 A. Fels, Monopolies, mergers and media, speech to the Melbourne Press Club, July 16, 1996, https://www.accc.gov.au/speech/monopolies-mergers-and-media (accessed December 18, 2018).

partnership between Seven, Nine, and Britain's BSkyB, in which News Corporation had an interest. News Corporation now owns all of the channel and uses it to cross promote News Corporation publications. Its reach is limited by the limited reach of Foxtel, about 3 million of Australia's 10 million households in 2018.

It has long been argued that having only so few big players in many important industries is a price Australia has to pay for its small population and remote location. Australia has two main airlines, two main supermarket chains, two main liquor chains, two main real estate advertising platforms, three main phone companies, and four main banks; as well as two main newspaper publishers and three private television networks, some of who are now merged with each other.

It has even been suggested that Australia needs bigger and fewer firms than other countries in order to achieve the economies of scale necessary to compete on a global stage - the co-called "national champions" argument.

Whether or not that argument has merit, and the Australian Competition & Consumer Commission has rarely, if ever, given it credence.

V. A SMALL NUMBER OF VOICES HAS THE POTENTIAL TO DISTORT DEMOCRACY

Journalism is a public good in more than a formal sense. Formally, once a newspaper or television report has been prepared for one person, it is available to all people, not only because much of it is now free to access via the internet, but also because even where paywalls are erected or people have to pay for physical copies, once information has been produced, it spreads. News is necessarily available to more people than the people who pay for it.

Less formally but more importantly, journalism is a public good because even people who can't consume it or don't want to consume it benefit from it. Without the threat of exposure, politicians, banks, employers, trade unions, services providers and all other kinds of entities will behave less properly.

The argument can be overstated. People will always be curious, and people will always want to publicize things. They will never be without journalism. But without journalism on its traditional grand scale, they might be worse off.

Sometimes called the 'fourth estate' in recognition of its role along with parliament, the government and the judiciary in creating a functioning society, journalism is an unusual public good in that it works best if much of it is privately provided. In the words of Greg Hywood, Fairfax Media's chief executive from 2011 until the Nine takeover in 2018, journalism is "a public good in a commercial model."

---

10 Australian Competition & Consumer Commission, ACCC will not oppose Nine-Fairfax merger, media release November 8, 2018, https://www.accc.gov.au/media-release/accc-will-not-oppose-nine-fairfax-merger (accessed December 18, 2018).

VI. DIGITISATION HAS MADE JOURNALISM CHEAPER, BUT LESS COMMERCIAL

The early years of the digital age improved the commercial model. Hywood estimates the company shed a third of its workforce when computer technology enabled it to move from printing with hot metal to computer-set cold type in the 1980s. An entire class of workers known as compositors was no longer needed.[11]

Later, digital technology allowed Fairfax and News Corporation to contract out much of their editing and production work to off-site locations, one of which was in lower-wage New Zealand.[12] OECD estimates suggest that around half the cost of producing a physical newspaper is the raw materials – paper and ink – distribution, with Australia's costs high compared to those in other countries.[13] Importantly, those costs remain high for each additional newspaper sold. As circulation of physical papers has declined and their online readership soared, those costs have collapsed, and extra readers became almost costless to service.It has also become possible to develop direct relationships with them and upsell and tailor services to them, something that wasn't usually possible in the days of physical papers when third-party delivery agents known as newsagents stood between publishers and their customers.

And reporting itself has become cheaper. Online sources of data mean there is less need for phone calls and checking and have made it possible to do major investigations on a scale that would behave once been daunting.

In another plus for journalism, new operators can set up cheaply. Guardian Australia, Daily Mail Australia, The Conversation and The New Daily are among the new sources of daily news that wouldn't once have been commercially viable.

Even broadcasters, previously unable to directly compete with newspapers, are offering text-based online products that are hard to distinguish from newspapers. The government-owned ABC News website had 8.3 million unique readers in 2018, not too many less than "news.com.au," owned by News Corporation, with 10.3 million. Fairfax Media's two main papers, the *Sydney Morning Herald* and *The Age* had 7.5 million and 3.8 million readers. The newly-arrived Daily Mail had 5.1 million and Guardian Australia 4.5 million.[14] And ABC News wasn't merely a secondary source of news for people who treated newspapers more seriously. The same figures show that the average visitor to the ABC News site lingered longer on its stories than visitors to any of the newspaper sites.

---

11 G. Hywood, *The Fourth Estate*.

12 AAP, Sub-editing positions to go at Fairfax, *news.com.au* January 23. 2013, https://www.news.com.au/finance/business/sub-editing-positions-to-go-at-frg/news-story/75e35ca3018a9d8badaf04d4d984d694 (accessed December 18, 2018).

13 Organization for Economic Co-operation and Development, *The evolution of News and the Internet*, June 11, 2010, http://www.oecd.org/sti/ieconomy/45559596.pdf (accessed December 18, 2018).

The ABC is owned and funded by the government, through an appropriation of about A$1 billion per year. It doesn't accept advertisements. Unlike the BBC, which is funded by license fees, or the United States public radio, which is funded by donations and grants, its budget is dependent on the whims of the governing political party. But the governing party is constrained in how far it can trim the ABC's budget by overwhelming public support for the ABC.

VII. DIGITISATION HAS MADE JOURNALISM CHEAPER BUT LESS COMMERCIAL

A 2018 public opinion poll found the ABC to be the fourth most trusted institution in Australia, behind only the state and federal police forces and the High Court. It was more trusted than the Reserve Bank, charities, and the public service, and far more trusted than parliaments and political parties.[15]

Another survey found it to be Australia's most trusted source of news, believed by 69 percent of the population, well above the range of 39 to 59 per centpercent for newspapers and other online news sites.[16] Yet its comparatively cheap repurposing of journalism prepared for broadcast has come under attack from the dominant newspaper chains for undermining their business model. They charge for content and sell advertising. The ABC does neither, and was originally set up in 1932 to fill gaps in national radio coverage. A submission from Fairfax Media to a 2018 inquiry into the ABC's impact on newspapers noted that its original charter made clear "that the ABC's remit was broadcasting."[17] The charter wasn't formally expanded to include online media services until 2013, 15 years the birth ABC News Online. The inquiry gave short shrift to the concerns of the newspaper publishers, noting that the ABC was "established and funded to provide free services."[18] The publishers' deeper concerns about the digital age relate to the competition it has brought them for readers (originally competition from foreign publications, previously not readily available) and for advertising (increasingly from advertising-only or specialist news sites dealing with cars, jobs and real estate) and to the control of advertising and what gets read, which has shifted away from them towards platforms such as Google and Facebook.

---

14 Nielsen Australia press release, "Digital content ratings November 2018," December 11, 2018, https://www.nielsen.com/au/en/press-room/2018/nielsen-digital-content-ratings-november-2018-tagged-rankings.html (accessed December 18, 2018).

15 Essential Media Communications, Trust in Institutions, Essential Report, September 25, 2018 https://www.essential-vision.com.au/trust-in-institutions-11 (accessed December 18, 2018).

16 *Id*.

17 Fairfax Media, *Response to Issues Paper*, submission to Expert Panel Inquiry into the Competitive Neutrality of the National Broadcasters, June 22, 2018, https://www.communications.gov.au/sites/default/files/submissions/fairfax_media_-_25_june_2018.pdf (accessed December 18, 2018).

18 Expert Panel, *Inquiry into the Competitive Neutrality of the National Broadcasters*, Department of Communications, September 2018, https://www.communications.gov.au/documents/inquiry-competitive-neutrality-national-broadcasters-report-expert-panel (accessed December 18, 2018).

At the dawn of the internet age in 1999 the Fairfax Media city papers brought in A$800 million of advertising revenue. By 2017 they brought in only A$225 million from both print and digital advertising, a comparison that takes no account of the effects of inflation.[19] Much of the contraction was due to the loss of classified advertising to specialist sites. Classified advertising had been much more valuable to newspapers than display advertising because they had been able to charge much more for it per column inch. Although display advertising did move online, newspapers were able to charge much less for advertisements on websites than they had for advertisements in their physical papers. Online advertisers had a choice of many more outlets in which to place ads.

Estimates prepared by the Australian Competition & Consumer Commission for its inquiry into the effect of digital platforms on traditional news providers show that in 1996 printed newspapers took in 65 percent of the money spent on advertising in Australia, with television taking in most of the rest. By 2017 they took in just 12 percent. Online advertising, insignificant in 1996, took in almost half.

VIII. ON LINE, NEWSPAPERS HAVE LOST CONTROL OF THEIR FRONT DOORS

Analysis prepared for the inquiry found that less than half of the readers of online news sites went there directly. Fifty-seven percent went via Google or Facebook or another intermediary.[20] A study of UK internet users by the Reuters Institute quoted by News Corporation in its submission to the digital platforms inquiry[21] found that only 37 percent of readers who had reached a news site via a search engine or social media platform couldn't remember the name of the site.[22] However, most could remember the name of the search engine or platform.News Corporation points out that Google, the dominant search engine, does not own the content it displays or directs people to. "Instead, it scrapes content from third party publishers which it displays in its own search results without compensating publishers for doing so."[23] Publishers are able to opt out, but it renders their content unsearchable. "Threatened with digital invisibility, a publisher therefore has no choice but to permit Google to scrape its content without being Compensated," News Corporation says.

---

19 Fairfax Media, *Response to Issues Paper.*

20 Australian Competition & Consumer Commission, *Preliminary report* 2018 (p. 62).

21 News Corporation Australia, Submission 2 to the ACCC Digital platforms inquiry, September 7, 2018 (p. 9), https://www.accc.gov.au/system/files/News%20Corp%20Australia%20Submission%202.pdf (accessed December 18, 2018).

22 Nielsen Australia press release, "Digital content ratings November 2018," December 11, 2018, https://www.nielsen.com/au/en/press-room/2018/nielsen-digital-content-ratings-november-2018-tagged-rankings.html (accessed December 18, 2018).

23 News Corporation Australia, Submission 2 to the ACCC Digital platforms inquiry, (p. 5).

By displaying headlines and sometimes snippets of news arranged in the format of a newspaper homepage, Google's Google News service creates "the expectation that journalism should be free."

From 2008 to 2017 it enforced that expectation through a regime known as First Click Free ("FCF"), which required owners of locked content to give readers who came there via Google access to a certain number of free articles per day. News Corporation says in practice this meant only three percent of Google users saw paywalls.

"Through First Click Free, Google in effect forced subscription publishers to choose between two unattractive options: Either submit to FCF, allowing users to access much or all their content for free and thereby blunting their incentive to subscribe; or withdraw from it and suffer an immediate decline in visibility on Google search that would result in a loss of traffic and revenue from subscription conversions," News Corporation said.

In October 2017 Google retracted the First Click Free policy and replaced it with Flexible Sampling, which allowed publishers to select the number of paywalled articles they wanted to provide to Google users for free. But it continued to prioritize free articles in another way, by displaying in a carousel above the standard search results articles provided in its Accelerated Mobile Pages format. Hosted by Google and therefore quick to load, so-called AMP articles can be quickly swiped between, regardless of the publisher.

News Corporation says the format undermines the brand value of publishers, undermines the ability of consumers to identify sources, and gives the impression that all sites/content on the carousel are in some sense "Google approved." It says articles not supplied in the format are demoted in search results, regardless of their relevance to the user's search query.[24] Google denies this, saying it "does not rank news sites based on their business model." Many news sites that charge subscriptions such as *The Australian* and *The Australian Financial Review* feature prominently in its search results.[25] News Corporation also complains about Google changing its search algorithms with little to no notice and refusing to supply publishers with information on how they work. Google counters that it doesn't reveal the specific details of its algorithm changes because it is engaged in a constant cat and mouse game against sites that try to "game" its algorithms to get higher rankings in search results without providing value.[26] Facebook also changes its algorithms without notice, announcing on January 12, 2018 that it had prioritized the amount of content users saw from friends and family, cutting news content by 20 percent.[27] News

---

24 News Corporation Australia, Submission 1 to ACCC Digital platforms inquiry, April 20, 2018, https://www.accc.gov.au/system/files/News%20Corp%20Australia%20%28April%202018%29.pdf (accessed December 18, 2018).

25 Google, Submission 2 to ACCC Digital platforms inquiry, October 19, 2018, https://www.accc.gov.au/system/files/Google%20Submission%202%20%28October%202018%29.pdf (accessed December 18, 2018).

26 Google, Submission 2 to ACCC Digital platforms inquiry, (p. 5).

27 Mark Zuckerberg, Facebook announcement, January 11, 2018, https://www.facebook.com/zuck/posts/10104413015393571 (accessed December 18, 2018).

Corporation suggested the ACCC recommend an Algorithm Review Board to analyze and remedy algorithmic distortions of competition.[28] The ACCC put forward such a draft recommendation in its preliminary report, proposing that the authority have jurisdiction over digital platforms that generate more than A$100 million per annum in revenue in Australia and disseminate news and journalistic content, including by providing hyperlinks or snippets of such content.[29] It would make Australia the first country in the world to submit Google and Facebook's algorithms to a public interest test.

The publishers are also concerned that Google knows more about their customers than they do, being in an "unprecedented position" to identify potential targets for advertising[30], which is one of the reasons why Fairfax has subcontracted much of its advertising sales to Google in a relationship it says is "mutually beneficial."[31] The ACCC preliminary report proposes a range of amendments to the Privacy Act to better enable consumers to make informed decisions about and have greater control over the collection of their personal information, alongside increased legal remedies for serious breaches of privacy and an enforceable privacy code of conduct for digital platforms.

It also proposes a separate, independent review to design a "level playing field" regulatory framework that would apply the same rules to all entities that perform comparable functions in the production and delivery of content, whether they are publishers, broadcasters, other media businesses, or digital platforms.

It is considering recommending that digital platforms such as Facebook and Google be required to give it advance notice of the acquisition of any business with activities in Australia and to provide it with sufficient time to enable a thorough review of their likely consequences. It wants the merger law be reworded to make clear that it can consider the likelihood that an acquisition would result in the removal of a potential competitor and the amount and nature of data that the acquirer would get access to.

It acknowledges publishers concerns about the atomization of news and, for some consumers, a disconnect between news and its source. "These consumers may not know where their news comes from and whether the creator of that news content has committed to journalistic processes, such as fact checking and accuracy," it says. "Combined with the algorithmic selection of news, this potentially exposes individuals/consumers to the risk of filter bubbles or echo chambers, as well as the risk of unreliable information."[32] It has sought comment on a proposal to require digital platforms to signal, in their display of journalistic content to consumers, content from media businesses that have signed up

---

28 News Corporation Australia, Submission 1, (p. 6).

29 Australian Competition & Consumer Commission, Preliminary report, Digital platforms inquiry 2018, (p. 11)

30 News Corporation Australia, *Submission* 1, p 51.

31 G. Hywood, *The Fourth Estate*.

32 Australian Competition & Consumer Commission, Preliminary report, Digital platforms inquiry 2018, (p. 14).

to certain standards, perhaps by way of a "badge" on news content as it appears in search results or a user's news feed.[33] It is also open to ideas about how to support journalism where it is in danger of vanishing, including extending the A$60.4 million short-term Regional and Small Publishers Jobs and Innovation Package announced in 2017 as part of the deal that allowed non-government members of parliament to support the withdrawal of the cross-media ownership rules.[34] The package includes a regional journalism scholarships program, a regional and small publishers cadetship program, and a regional and small publishers innovation fund but expires after three years.

Other options canvassed by the ACCC include tax offsets for the costs incurred by news organizations in producing journalism with high public benefits, and tax deductibility for subscriptions to publications that are signatories to a code of practice.

An option not canvassed in the ACCC report, but raised with it,[35] is redirecting some of the A$1.3 billion per year allocated to the ABC and SBS to fund regional journalism in places where it is at risk along the lines of an £8m per year program to redirect BBC license fees to pay for 150 regional newspaper reporters in the UK.[36]

The ACCC recognizes the definitional difficulties in implementing any such programs and also the risk that the recipients might no longer be independent from the government.

It acknowledges that it has not yet been established that Australia doesn't have enough high quality journalism. There might not be as much as there could be, but it points out that falling short of "perfection" is not usually regarded as a sufficient reason for government intervention.[37] Australia continues to be supplied with high quality Australian music decades after the industry warned that digitization was going to destroy the local music industry.

For the moment Fairfax Media and News Corporation claim to have sustainable funding models. Fairfax will be supported by Nine and other businesses it owns including the nation's second-biggest real estate portal Domain, with whom it has a symbiotic relationship. It says its newspaper and online news business is making money. News Corpora-

---

33 Australian Competition & Consumer Commission, Preliminary report, Digital platforms inquiry 2018, (p. 15).

34 Department of Communications and the Arts, Regional and Small Publishers Jobs and Innovation Package Fact Sheet   https://www.communications.gov.au/what-we-do/television/regional-and-small-publishers-jobs-and-innovation-package (accessed December 18, 2018).

35 H. Ergas, J. Pincus & S. Schnittger, Public Interest Journalism, the Internet, and Competition for Advertising, CPI Antitrust Chronicle, September 2018, (p. 6), https://www.competitionpolicyinternational.com/wp-content/uploads/2018/09/CPI-Ergas.pdf (accessed December 18, 2018).

36 BBC News, BBC-funded local reporters to be spread across UK, February 2, 2017, https://www.bbc.com/news/uk-38843461 (accessed December 18, 2018).

37 Australian Competition & Consumer Commission, Preliminary report, Digital platforms inquiry 2018, (p. 291).

tion's newspapers are heavily supported by Foxtel which continues to make profits notwithstanding the encroachment of on demand video from competitors including Netflix and an Australian-owned firm Stan set up by Nine and Fairfax.

IX. PRIVATE BENEFACTORS APPEAR READY TO HELP

News Initiative program offering funding of up to A$300,000 for projects that would inject new ideas into the media industry.[38]

Also, in November 2018 an Australian philanthropist Judith Neilson announced a commitment of A$100 million to create a Sydney-based world-leading institute to support "evidence-based journalism and the pursuit of truth." "The institute will be independent, non-partisan and open to all who want to take up the challenge of contemporary journalism with goodwill and in good faith," she said. "I want it to sit right in the middle of the public square. From time to time it will be involved in controversy: so be it. It will be a forum for ideas, but an advocate of none." "I will play no role in its governance. I have no political or ideological agenda, and I will rely on experienced and respected journalists, practitioners and scholars to guide the institute's work."[39]

"I will play no role in its governance. I have no political or ideological agenda, and I will rely on experienced and respected journalists, practitioners and scholars to guide the institute's work."[40]

X. IT'S ONE SIGN, AMONG MANY, THAT JOURNALISM HAS A FUTURE IN AUSTRALIA

But no industry has a right to survive forever, and no industry has a right to survive without change. Australia's media industry has been slow to adapt to change, in part because it had been complacent and highly concentrated. It's catching up.

---

38 P. Wallbank, Google launches Asia-Pacific innovation challenge offering up to $300,000 for publishers' projects, *Mumbrella*, November 22, 2018, https://mumbrella.com.au/google-launches-asia-pacific-innovation-challenge-offering-up-to-300000-for-publishers-projects-553486 (accessed December 18, 2018).

39 J. Neilson, Why I'm spending $100 million on 'the pursuit of truth, *Sydney Morning Herald*, December 3, 2018, https://www.smh.com.au/national/why-i-m-spending-100-million-on-the-pursuit-of-truth-20181202-p50jnv.html (accessed December 18, 2018); P Wallbank, Sydney philanthropist Judith Neilson launches $100m journalism fund, *Mumbrella*, November 28, 2018, https://mumbrella.com.au/sydney-philanthropist-judith-neilson-launches-100m-journalism-fund-554654 (accessed December 18, 2018).

40 J. Neilson, Why I'm spending $100 million on 'the pursuit of truth, *Sydney Morning Herald*, December 3, 2018, https://www.smh.com.au/national/why-i-m-spending-100-million-on-the-pursuit-of-truth-20181202-p50jnv.html (accessed December 18, 2018).

EMPOWERING AND PROTECTING EUROPEAN CITIZENS IN AN EVOLVING MEDIA LANDSCAPE

By Johannes Laitenberger[1]

ABSTRACT

Director-General Laitenberger illustrated the main trends in media markets as observed from the vantage point of the enforcement of EU competition law. Such trends include the rise of digital giants on a global scale, the progressive integration of content producers, aggregators, and distributors along the value chain, such practices as geo-blocking that may undermine the integrity of the single market, looking into cases that hinge on factors other than price, and the implications of the accumulation of large amounts of data. The media landscape is broad and diverse. To organize it and focus on the parts that are most relevant to competition policy and enforcement, Director-General Laitenberger made two distinctions: (i) Challenges that are best dealt with by competition law enforcement and challenges that are best dealt with by regulatory measures and (ii) Challenges that belong with the national level and those that belong with the EU level. The Digital Single Market strategy is the overarching policy framework that allows actors in the four resulting squares to work together and produce the best results. Director-General Laitenberger used a review of enforcement action in media markets across all instruments – antitrust, merger review and State aid control – to bring to the fore enforcement priorities and their underlying logic. A look into the future closed his address.

Keynote speech at the 2018 Jevons Colloquium on "Future Perspectives on Media Markets" Rome, May 22, 2018.

I. INTRODUCTION

I would like to thank Antonio Bavasso for the kind invitation to speak at the Jevons Colloquium and Giovanni Pitruzzella and the *Autorità Garante* for hosting us today. It is a pleasure to be once again at a Jevons event.

---

1 Director-General for Competition, European Commission.

It is a privilege to be back in Rome and at the *Autorità Garante*, which under Giovanni's leadership has contributed to debate with such energy in our European Competition Network and beyond.

And it is both a pleasure and a privilege to come back to some of the issues that got me started many years ago – in fact, two decades ago – first as case-handler in what was then called DG IV in the European Commission, later as a member of the cabinet of the then Commissioner responsible for audiovisual policy, Viviane Reding.

I had more hair at the time – and I knew a lot more detail about the media sector than I know today.

But you can imagine how much I look forward to exchanging views with such a distinguished audience on our ever-changing media landscape and the implications of its development for the enforcement of EU competition rules and other public policies.
Even if my remarks will necessarily be broad brush and far from exhaustive, I still hope they will show the wood composed by the many trees that we will examine together today.

II. CHANGING MEDIA MARKETS

Now saying that the media landscape is ever-changing has been a bit of an understatement for quite some time. Over the past thirty years or so, we have witnessed one revolution after the other in the way people read, listen to speech and music or watch pictures and films. And the trend shows no signs of abating.

Let me mention some of the developments in today's media markets that we are observing in our practice at DG Competition.

One obvious development is that many digital products and services reach end-users at no monetary cost. They are rather "paid for" with attention and personal data. This is, of course, a feature we can observe both in media markets and other markets.

As large digital players amass vast amounts of data, competition policy and enforcement must be on the lookout to make sure that the data is not used in anti-competitive ways.

As Commissioner Margrethe Vestager said a few months ago, "controlling large amounts of data shouldn't become a way to shut rivals out of the market," adding that "if data does become an obstacle to competition, we have the tools we need to stop that".[2]

Another feature we have noticed is geo-blocking in the Single Market. Many users find this baffling or outright irritating. While the digital distribution and consumption of

---

[2] Speech on "*Clearing the path for innovation*", Web Summit, Lisbon, November 7, 2017, available at https://ec.europa.eu/commission/commissioners/2014-2019/vestager/announcements/clearing-path-innovation_en.

content in principle knows no borders, media organisations have adapted digital tools to manage or limit the content that users can access based on where their devices are located. But since the action of the EU's competition enforcers is predicated on a seamless single market, digital barriers erected by companies through collusion or anti-competitive uni-lateral conduct by dominant firms cannot be out of our focus.

Another market trend we are observing is of immediate interest for merger review – but of course not only for merger review.

This is the progressive integration of traditional and new players, such as content produc-ers, content aggregators and content distributors across different levels of the value chain.

And yet another trend is the emergence of new players, new channels and new offers, such as – to name three companies in separate markets – Facebook, Amazon and Netflix, that offer services to end users on the basis of different business models.

III. TACKLING ONLINE DISINFORMATION AND PRESERVING MEDIA PLURALITY

We are also noticing a trend that can not only disrupt whole industries but also have implications for society at large. A growing number of users receive their news and enter-tainment from only a handful of large digital hubs.

To gauge the size of this shift, consider that for the first time last year U.S. consumers spent more on entertainment that was streamed to their TVs and digital devices than to buy tickets to go to the cinema.[3] A recent study by the European Commission's Joint Research Centre points out that two thirds of consumers of online news prefer to access it through algorithm-driven platforms, such as search engines, news aggregators or social media websites. The study also finds that market power and revenue streams have shifted from news publishers to platform operators who have the data to match readers, articles and advertisements.[4]

This trend has obvious consequences for traditional media. The printed press, broadcasting and television must all – at least to a point – reconsider their business model and societal role. And it has obvious consequences for present and future generations of users. Past parameters for distinguishing trustworthy from untrustworthy information and content do not translate seamlessly from the analogue to the digital environment.

---

3 Motion Picture Association of America, *A comprehensive analysis and survey of the theatrical and home enter-tainment market environment (THEME) for 2017*, available at: https://www.mpaa.org/wp-content/uploads/2018/04/MPAA-THEME-Report-2017_Final.pdf.

4 Martens, B., Aguiar, L., Gómez-Herrera, E. & Mueller-Langer, F. (2018), *The digital transformation of news media and the rise of disinformation and fake news*, Digital Economy Working Paper 2018-02, JRC Technical Reports, European Commission, available at https://ec.europa.eu/jrc/sites/jrcsh/files/jrc111529.pdf.

In contrast, the amount of unreliable and sometimes artful news in circulation – and the efficiency of this circulation – appears to be growing at a fast clip. And with it grow our concerns that people's views can be manipulated and the democratic process meddled with. This is worrying for reasons that far exceed competition control.

The most recent policy response at the EU level is the initiative presented by the European Commission in April this year. Inserted into the wider policy, regulatory and enforcement agenda of the Juncker Commission, it comprises inter alia a set of measures specifically tailored to tackle online disinformation.[5]

The Communication includes the idea of an EU-wide Code of Practice on Disinformation. But it also reminds of the competence and responsibility of EU Member States to ensure the access to and the support for quality and diversified information and content.

Member States have a wide margin to foster the production and distribution of content by supporting public broadcasters, film production and press activities, without falling foul of State aid rules.

And Member States have the faculty – recognized by Art. 21 (4) of the EU Merger Regulation – to assess media plurality concerns in addition to and independently of competition concerns. The ongoing public interest probe by the UK into the Fox/Sky transaction cleared on competition grounds by the European Commission quite some time ago is just one example.[6] Reliable information, free and diverse cultural expressions, and media pluralism are non-negotiable values in the European Union. Indeed, the Amsterdam Treaty's statement that "public broadcasting in the Member States is directly related to the democratic, social and cultural needs of each society and to the need to preserve media pluralism" is but one expression of these principles.[7]

I will come back to this again in a moment.

---

5 Communication from the Commission to the European Parliament, the Council, the European Economic and Social Committee and the Committee of the Regions, *Tackling online disinformation: a European Approach*, 26 April 2018, COM(2018) 236 final. Available at https://ec.europa.eu/digital-single-market/en/news/communication-tackling-online-disinformation-european-approach.

6 Case M.5932, *News Corp / BSkyB*, available at http://ec.europa.eu/competition/elojade/isef/case_details.cfm?proc_code=2_M_5932.

7 Treaty of Amsterdam amending the Treaty on European Union, the Treaties establishing the European Communities and certain related acts - Protocol annexed to the Treaty of the European Community - Protocol on the system of public broadcasting in the Member States, OJ C 340, 10.11.1997, p. 109. Available at https://eur-lex.europa.eu/legal-content/EN/TXT/?uri=uriserv:OJ.C_.1997.340.01.0001.01.ENG.

IV. POLICY TEAMWORK

From what I have just said, it is clear that public policy in media markets is carried out by different actors at different levels. We can try to systematise it using two distinctions.

The first is between the issues in the media landscape that belong with competition policy and enforcement and those that belong with other regulation and legislation – both at EU and national level.

This distinction runs across all media markets and all sectors, particularly those subject to sector-specific regulation, such as telecommunications.

The second distinction runs between the issues that belong with the EU level, notably the European Commission, and those that belong with the national level, notably the national competition authorities in the EU Member States.

So, we have a simple two-by-two table: other regulation and competition control on the two rows, and EU and national level on the two columns.

How can we draw the table so that the different policies dovetail and, together, produce the best results?

The current, overarching policy framework is provided by the Digital Single Market strategy, which sits among the top priorities of the Juncker Commission.[8]

The strategy can be described as a concerted effort to put the Single Market online in a coherent and comprehensive fashion for the benefit of consumers, businesses and society at large.

The Digital Single Market covers the essential areas, including e-commerce, copyright rules, audiovisual rules, cybersecurity, free circulation of data, fast internet connections, privacy and the fostering of digital skills.

A number of directly media-related regulatory measures fall under its broad umbrella. Let me mention the main ones for our purposes, starting with the Audiovisual Media Services Directive.

The Commission's proposal to amend the Directive updates for today's Internet-centred environment rules that were written for a landscape dominated by TV. Indeed, the original name of this legal instrument was "Television without borders."

---

8 Communication from the Commission to the European Parliament, the Council, the European Economic and Social Committee and the Committee of the Regions, *A Digital Single Market Strategy for Europe*, 6 May 2015, COM(2015) 192 final. Available at https://eur-lex.europa.eu/legal-content/EN/TXT/?uri=CELEX:52015DC0192.

9 European Commission (26 April 2018), *Audiovisual media services: breakthrough in EU negotiations for modern and fairer rules*, Press Release IP/ 18/3567, available at http://europa.eu/rapid/press-release_IP-18-3567_en.htm.

The goal is building a more level regulatory environment for the entire audiovisual sector, including on-demand services and video-sharing platforms. The proposal's fundamental elements were agreed by the European Parliament, the Council and the Commission last April. After formal confirmation by the Council and the European Parliament's plenary vote, its rules will soon be ready to be transposed into national law.[9] Secondly, the Regulation on Cross-border Portability of Online Content Services that was adopted in 2017. It ensures that consumers who buy or subscribe to films, sport broadcasts, music, e-books and games can access them when they travel to other EU countries.[10]

This legal text belongs to the wider field of copyright regulation, which also includes the Commission proposals for the Copyright Directive[11] and the "SatCab" Regulation proposal[12], which are still pending in the legislative process.

The Copyright Directive concerns inter alia copyright rules for text and data mining for scientific purposes, a negotiation mechanism to facilitate the availability of audiovisual works on video-on-demand platforms and the introduction of a right to fair remuneration and to information claims of authors against contract partners and, where Member States foresee so, distributors. Particularly debated are provisions on ancillary copyright for news publishers for so-called "snippets" and monitoring and filtering obligations of online service providers.

The "SatCab" Regulation would extend the so-called "country of origin" principle, already applicable to satellite transmissions for about two decades, to ancillary online broadcasts. Rights would only need to be cleared for the broadcaster's country of establishment, covering simulcast and catch-up services, but not video-on-demand services.

Also, this proposal is hotly debated, which is why narrowing the scope of the "country of origin" principle to e.g. news and current affairs is being considered in the European Parliament, as well as in the Council.

This being said, the adoption of the Commission proposals would undoubtedly foster the further emergence of a European public sphere. This in turn could open up business and debating dynamics hitherto thwarted by the fragmentation of the Single Market for audiovisual content.

---

10 Regulation (EU) 2017/1128 of the European Parliament and of the Council of 14 June 2017 on cross-border portability of online content services in the internal market, OJ L 168, 30.6.2017, p. 1–11. Available at https://eur-lex.europa.eu/legal-content/EN/TXT/?uri=uriserv:OJ.L_.2017.168.01.0001.01.ENG.

11 Proposal for a Directive of the European Parliament and of the Council on Copyright in the Digital Single Market, 14 September 2016, COM(2016) 593 final. Available at http://eur-lex.europa.eu/legal-content/EN/TXT/?uri=CELEX:52016PC0593.

12 Proposal for a Regulation of the European Parliament and of the Council laying down rules on the exercise of copyright and related rights applicable to certain online transmissions of broadcasting organisations and retransmissions of television and radio programmes, 14 September 2016, COM(2016) 594 final. Available at http://eur-lex.europa.eu/legal-content/EN/TXT/?uri=CELEX:52016PC0594.

Last but by no means least, all of this is complemented by the Geo-blocking Regulation, devoted to ending the geo-blocking practices, that will enter into force in December.[13]

I would also add a number of measures which, although not exclusively linked to media markets, deal with core issues for digital players – especially platforms and social media.

I am referring, for example, to the EU net neutrality rules adopted in 2015[14] and the General Data Protection Regulation, which is putting privacy rights and interests of European citizens at the centre, which will come into effect later this week.[15] And also to the Commission's latest proposal for new rules on online platforms' terms and transparency[16], in particular vis-à-vis small businesses, presented at the same time as the afore-mentioned initiative on tackling online disinformation, that is complementary to the user-oriented "New Deal for Consumers" proposals presented earlier, also in April.[17]

Crucially, no overview would be complete without the work on the regulatory framework for the communication infrastructure. Its centre-pieces are the Commission proposals for the European Electronic Communications Code[18], connectivity[19] and the 5G Action Plan.[20] Without the right framework for the infrastructure, new and enhanced content will simply not reach the user.

---

13 Regulation (EU) 2018/302 of the European Parliament and of the Council of 28 February 2018 on addressing unjustified geo-blocking and other forms of discrimination based on customers' nationality, place of residence or place of establishment within the internal market and amending Regulations (EC) No 2006/2004 and (EU) 2017/2394 and Directive 2009/22/EC, OJ L 60I, 2.3.2018, p. 1–15. Available at https://eur-lex.europa.eu/legal-content/EN/TXT/?uri=CELEX:32018R0302.

14 Regulation (EU) 2015/2120 of the European Parliament and of the Council of 25 November 2015 laying down measures concerning open internet access and amending Directive 2002/22/EC on universal service and users' rights relating to electronic communications networks and services and Regulation (EU) No 531/2012 on roaming on public mobile communications networks within the Union, OJ L 310, 26.11.2015, p. 1–18. Available at http://eur-lex.europa.eu/eli/reg/2015/2120/oj.

15 ERegulation (EU) 2016/679 of the European Parliament and of the Council of 27 April 2016 on the protection of natural persons with regard to the processing of personal data and on the free movement of such data, and repealing Directive 95/46/EC (General Data Protection Regulation), OJ L 119, 4.5.2016, p. 1–88. Available at http://data.europa.eu/eli/reg/2016/679/oj.

16 Proposal for a Regulation of the European Parliament and of the Council on promoting fairness and transparency for business users of online intermediation services, 26 April 2018, COM(2018) 238 final. Available at http://ec.europa.eu/newsroom/dae/document.cfm?doc_id=51803.

17 European Commission (11 April 2018), A New Deal for Consumers: Commission strengthens EU consumer rights and enforcement, Press release IP/18/3041, available at http://europa.eu/rapid/press-release_IP-18-3041_en.htm.

18 Proposal for a Directive of the European Parliament and of the Council establishing the European Electronic Communications Code, 12 October 2016, COM(2016) 590 final/2. Available at http://eur-lex.europa.eu/legal-content/EN/ALL/?uri=comnat:COM_2016_0590_FIN.

19 Communication from the Commission to the European Parliament, the Council, the European Economic and Social Committee and the Committee of the Regions, Connectivity for a Competitive Digital Single Market - Towards a European Gigabit Society, 14 September 2016, COM(2016) 587 final. Available at http://ec.europa.eu/newsroom/dae/document.cfm?doc_id=17182.

20 Communication from the Commission to the European Parliament, the Council, the European Economic and Social Committee and the Committee of the Regions, 5G for Europe: An Action Plan, 14 September 2016, COM(2016) 588 final. Available at http://ec.europa.eu/newsroom/dae/document.cfm?doc_id=17131.

The updated "Significant Market Power" guidelines[21] will orient national regulatory authorities when they analyze telecoms markets. They contribute to competitive markets through reflecting the latest developments and addressing issues previously not included.

Examples are the competitive impact of online service providers who have started to offer internet-based services, increased provision of bundled services at retail level, competitive pressure of cable-based services as well as the transition from monopolistic to oligopolistic market structures in some countries.

I am mentioning these measures because I believe that, at this point in time, there is an obvious sensitivity among the European public: the desire to keep or regain control of the news, media and online experience in a level, safe and open digital environment.
The EU institutions are delivering on this in a joined-up fashion.

V. A COHERENT APPROACH FOR COMPETITION POLICY AND ENFORCEMENT IN MEDIA MARKETS

After this summary review of the EU's regulatory work in media markets, I will now try to show how the action of DG Competition dovetails with it. Let me start with a statement of principle. The function of competition policy and enforcement is not to duplicate or correct other regulation. It is to address and prevent – taking account of the regulatory framework – specific failures resulting from the behaviour of firms that collude, abuse market power or could, if merged, significantly impede effective competition.

I am stressing what to this audience must seem to be a truism because in the fast-moving reality just described, a lot of expectations are focussed on competition law. The Commission uses its remit under competition law in full, but in the full respect of its limits.

Or, as Commissioner Vestager recently put it: "Just because you have a wonderful hammer, it does not mean that everything is a nail."[22] The central objective of our approach to media markets is keeping the market for the provision of content open, innovative and well-functioning, including across borders in the Single Market.

I have already mentioned one of the practices that fragment the Single Market in digital industries; geo-blocking. The prevalence of geo-blocking was one of the main findings of our e-commerce sector inquiry.[23] Our analysis showed that as much as 70% of distribu-

---

21 Communication from the Commission, Guidelines on market analysis and the assessment of significant market power under the EU regulatory framework for electronic communications networks and services, OJ C 159, 7.5.2018, p. 1–15. Available at https://eur-lex.europa.eu/legal-content/EN/TXT/?uri=CELEX:52018XC0507(01).

22 Remark by Commissioner Vestager reported by the press at the American Enterprise Institute, Washington D.C., 18 September 2017. Published speech available at https://ec.europa.eu/commission/commissioners/2014-2019/vestager/announcements/how-competition-can-build-better-market_en.

23 Report from the Commission to the Council and the European Parliament, *Final report on the E-commerce Sector Inquiry*, 10 May 2017, COM(2017) 229 final. Available at http://ec.europa.eu/competition/antitrust/sector_inquiry_final_report_en.pdf.

tors in digital content markets used it to prevent cross-border access to digital content. When geo-blocking is based on contractual restrictions or on the unilateral conduct of dominant firms, there is a role for competition law enforcement to verify whether they are justified or not.

We also make sure that the playing field is level for both public and private operators, and for incumbents and new market entrants. This is crucial for innovation.

Incumbents should not prevent entrepreneurs with fresh business ideas from bringing them to the market.

Another consistent aim – especially pertinent in merger review – is making sure that the value chain over which content is produced and delivered to end users remains competitive.

This includes both fixed and mobile infrastructure, which are increasingly our preferred means to access content.

For example, in the *Orange/Jazztel* transaction[24], we identified competition concerns in relation to the delivery of fixed services – including TV – to Spanish consumers. In the end, we approved the deal only subject to the divestiture of Orange's fiber network in Spain, among other things.

In the *Hutchison/Wind*[25] merger in Italy, the Commission approved the deal subject to a remedy that would pave the way for a new fourth mobile network operator in Italy, Iliad.

The company has just announced its commercial launch in the coming weeks. Again, the goal was ensuring sustained infrastructure competition, here in the country's mobile sector. We also assist EU countries in their efforts to remedy market failures when it comes to the underlying infrastructure with the shared objective of offering citizens the backbone connectivity needed for data-intensive products and services.

Given the significant roll-out of infrastructure in recent years, the potential for market distortive effects of State aid in this area has increased, which is why the complementarity of the General Block Exemption Regulation ("GBER")[26] and the specific State aid guide-

---

24 Case M.7421, *Orange/Jazztel*, available at http://ec.europa.eu/competition/elojade/isef/case_details.cfm?proc_code=2_M_7421.

25 Case M. 7758, *Hutchison 3G Italy/Wind/JV*, available at http://ec.europa.eu/competition/elojade/isef/case_details.cfm?proc_code=2_M_7758.

26 Commission Regulation (EU) No 651/2014 of 17 June 2014 declaring certain categories of aid compatible with the internal market in application of Articles 107 and 108 of the Treaty, OJ L 187, 26 June 2014, p. 1, as amended by Commission Regulation (EU) 2017/1084 of 14 June 2017 amending Regulation (EU) No 651/2014 as regards aid for port and airport infrastructure, notification thresholds for aid for culture and heritage conservation and for aid for sport and multifunctional recreational infrastructures, and regional operating aid schemes for outermost regions and amending Regulation (EU) No 702/2014 as regards the calculation of eligible costs, OJ L 156, 20.6.2017, p. 1-18. Both available at http://ec.europa.eu/competition/state_aid/legislation/block.html.

lines for broadband[27] offer a targeted and adapted framework to assess public support to broadband roll-out.

Using our State aid guidelines, we have applied a pro-competitive philosophy in more than 150 positive decisions over the past ten years, including in Italy's multi-billion Banda Ultra Larga project.

EU Member States are also keen to use the flexibility of the General Block Exemption Regulation: as many as 113 cases in the last four years have been reported.

Under the GBER, aid can be granted in support of the objectives of the Digital Single Market. At the same time, public tenders and the requirement of open access to the subsidized networks prevent that taxpayers' money goes into expensive and closed monopolies. So, we try to always find the right balance between addressing market failures in underserved areas and keeping private market incentives intact, avoiding the overbuilding of commercially funded infrastructure, notably in well-served areas.

Moving from the infrastructure heading to the content heading, let me give you a few other examples drawn from our practice.

To make sure that users have access to content and service irrespective of where they happen to be within the Single Market, we are looking into contractual restrictions on cross-border sales.

Some cases concern the distribution of goods, such as consumer electronics and licensed merchandise, while others relate to services such as Pay-TV[28] or PC video games[29]. All these investigations tackle potential barriers to cross-border trade, including on-line.

Two cases featuring e-books exemplify our approach *vis-à-vis* large platforms.

One is the *Amazon* e-books case decided last year[30], where we came to the preliminary conclusion that Amazon may have abused its dominant position in the distribution of e-books to European consumers.

---

27 *Communication from the Commission, EU Guidelines for the application of State aid rules in relation to the rapid deployment of broadband networks*, OJ C25, 26.01.2013, p.1-26. Available at https://eur-lex.europa.eu/legal-content/EN/TXT/?uri=uriserv:OJ.C_.2013.025.01.0001.01.ENG.

28 Case AT.40023, *Cross-border access to pay-TV*, available at http://ec.europa.eu/competition/elojade/isef/case_details.cfm?proc_code=1_40023.

29 Cases AT.40413, *Focus Home;* AT.40414, *Koch Media;* AT.40420, *ZeniMax,* AT.40422, *Bandai Namco,* and AT.40424, *Capcom*. For further information see IP/17/201 of 2 February 2017, available at http://europa.eu/rapid/press-release_IP-17-201_en.htm.

30 Case AT.40153, *E-book MFNs and related matters (Amazon)*, available at http://ec.europa.eu/competition/elojade/isef/case_details.cfm?proc_code=1_40153.

We were concerned that by imposing so-called "Most Favored Nation" (or "Most Favored Customer") clauses on publishers, Amazon was preventing competitors from launching competing new and innovative business models.

To address our concerns, Amazon offered not to enforce or put in place such clauses during a period of five years.

Its commitments were made binding last year until 2022.

Before the *Amazon* case, already in 2012-2013, we had investigated alleged horizontal collusion between Apple and e-books publishers affecting the prices charged to consumers.[31]

At the time, the e-book market was still nascent in most of Europe but also highly dynamic and the Commission felt bound to intervene.

Apple and the publishers also offered commitments for a duration of five years that addressed these concerns.

I would like to add that our *Google Search/Comparison Shopping Services*[32] and our ongoing investigations into *Google Android*[33] and *Google AdSense*[34], whilst of course not media-specific, offer insights on the working of digital markets that are valuable beyond these cases. We will check the lessons learned from these cases carefully against the specific facts of other cases, including in the media field.

To complete the above-cited two-by-two table, I must stress that many media-related issues are handled at the national level – for instance the sale and licensing of rights, e.g. sports rights or film rights.

The *Autorità Garante* and many other national competition authorities have also detected and addressed possible abusive conduct by collecting societies.

In some instances, they opened up newly liberalised markets to new entrants.[35] In others, they brought the pricing practices of collecting societies to the attention of the Court of Justice.[36]

---

31 Case AT.39847, E-books, available at http://ec.europa.eu/competition/elojade/isef/case_details.cfm?proc_code=1_39847.

32 Case AT.39740, *Google Search (Shopping)*, available at http://ec.europa.eu/competition/elojade/isef/case_details.cfm?proc_code=1_39740.

33 Case AT.40099, *Google Android*, available at http://ec.europa.eu/competition/elojade/isef/case_details.cfm?proc_code=1_40099.

34 Case AT.40411, *Google Search (AdSense)*, available at http://ec.europa.eu/competition/elojade/isef/case_details.cfm?proc_code=1_40411.

35 AGCM Decision n. 26497 of 22 march 2017, A489 - NUOVO IMAIE-CONDOTTE ANTICONCORRENZIALI, *Bollettino* n. 13/2017.

36 Case C-177/16, Biedrība „Autortiesību un komunicēšanās konsultāciju aģentūra - Latvijas Autoru apvienība" v Konkurences padome. Request for a preliminary ruling from the Augstākā tiesa, judgment of the Court of 14 September 2017, ECLI:EU:C:2017:689; and Case C-525/16, MEO — Serviços de Comunicações e Multimédia S.A. v Autoridade da Concorrência, judgment of the Court of 19 April 2018, ECLI:EU:C:2018:270.

Following the implementation of the 2014 Directive on collective rights management, DG Competition is also closely monitoring newly created opportunities for licensing on a cross-border basis.

We are also working through State aid rules with EU Member States in their efforts to support quality information and creation, media literacy or linguistic diversity, as emphasised in the already mentioned initiative to tackle online disinformation.

The Commission approved individual national measures for news agencies – Agence France Presse in France and Agencia EFE in Spain – as guarantors of independent and impartial quality journalism and providers of reliable news.[37]

Let me stress that EU Member States may also channel aid away from beneficiaries that would do not meet certain standards.

For instance, we have recently approved a national aid scheme in France for the distribution of smaller publications.[38]

The scheme specifically excludes companies that have been found guilty to disseminate hate speech.

Examples concerning the value chain spanning content, aggregation and distribution come from merger control.

Transactions combining different levels of the value chain can raise input and/or customer foreclosure concerns.

In the 2014 *Liberty/De Vijver* transaction in Belgium[39], the company that resulted from the merger was going to be present in the production of TV content, the wholesale of TV channels and the retail distribution of TV services.

In the 2017 *Discovery/Scripps* transaction[40], competition concerns arose with respect to the Polish market, where the transaction risked increasing Discovery's bargaining power vis-à-vis TV distributors, because of the acquisition of certain channels.

In both decisions, the Commission accepted remedies from the merged entities.

---

37 Case SA.30481, *State Aid in favour of Agence France-Press* (AFP), available at http://ec.europa.eu/competition/elojade/isef/case_details.cfm?proc_code=3_SA_30481; Case SA.35474, *State aid to news agency EFE*, available at http://ec.europa.eu/competition/elojade/isef/case_details.cfm?proc_code=3_SA_35474.

38 Case SA.47973, *French Press Aid 2015 Decree*, available at http://ec.europa.eu/competition/elojade/isef/case_details.cfm?proc_code=3_SA_47973.

39 Case M.7194, *Liberty Global/Corelio/W&W/De Vijver Media*, available at http://ec.europa.eu/competition/elojade/isef/case_details.cfm?proc_code=2_M_7194.

40 Case M.8665, *Discovery/Scripps*, available at http://ec.europa.eu/competition/elojade/isef/case_details.cfm?proc_code=2_M_8665.

In *Liberty/De Vijver*, the concerns were removed by a combination of "supporting actions" and formal commitments submitted by Liberty. Competing TV distributors were guaranteed access to the "must have" channels Vier and Vijf under fair, reasonable and non-discriminatory ("FRAND") terms for seven years, which removed the input foreclosure concerns. Competing TV channels were guaranteed access to the merged entity's distribution operation, Telenet, through amended terms offering protection against a possible customer foreclosure strategy. Discovery committed to make Scripps's crucial TVN24 and TVN24Bis flagship news channels available to TV distributors for a reasonable fee determined by reference to comparable agreements for a period of seven years.

Another vertical media merger we handled was *AT&T/Time Warner*, which we cleared unconditionally under the simplified procedure in March last year.

That was admittedly a much less eventual affair than the U.S. case, which we are following with obvious interest.

The main factor that accounts for this difference is that AT&T has a very limited presence in the EU, other than in certain specific business-services markets where the link with Time Warner would not give rise to competition concerns.

The story is actually instructive. When different competition authorities take different decisions in the same case, it is often because of different market conditions.

Different decisions do not automatically mean divergent approaches. Conversely, two authorities may take the same approach and still arrive at different outcomes when market conditions are not the same.

VI. A LOOK INTO THE FUTURE

These examples paint a quick sketch of our present action. As we look into the future, we cannot avoid certain looming questions. First, which media outlets will survive and thrive? Second, who will ultimately pay – and how – for production and distribution of content? Third, what are the further implications of the developments we are witnessing for regulators and competition enforcers at EU and national level and for society as a whole?

One can argue that traditional models are under threat with the emergence of new production and distribution outlets and platforms. Several players in these markets, e.g. certain newspaper publishers, struggle to monetise content. Others, in contrast, have undertaken major shifts towards subscription-based services and online advertising, and prosper.

For now, no global or pan-European business model has emerged that would specifically build around Europe's values and rich cultural and linguistic diversity. Instead, more often than not, national and even relatively small players are up against players that capitalise their global reach.

This being said, in the music sector, certain European streaming services paved the way for an industry rebound.

What can be drawn from this is the fact that open and level markets carry a diversity of opportunity whose outcomes are not pre-determined. One thing is certain. We will continue to nurture and build upon our tradition, our values and our cultural and linguistic diversity, accompanying EU Member States in their support of quality and diversified news and creation.

At the same time, there is a clear need to remove ever more decisively unjustified regulatory or contractual barriers to the emergence of successful new business models and operators active across Europe and world-wide.

But let us not forget that, while competition enforcement may contribute to broader policy objectives, it is fact- and case-specific, hence by its nature pointillist. A picture emerges once you have taken some distance and connected all the spots on the media-landscape canvass.

We can see strong trends on this canvass, in content and distribution and advertising. There are important moves towards immediacy, proximity and customisation.

Services and infrastructure convergence is as steadfastly continuing as its concrete deployment is enigmatic.

At the same time, multi-homing blurs the boundaries between different ways to access content and advertising.

Non-price dimensions such as quality, innovation and availability are increasingly important.

Certain markets in certain countries may become more concentrated as a consequence of a drive towards consolidation.

But none of this limits the ability of the European Commission and of the national competition authorities to intervene if there is evidence that certain firms do not compete on the merits.

This is also true for the digital sphere and is attested by the broader story told by enforcement in past and recent years.

From the *Microsoft* cases[41] to our Google investigations mentioned above, we incorporated analysis relating to, inter alia, intellectual property, network effects, "free products", zero marginal costs or the importance of data.

In our *Amazon MFN* case just described, for the first time we dealt with a novel issue – non-price MFNs – in less than two years, thus providing guidance on how to deal with MFNs by dominant companies.

---

41 Case AT.37792, *Microsoft*, available at http://ec.europa.eu/competition/elojade/isef/case_details.cfm?proc_code=1_37792; Case AT.39530, *Microsoft (Tying)*, available at http://ec.europa.eu/competition/elojade/isef/case_details.cfm?proc_code=1_39530.

In past sports rights cases, we addressed rights licensing issues.[42] And for a long time, we have struck the balance between public service and private business, e.g. in broadcasting.[43] Our market definitions and competitive assessments are in tune with the times.[44]

To preserve this ability, we must nurture our capacity to take rapid and decisive action, in terms of resources, technological capacity, intelligence, analysis and procedures.

We need to monitor developments with extreme care so that the next concern – if and when it materialises – will find us prepared to protect the rights and interests of our fellow European citizens.

And we have seen that developments in the media landscape may have implications in different areas: competition in the Single Market, information and creation, even for democracy.

This means that lawmakers, regulators and competition enforcers – both at EU and national level – should continue to cooperate openly and effectively, because change is fast and the balance between the various public authorities concerned will likely remain shifting.

All actors involved should play as a team guided by the wellbeing of the citizens of the EU as their shared, ultimate goal.

At a time when it seems that our lives are overseen by devices that are ever more powerful; software that becomes ever smarter; and companies that grow ever bigger and more influential, I believe that this is what Europeans expect of their public authorities. So that the opportunities out there, manifold and precious, can be enjoyed by all, not just a few.

In delivering this task, the dialogue and exchange with our global partners is of the essence – for example with our partners from the USA present here today and whose presence I salute.

This conference contributes to dialogue, understanding and hence excellence in the pursuit of regulation, and competition policy and enforcement.

So, thank you, again, for having me today.

And thank you for what money cannot buy – your attention.

---

42 Case AT.37398, *UEFA*, available at http://ec.europa.eu/competition/elojade/isef/case_details.cfm?proc_code=1_37398; Case AT.37214, *DFB*, available at http://ec.europa.eu/competition/elojade/isef/case_details.cfm?proc_code=1_37214; Case AT.38173, *The Football Association Premier League Limited*, available at http://ec.europa.eu/competition/elojade/isef/case_details.cfm?proc_code=1_38173.

43 Communication from the Commission on the application of State aid rules to public service broadcasting, OJ C 257, 27 October 2009, p.1-14. Available at https://eur-lex.europa.eu/legal-content/EN/TXT/?uri=celex:52009XC1027(01).

44 See, for example, Case M.5932, *News Corp / BSkyB*, available at http://ec.europa.eu/competition/elojade/isef/case_details.cfm?proc_code=2_M_5932; Case M.7217, *Facebook / WhatsApp*, available at http://ec.europa.eu/competition/elojade/isef/case_details.cfm?proc_code=2_M_7217; and Case M.8124, *Microsoft / LinkedIn*, available at http://ec.europa.eu/competition/elojade/isef/case_details.cfm?proc_code=2_M_8124.

MEDIA AND TWO-SIDED MARKETS

By Bruno Jullien[1]

ABSTRACT

This article presents recent evolutions in the economic analysis of media competition, based on the two-sided market approach to media, and some implications for competition policy. It discusses the effect of multi-homing by consumers (consumption of multiple media content), the competition to attract and retain consumers' attention, as well as potential pro and anti-competitive effects of bundling. Conflicting effects on the two sides of the market of mergers and contractual agreements may also require reconsidering the traditional approach to competition policy.

"What we're selling ... is available human brain time."
Patrick Le Lay – former CEO of TF1 (translated)

I. INTRODUCTION

The theory of "two-sided markets" that emerged 15 years ago has established itself as a leading paradigm for the competitive analysis of many activities involving intermediation services. Among the many applications of the theory, adaptation of the two-sided market model to media industries led to better rationalization of the media activities by modeling explicitly the media business as enabler for interactions between advertisers and consumers. Media are then viewed not only as distributors of content such as videos, news, magazines, TV programs, or music, but also as contributors to the process of matching consumers and products available on the market, through advertising. This helped clarify the nature of competition in media markets and provided a framework for analysis that can account for instance for free media, premium content, or bundling.

At the same time, Internet and the emergence of the digital economy have been the source of a major disruption in media markets. New online media such as social networks, video streaming services, or news aggregators have emerged, while traditional media have moved their activities online. The new digital media constitute a challenge for competition authorities who sometime lack the conceptual tools to address the questions raised by new online practices. The antitrust treatment of two-sided markets is one of the challenges faced by competition authorities as traditional wisdom regarding market power

---

1 Toulouse School of Economics, CNRS, Toulouse, France. The author thanks Xavier Lambin for very valuable comments.

and its consequences have to be reconsidered in this context. For instance, the theory of two-sided market has shown that margins are not good indicators of the exercise of market power when the activity of a firm is two-sided.[2]

New research on the topic should aim at helping authorities and legal counsels to build adequate frameworks and develop the relevant concepts. The research on the two-sided market approach to media is still young and fast-evolving, but has already demonstrated that the two-sided market model can deliver useful insights for competition policy.

The objective of this article is to discuss some recent evolutions of the economic literature on media. It focuses its attention on the two-sided nature of media markets and its implications for competition on media markets. The discussion is not intended to be exhaustive, rather, I aim at pointing some of the main developments that are of interest for the conduct of competition policy.

After a brief introduction to the seminal modeling of two-sided media, the article discusses the role of multi-homing, i.e. consumption of multiple similar information goods, the new focus on attention, and the role of bundling and potential conflicts between the interests of different sides.

II. THE TRADITIONAL MODEL OF MEDIA MARKETS

The leading model for media that emerged in the economic literature of the 2000s was one of a "two-sided market" involving mainly two groups of actors: Viewers/readers/listeners on one side and advertisers on the other side.[3] As developed in the work of Anderson & Coates on TV media, media outlets compete to attract consumer's attention and sell it to advertisers.[4] Attracting consumers is achieved by proposing valuable content which may be produced in-house or acquired from third parties. This content is then bundled with advertising space that is sold to advertisers. The revenue per consumer that is generated depends on the quality of advertising, in particular in terms of final product sales or image building, which determines the price charged to advertisers.

In this traditional view of media, it was assumed that each individual consumer focused her consumption on one media outlet while advertisers could diffuse their ads over all outlets. In the two-sided market jargon, consumers single-home while advertisers multi-home. This view has several consequences for the functioning of media markets and the

---

2 See Jean Tirole's Nobel lecture, "Market Failures and Public Policy," December 8, 2014.

3 Caillaud, Bernard & Bruno Jullien, "Competing cybermediaries," *European Economic Review* 45.4-6 (2001): 797-808 and "Chicken & egg: Competition among intermediation service providers," *RAND Journal of Economics* (2003): 309-328; Jean-Charles & Jean Tirole, "Platform competition in two-sided markets," *Journal of the European economic association* 1.4 (2003): 990-1029.

4 Anderson, Simon P. & Stephen Coate, "Market provision of broadcasting: A welfare analysis," *The Review of Economic Studies* 72.4 (2005): 947-972.

locus of competition. As each consumer was unique to one outlet, the outlet became a bottleneck to access consumer's attention. And as advertisers could spread ads in all outlets, this access was not competing with access to other consumers. Absent any diseconomy of scale for advertisers or congestion effects that would induce interdependency of the values of ads across outlets, each media outlet could choose it advertising volume and rate with no competitive constraint. The consequence was a relatively high ads revenue per consumer which translated into intense competition to attract consumers. This model, that resulted in high prices on one side and intense competition on the other side, was sometime referred to as a "competitive bottleneck."

This model was very successful in particular in rationalizing free media (free newspapers, radio, TV stations). Indeed, when the advertising revenue is larger than the service cost, optimal prices may be negative in competitive as well as oligopolistic markets, resulting in zero prices if negative prices are not feasible.

The model also had implications for competition policy. First, any market power on the advertising side is derived from the strength on the consumer side and the population of consumers a media outlet can provide access to. Second, provided that there is enough competition on the consumer side, the model predicted that the two-sided nature of media would function to the benefits of consumers. Indeed, a media outlet would determine its advertising strategy to maximize the joint surplus of the outlet and its consumers, and pass-through this surplus to consumers through low prices and high-quality content. Hence, concerns about excessive market power and abuse of dominant position should be focused on the consumer side.

This view seems to have influenced some decisions. For instance, these considerations have been mentioned in several decisions by the French *Autorité de la Concurrence* concerning the media industries.[5]

III. MULTI-HOMING IN MEDIA MARKETS

The above view of media was challenged during the last decade for its inability to explain some evolutions related to the digital economy. With the internet, the media industries undertook major changes with a large part of the activity moving online and many innovative services emerging. Among unexplained phenomena were the global decline in advertising revenue, despite a boom in advertising possibilities and the emergence of very large outlets charging higher prices per consumer for advertising. This led to reconsideration of two key assumptions of the competitive bottleneck model.

---

5 Décision n° 15-DCC-139 du 20 octobre 2015 relative à la prise de contrôle exclusif de l'activité d'édition et de commercialisation des journaux Le Parisien et Aujourd'hui en France par le groupe LVMH – Moët Hennessy – Louis Vuitton, avis 05-A-18 du 11 octobre 2005 relatif à l'acquisition du pôle Ouest de la Société Socpresse et de fonds de commerce de la SEMIF par la Société SIPA, décision du Conseil de la concurrence 06-D-18 du 28 juin 2006 relative à des pratiques mises en oeuvre dans le secteur de la publicité cinématographique.

First, advertisers may face campaign budgeting constraints and diseconomy of scale which would imply some degree of competition for advertisers between media outlet, even when they give access to different consumers. Moreover, the assumption of "single-homing" consumers does not fit with new behaviors online, as consumers can easily switch from one media outlet to another and rely on content aggregators. The predictions of the competitive bottleneck model both in terms of revenue on the advertising side and the nature of competition change quite radically if consumers "multi-home," i.e. if viewers watch multiple channels or readers read multiple newspaper over a relatively short period of time. Consumers multi-homing affects the advertising market in several ways. Advertisers have several alternatives to reach a consumer which generates competition between media outlet.

Second an advertiser spreading its ads over several outlets may not be able to target precisely consumers and cannot predict precisely when and how a given consumer will be exposed to the ad.[6] With imperfect tracking technologies and assuming that the value of the impression of a consumer declines after the first impression, advertisers will be concerned that ads put on several media outlets would reach the same consumers. It follows that the value of two ads displayed in two distinct outlets with a similar size of audience is less than twice the value of one ad displayed in any of the two outlets. The consequence is that media outlets are not able to charge the advertiser the full value of the two ads, because if they do, the advertiser will prefer to deal with only one of the two outlets.

Hence consumer multi-homing reinstates competition for advertisers. Either only one outlet deals with the advertiser and there is direct competition for advertisers or both outlets deal with the advertiser and in this case the price charged by each outlet cannot exceed the "incremental value," that is the additional value created for the advertisers by using a second outlet.[7] The sum of the incremental values of the media outlets is less than the total value of the ads on the outlets, leading to rent dissipation. This type of competition then leads to total revenue that is lower than the competitive bottleneck model, which can explain a decline in total advertising revenue.

According to this logic the consequence is that competition on the consumer side becomes mostly a competition for "unique eyeballs," i.e. consumers who focus their attention on one outlet. Consumers who surf a lot across outlets may dilute the value and even reduce the profit due to lower ads revenue per user.

As media outlets giving access to more unique consumers can charge higher prices, a larger audience also gives rise to higher advertising revenue per consumer. This advantage for larger outlets can generate increasing concentration in the media markets, in particular

---

6 See Athey, Susan, Calvano, Emilio & Joshua S. Gans, "The impact of consumer multi-homing on advertising markets and media competition," *Management Science* 64.4 (2016): 1574-1590.

7 See Anderson, Simon P., et al. "Media market concentration, advertising levels, and ad prices," *International Journal of Industrial Organization* 30.3 (2012): 321-325.

if the cash is reinvested to raise the quality to consumers (such a view implies that access to capital market is imperfect). From a competition policy perspective this may result in some form of barrier to entry as a new entrant may not be able to generate enough cash to cover its cost for a long period of time.

IV. COMPETING FOR ATTENTION

Attention is a scarce resource: Consumers have limited time and attention capacity that they need to spread over multiple activities. In the two-sided view of media, a media controls access to a share of this resource and monetizes it by selling advertising. There is however little understanding of the economic consequence of the rise of the "market for attention" that became prominent in the Internet.

As emphasized by Boik et al., a special feature of competition for the attention of consumers in online markets is that, unlike more traditional markets, prices are not effective in allocating the scarce resource.[8] Due to the two-sided nature of the activity, consumers often face zero prices and even when they face positive prices, theses prices are not well tailored to attention, which is hardly quantifiable. In markets where firms compete to attract attention, competition takes place by offering subsidized content to consumer. This leads many media to become multi-sided platforms by hosting third party content. And, of course, the contest to attract the attention of unique consumers discussed above leads to a race to attract premium content, content that generates large audience and often unique audience. In a recent work, Anderson, Foros, Kind & Peitz (2016) argue that competition for attention leads to proliferation of content.[9]

Moreover, attention is subject to congestion, as increasing attention on one content reduces the capacity available for others. Proliferation of content then results in excessive congestion and inefficient supply of content. A traditional economic answer is to introduce a tax on content (a "Pigouvian" tax) as it is done for traffic or pollution for instance. In the context of attention congestion, it is hardly conceivable however as we know little about how attention is allocated. A consequence is that excessive competition may harm consumers.

Thinking about the media industry as trying to capture and resell consumer's attention leads to questioning the notion of relevant markets. The recent study by Boik et al. suggests that consumers optimize both the set of services they devote attention to and the level of attention within each service. Moreover, they find that information products that have attracted a significant share of consumer's attention have evolved over the recent period. The existence of intensive margins for attention raises the possibility that seemingly unrelated services constrain each other, if an increase in the attention on one service

---

8 Boik, Andre, Greenstein, Shane & Jeffrey Prince, "The empirical economics of online attention," No. w22427, *National Bureau of Economic Research*, 2016.

9 Op. cit.

comes at the expense of attention in the other service. This may lead to move the cursus of market definition from product characteristics to the type of attention they generate.

V. BUNDLING

As mentioned, the typical activity of a media involves some form of bundling, such as TV channels, e-book libraries, and subscription-based video-streaming. Indeed, bundling of content is ubiquitous in media industries. While the competitive assessment of bundling of similar contents can follow standard analysis, some new practices in online media raises new issues. In particular, it is common that media platforms seek growth by incorporating in their platforms new services seemingly not related to their initial media offer, either by external acquisition or in-house development. Well-known examples are Google offering email and storage services, or Facebook offering news services.

The traditional economic analysis of bundling emphasizes either price discrimination or dynamic leverage. According to the first view, firms offer several bundles targeted at different types of consumers so as to extract more profit. The alternative view is that bundling is a strategy that entails some short-term loss but allows the firm to prevent the emergence of a future competitor.

In the context of a two-sided market, bundling may however have a different motivation. One motivation is to increase the reach and retain attention of consumers, by raising the value of a free offer.[10] This is because a media outlet may be constrained to charge non-negative prices and would be willing to subsidize consumer's participation to raise advertising revenue. Expanding the offer is then a way to provide such subsidy. Underlying such a strategy is the property that consumers face fixed participation costs of adhering to the media platform (shopping costs) which explains why offering a new product at a subsidized rate on an online platform raises the sales of other products, and thus the attention devoted by consumers to the platform and advertising revenues.[11]

At first glance such a practice should not raise concerns, and indeed it is welfare enhancing when used by a monopoly media platform. In a competitive context, such bundling strategy, that allows to raise the value to consumers and thereby the attractiveness of the media for advertisers is in general procompetitive. However, one may be concerned that it induces barriers to entry as large platforms will be difficult to challenge for a new entrant and the largest outlets will attract most advertising revenues.

For example, de Corniere & Sarvary have argued that bundling user-generated content and news on a social media may harm newspapers and may reduce total investment in news

---

10 Amelio, Andrea & Bruno Jullien, "Tying and freebies in two-sided markets," *International Journal of Industrial Organization* 30.5 (2012): 436-446.

11 An alternative motive for expanding the offer to new services is to collect more data on the consumers.

quality.[12] This is because, while bundling allows to promote news content by showing it on the social media platform, it also diverts some advertising revenue away from news outlets and reduces their incentive to keep the attention of readers with high-quality content.

The tied good is sometimes a free information good financed through advertising revenue. In that case, it has been shown that the market mechanism that (should) cancel the short-run value of tying as an exclusion tool is ineffective.[13] The reason is that competitors cannot react by reducing their price beyond gratuity. This allows a media outlet leveraging its market power on some content by tying it with another competitive content, thereby capturing the advertising rent without fearing that competition will erode its profits. This implies instant recovery of the profit sacrifice on the consumer side with larger advertising revenue. Total welfare is then lower as consumers are diverted away from the most valuable content.

VI. SEE-SAW EFFECTS

In a media context, several recent contributions have emphasized that structural changes or other forms of market intervention (such as a ban on some contractual practices by media platforms or a price-cap) may result in a see-saw effect: A measure that hurts advertisers may benefit consumers (and *vice-versa*).

When consumers dislike facing more advertising, a reduction in advertising price benefits advertisers, but the resulting inflation of ads harms consumers. While a better targeting technology seemingly benefits both side of the market, it may result in lower consumer surplus if it is countervailed by higher ad volume.

See-saw effects have been found in the analysis of mergers, for instance.[14] Indeed, a merger may benefit or harm consumers depending on whether the merged entity can better monetize the eyeballs on the advertising market, suggesting an increase in advertising level. As coordinating two media platforms' offers to advertisers may raise the revenue per eyeball, incentives to attract new consumers will be higher for the merged entity, which may choose to reduce the prices and to raise the quality of the information goods offered to consumers. The (sparse) empirical literature suggests that the mergers investigated (between radio stations or TV distributors) have raised the price of ads. It is less conclusive for the consumer side although the audience is found to increase in some studies.

A see-saw effect may also result from contractual practices on the advertising side. A restriction imposed to advertisers that could be considered as abusive in a one-sided view of the market may be justified by substantial benefits to consumers.

---

12 de Cornière, Alexandre & Miklos Sarvary, "Social Media and News: Attention Capture via Content Bundling," *Mimeo* (2018).

13 Jay Pil Choi & Doh-Shin Jeon, "A Leverage Theory of Tying in Two-Sided Markets," *TSE Working Paper*, n. 16-689, September 2016, revised March 2018.

14 Anderson, Simon P. & Martin Peitz, "Media see-saws: winners and losers on media platforms," No. 15-16. *Working Paper Series*, Department of Economics, University of Mannheim, 2015.

In any competition decision involving a see-saw effect, antitrust authorities will have to take a stance on how to balance the interests of the two sides of the market. Notice that by the nature of the problem, it will not be possible to address a competitive concern on the advertising side without affecting the consumer side. Hence the balancing exercise seems unavoidable, either explicitly or implicitly.[15]

Another factor that is rarely mentioned in competition cases and in the economic literature on this subject, but that should be factored in the balancing exercise, is that advertising is not a standard consumption good. Advertising provides information to consumers, changes their taste and signals quality through wasteful spending. The welfare analysis of advertising has in particular shown that a competitive market may provide an excessive amount of advertising. From this perspective some concentration that reduces the volume of advertising by raising the advertising price and reducing multiple impressions may be welfare-enhancing.

VII. CONCLUDING COMMENTS

This article discussed a few recent contributions from a burgeoning literature. The traditional view of media competing to attract consumers and exploiting exclusive access to attention has been replaced by a more balanced view of the two sides. With multi-homing consumers, attention is a key driver of competition between media outlets, while this factor can often be neglected in the analysis of other platforms.

As is often the case in the analysis of two-sided markets, conclusions on bundling/tying practices depend on the context. While it raises the value offered by one media outlet to consumers, it also raises exclusionary concerns when performed by a strong media that leverages its market power.

Accounting for two-sidedness in merger analysis may be challenging as competition authorities are not used to balance the interests of several parties. As is well known, it also raises issues of market definition as the market is a locus for the interaction of several demands. Moreover, platforms that compete with each other may adopt very different business models. For instance, some media rely on subscription, others on advertising and gratuity, many newspapers use a mixture of the two.

To conclude this discussion, it is worth mentioning that I have set aside the issue of data, which may become prominent for media. As access to large and unique data may allow to offer better personalized services, better advices, and better targeting of advertising, the induced network effect may result in concentration and ultimately raise antitrust concerns.

---

15 The recent ruling by the U.S. Supreme Court on the *American Express* case appears to be a first step in this direction. *Ohio v. American Express Co.*, 585 U.S. (2018).

MEDIA IN COMPETITION LAW ENFORCEMENT BY THE BELGIAN COMPETITION AUTHORITY

By Prof. em. Dr. Jacques Steenbergen[1]

ABSTRACT

The Belgian Competition Authority has mainly dealt with three types of media related cases: Television rights for sports competitions, mergers, and online subscriptions for newspapers and magazines. It regularly screens whether the terms and conditions in the requests for proposals for the auctioning of television rights for Belgian premier league football are compatible with competition law, and it imposed interim measures in respect of a long-term exclusive contract for cyclo-cross television rights. The merger cases were mainly driven by efforts of publishers of printed press to reposition themselves in a rapidly changing environment, and by the search for vertical integration between network and content providers. In these cases, the BCA requalified media plurality as consumer choice concerns; and, in 2011, the BCA reached an informal settlement with Apple on the term and conditions for online subscriptions for newspapers and magazines.

I. INTRODUCTION

The Belgian Competition Authority has mainly dealt with three types of media related cases: Television rights for sports competitions, mergers, and online subscriptions for newspapers and magazines.

II. TELEVISION RIGHTS

A. *Premier League Football*

Since 2005, the Pro League (the organization of football clubs playing in the Belgian Premier League) checked regularly with the Investigation and Prosecution Service (*Auditorat*) of the Belgian Competition Authority whether the terms and conditions for the auctioning of television rights are compatible with competition law.

---

1 President of the Belgian Competition Authority.

Constructive discussions have resulted in 2011 in a set of terms and conditions that has since been used for requests for proposals (*cahier des charges*). The rights are granted for three seasons (three years).

This informal settlement makes it easier for potentially interested parties to bid for the rights and facilitates the regular screening of auction processes.

B. Cycle-Cross

On November 5, 2015, the Competition College of the Belgian Competition Authority granted interim measures at the request of Proximus NV against Telenet NV.[2] Proximus is the incumbent telecom operator and also offers television access nationwide, often as part of its triple play offer. Telenet, part of the Liberty Global group, is the main cable operator and broadband supplier in Flanders where it has a very high market share and where it is also a significant player for fixed line telephony. In 2015, it acquired Base, one of the three mobile operators and it expanded its geographic footprint.

Proximus filed a complaint with a request for interim measures against Telenet. Proximus argued that Telenet infringed Articles IV.1 and 2 of the Belgian Code of Economic Law ("CEL") and Articles 101 and 102 TFEU by obtaining exclusive rights for the transmission of cyclo-cross competitions for a period of five years in a bilateral agreement with the cyclo-cross association without offering other interested parties any opportunity to make an offer. Cyclo-cross competitions are very popular with television viewers in Belgium.

In order to grant interim measures, the Belgian Competition Authority has to establish (i) a prima facie case; and (ii) the urgent need to avoid a prejudice that is serious, immediate, difficult to repair, and that is caused by the behavior that constitutes the prima *facie case*.[3] The standard to establish a prima *facie case*, as confirmed by consistent case law, is that it should not be manifestly unreasonable to consider that the facts constitute an infringement of the rules of competition.[4]

There is prejudice when the complainant would have been in a more favorable position without the alleged infringement. In order to decide whether the prejudice is serious and immediate, the authority examines primarily whether the prejudice can be compensated *ex post* by granting damages, and whether the prejudice can still be avoided or limited for the period between the decision on interim measures and the decision on the complaint in the main case. The interim measures need to be effective and proportional. In order to assess the proportionality, the authority needs to balance the impact of measures on the

---

2 Decision BMA-2015-V/M-15/0024.

3 Article IV.64 CEL.

4 See most recently the abovementioned judgement of the Court of appeal of Brussels June 28, 2017 in the *NV Alken-Maes v. NV Anheuser-Busch Inbev* case.

defendant in case no infringement is established in the main case, and the impact on the plaintiff in case no measures are imposed and an infringement is established.[5]

The College decided, referring *inter alia* to a decision of the French competition authority in a similar case concerning the transmission of rugby matches, that it was not manifestly unreasonable to consider that the agreement might constitute an infringement of Article IV.1 CEL and Article 101 TFEU.[6] The College concluded that there was therefore a *prima facie* case in the meaning of the provision on interim measures.

The College also decided that the alleged infringement caused a serious and immediate prejudice to the complainant that would be difficult to repair, if only because it would be difficult to establish the exact impact of the lack of cycle-cross coverage on the development of Proximus' client base for television access or triple play subscriptions.

The College gave the cycle-cross association the option between the organization of an auction (the remedy imposed by the French authority) or the suspension of the exclusivity clause, thus transforming the transmission rights from exclusive into non-exclusive rights until a final decision on the complaint. Parties chose (as we expected) the latter option. In its assessment, the College considered this remedy to be effective and proportional: It imposed no burden on the cycle-cross association (and could even provide them with additional income), and it did not need to result in a loss of transmission rights for Telenet.

The decision of the Belgian Competition Authority was appealed but upheld in court.[7]

III. MERGERS IN "MEDIA-LAND"

We have seen in recent years successive restructurings of the media industries. The transactions were mostly driven by efforts of publishers of printed press to reposition themselves in a rapidly changing environment, and by the search for vertical integration between network and content providers. Publishers buy titles from a player that wishes to refocus its portfolio or decides to exit the market. They also enter into joint ventures with each other, with cable companies or producers of television programs, and later reshuffle their shareholdings in order to obtain sole control over a refocused portfolio, etc. Some cases could be dealt with in a simplified procedure. But also, when the conditions for a simplified procedure were not met, the transactions did not always require remedies in order to be authorized.[8]

---

5 See further my contribution "Interim relief measures in competition cases – a European competition authority's perspective," in N. Charbit, C. Malhaldo & E. Yang (editors), *Douglas. H. Ginsburg Liber Amicorum - an antitrust professor on the bench*, Concurrences, Paris/New York, 2018, vol. I, pp. 545-560.

6 Decision 14-MC-01 of July 30, 2014 of the *Autorité de la Concurrence*.

7 Brussels, September 7, 2016.

8 See, e.g. Decision BMA-2018-C/C-07 of March 7, 2018, *Roularta Media, Rossel and Mediafin,* and BMA-2017-C/C-14 of April 26, 2017, *Mediahuis.*

A. *Relevant Product Markets*

The Belgian Competition Authority identified e.g. the following product markets: the markets for printed and digital general newspapers and for printed and digital financial newspapers, for magazines in a given language (leaving open whether a further distinction should be made between inter alia magazines with a focus on news, on a female, male, or youth audience); the markets for advertisement space in printed and digital national or printed and digital regional newspapers, for online advertisements, for TV advertisements, for the advertisements of jobs; and for the production of TV programs.

B. *The Development of Digital Products*

The development of digital products is obviously one of the main motives for restructuring and it has an increasing impact on market definitions and the assessment of competitive pressures.

The Belgian Competition Authority, often able to refer to European Commission decisions, has by now, in several decisions, considered that digital and printed newspapers are part of the same product market. It left open whether digital and printed magazines are also one product market. And the same applies for the markets for advertisements in digital or printed newspapers and in digital or printed magazines. The decisions left it open whether online news constitutes a distinct product market or is part of the market with other news channels. They also left it open whether the market for online advertisements constitutes a distinct product market. But even if these markets were to be seen as distinct product markets, the Competition College considered that they were subject to significant competition pressure from their respective neighboring markets for news or advertisements.[9]

C. *Merger Control and Media Plurality*

Belgium has no specific authority or merger control legislation aimed at the protection of media plurality. The Belgian Competition Authority has, however, considered that media plurality can be qualified as concerned with consumer choice. And it has thus taken a couple of decisions in which it imposed remedies in order to protect consumer choice as a competition concern.

In one of the first decisions of the present authority (re-established in 2013), the Competition College authorized an acquisition of newspapers by one of the two bigger Dutch language newspaper groups, provided the titles were maintained and each of them would have *inter alia* its own fulltime editor in chief and commentator.[10] The case could be seen as a three to two merger in respect of the Flemish market, but on a shrinking market for news-

---

9 See, e.g. the abovementioned Roularta/Mediafin decision and decision BMA-13-C/C-03 of October 25, 2015, *Mediahuis*.

10 The abovementioned *Mediahuis* decision.

papers. There also remained a strong player in one of the provinces (the seller) who had not succeeded in a turnaround of the target (but without developing a failing firm argument).

A later case was not concerned with newspapers but mainly with so-called people magazines.[11] Given the topics these magazines are expected to cover, the Competition College considered that there was limited scope for content diversification. It required that 20 percent of the editorial content in one of the magazines had to be different from another magazine in the group, and that the acquired magazines could not become identical under different titles. The case also presented some specific issues in respect of TV program magazines that were addressed in the remedies.

IV. NEWSPAPERS AND MAGAZINES ON IPAD: ON MOST FAVORABLE CUSTOMER CLAUSES AND DATA OWNERSHIP

In 2011, the Belgian Competition Authority received a complaint from publishers of newspapers that feared that Apple might impose as a condition for offering subscriptions in its Apple shop *inter alia* a most favored customer or even exclusivity clause for the subscription and access to newspapers and magazines on iPad, or that Apple would require a commitment that the publishers would not offer subscriptions at a price below the price charged in the Apple shop. They also objected to the commission Apple was expected to ask for sales in the Apple shop.[12] And it is in the context of today's debates on the ownership of (big) data also interesting to note that the publishers were very concerned that they risked to lose contact with their readers when subscriptions could be renewed in the Apple shop without a direct contact between the reader and the publisher.

As the conditions had not yet been fixed by Apple, we decided that the issue could be dealt with as an informal case.

Tablets and iPads were still new products for which other authorities had also already found it difficult to identify a dominant position. But we saw a potential infringement of Article 101 TFEU rather than an abuse of a dominant position in the meaning of Article 102 TFEU. We discussed this approach informally with the U.S. FTC. While Apple had not been very responsive as long as the public debate focused on a possible abuse of dominance, they immediately engaged in high level constructive discussions when informed that I wanted to discuss vertical issues under Article 101 and made them aware of the contacts with the U.S. antitrust authorities.

We considered that a distinction had to be made between the offering of the subscriptions (i.e. the digital newspapers and magazines) in the Apple shop, and the offering in the Apple

---

11 Decision BMA-2015-C/C-24 of August 4, 2015, *De Persgroep Publishing, Humo, Story et al.*

12 Annual Report of the Directorate General for Competition (in the previous authority) 2011, p.11.

shop of the apps of the publishers for access to digital newspapers and magazines. When selling the subscriptions in their shop, Apple could be seen as a distributor (agent or reseller).

We did not go into the price setting by Apple for its services (commission fee, services in respect of the renewal of subscriptions, etc.) or as a retailer. We considered that when Apple acts as a distributor, it should be free to charge for its services.

Our main concern was that the publishers should be free to determine the price of subscriptions whether selling to Apple as a reseller, asking Apple to act as an agent, or selling through any other channel or on any other platform. There was no indication that Apple intended to refuse to offer the apps of publishers in its Apple shop and not much discussion on the cost of apps in that shop (mostly free or at a low price).

With regard to the concern of the publishers about the contact with readers and the ownership of subscription data, we took the view that the ownership depended on the distribution model chosen by the publishers. In case Apple would act as a reseller, we saw Apple as the owner of the data. In case of an agency model, we would have to look at the agency agreement, and in case only the app would be offered in the Apple shop, the data and the contacts with readers would remain with publishers.

Apple agreed to apply conditions that met our concerns, and these apply, to our knowledge, still worldwide in respect of digital newspapers and magazines.

V. CONCLUSION

The television rights cases show that competition law enforcement in media industries still requires competition authorities to deal with issues that are probably as old and traditional as sport on television. The main contribution of the Belgian Competition Authority in this field is, however, that a well-designed interim measure procedure allows for a more effective protection of stakeholders by bringing forward the useful effect of its enforcement.

The experience of the Belgian Competition Authority in merger cases illustrates how the digital revolution impacts on smaller authorities as well as on the media industry. We never felt that we required new concepts. But especially when defining product markets, we clearly needed to look at, if not to predict, how the development of digital products changes both the demand and the supply side in media markets.

The *Apple* case also illustrates that it is unpredictable which competition authority, be its jurisdiction small or large, will be the first to be confronted with new issues. This only emphasizes the need for active and timely cooperation and exchange of experience among competition authorities as was e.g. the aim of the European Competition Network authorities in the European Union when setting up an early warning system in 2017.[13]

---

13 http://ec.europa.eu/competition/antitrust/ECN_meeting_outcome_17022017.pdf.

WHAT SHOULD EU COMPETITION POLICY DO TO ADDRESS THE CONCERNS RAISED BY DIGITAL PLATFORMS' MARKET POWER?

By Damien Geradin[1]

ABSTRACT

This paper shares some thoughts on what competition authorities could do to address the concerns that have been raised by the market power of digital platforms, and in particular those with an ad-funded business models. Some have suggested that pursuant to Schumpeterian competition, firms compete sequentially for the market as a whole and that antitrust intervention in digital markets is not only superfluous, but – because of the complexity of digital platform markets – it is also subject to type-II (over-enforcement) errors. This paper argues that the case against intervention has been overstated and that there are circumstances in which competition authorities need to step in to prevent digital platforms to engage in anticompetitive behavior. In particular, competition authorities should prevent *innovation-suppressing* conduct, i.e. dominant platform conduct that has the effect of making it harder for other companies to innovate. Ensuring healthy competition in online advertising markets is also critically important.

I. INTRODUCTION

The present paper is based on observations I submitted to DG Competition in response to its calls for observations made in the context of its decision to host a conference in Brussels in January 2019 on "*Shaping Competition Policy In The Era Of Digitisation*," as well as to the UK Digital Competition Expert Panel in response to its open consultation on the effects of digital markets.[2] Given the space limitation inherent to these exercises,

---

1 Professor of Competition Law & Economics and Member of the Tilburg Law & Economics Center (TILEC). Visiting Professor, University College London. All comments are made in my personal capacity.

2 See http://ec.europa.eu/competition/scp19/; See https://www.gov.uk/government/consultations/digital-competition-expert-panel-call-for-evidence/digital-competition-expert-panel.

my observations focused on platforms relying on a two-sided business model with a "free" side and a "monetization" side (i.e. "ad-funded platforms"), such as Google, Facebook, or Twitter, and the challenges they create for EU competition policy.[3]

This paper is also based on the research work I have carried out over the past decade on the digital economy, in the context of which I have authored papers on two-sided markets, intermediation platforms and the "sharing economy," mobile operating systems, big data, and business models based on the offering of "free" services.[4] While my scholarly work has generally cautioned against an over-extensive application of EU competition law, and in particular Article 102 TFEU, in recent years I have become increasingly concerned about the anticompetitive harm created by certain practices pursued by ad-funded platforms.[5]

While there is no consensus on what constitutes a "digital platform," for the purpose of the present paper, I consider that digital platforms comprise technology-enabled tools which facilitate exchanges between multiple groups – for example end users and producers – who do not necessarily know each other. Digital platforms are often lumped together under acronyms such as "FANG" or "GAFA," but the reality is that the business models of these companies can significantly vary. Google and Facebook operate a two-sided business model comprising the provision of free services, which are monetized through online advertising. Apple's strength is in the manufacturing of devices, such as the iPhone or the iPad. It also developed a highly profitable eco-system for the distribution of apps, music, and other products. Amazon is the world leader in e-commerce. But it also provides a range of other services, such as cloud computing. Thus, while these companies typically have market power on one or several core markets, the antitrust challenges they create may be different.

Against this background, Section II makes some general observations on the state of current knowledge with respect to digital platforms, as well as the schools of thought that have recently dominated the debate. Section III looks at the reasons why market power may be durable in digital platform markets. Section IV discusses why claims against antitrust intervention in digital platform markets are generally overstated. Section V addresses the competitive concerns linked to discrimination/self-preferencing, as well as the problems linked to the shaping of remedies to address these concerns. Section VI

---

3 Thus, my observations have no or limited application to digital platforms, which are not funded by ads, but by user subscriptions or commissions.

4 See, e.g. L. Filistrucchi, D. Geradin et al., "Identifying Two-Sided Markets," 36 (2013) *World Competition*, 33; L. Filistrucchi, D. Geradin et al., "Market Definition in Two-Sided Markets: Theory and Practice," (2014) (10)2 *Journal of Competition Law & Economics* 293; See, e.g. B. Edelman & D. Geradin, "Efficiencies and Regulatory Shortcuts: How Should we Regulate Companies like Airbnb and Uber," 19 (2016) *Stanford Technology Law Review* 29; See, e.g. B. Edelman & D. Geradin, "Android and Competition Law: Exploring and Assessing Google's Practices in Mobile," 12 *European Competition Journal* 159 (2016); See, e.g. D. Geradin & M. Kuschewsky, "Competition Law and Personal Data: Preliminary Thoughts on a Complex Issues," 2 (2013) *Revue Concurrences*; See B. Edelman & D. Geradin, "An Introduction to the Competition Law and Economics of 'Free,'" *CPI Antitrust Chronicle* (September 2018).

5 See D. Geradin et al., *EU Competition Law and Economics*, OUP, 2013 (Chapter 4).

discusses other potential forms of exclusionary abuses that may arise from the conduct of dominant platforms. Section VII discusses the risk of exploitative conduct by dominant platforms. Section VIII looks at potential competition concerns in the online advertising markets. Finally, Section IX provides some recommendations.

II. GENERAL OBSERVATIONS

First, it is important to recognize that no clear answers have been yet given to some questions of considerable importance to the application of competition rules in digital platform markets. For instance, is the success of some platforms essentially linked to their ability to acquire or process large troves of data or is it primarily due to superior engineering? Moreover, to the extent that data matters to the competitive process, could data-sharing remedies be envisaged considering technical and legal constraints? These are examples of questions that were already raised in competition policy circles a decade ago and on which the debate does not seem to have much progressed.

Second, digital markets are complex and publicly-available information on the inner workings of such markets is scarce. Thus, unless one obtains access to information privately-held by market actors (for instance on how first and second price auctions work in online display advertising markets), it is difficult to form an opinion – as an external observer – on the competition challenges created by certain practices and on the way these challenges can be successfully addressed. Thus, while there is a fair amount of commentary on the directions competition policy should take in digital markets, most observations made are unavoidably based on incomplete, and in most cases very incomplete, information.

Third, as a consequence of this "empirical uncertainty," debates have often been dominated – especially in the U.S. – by the extremes. For instance, some commentators have argued that most of the problems associated with digital platforms are not competition problems and, even if there were competition problems, competition authorities should refrain from intervening because market power is ephemeral and there is a significant risk of type-II errors.[6] But proponents of another school of thought, often labelled neo-Brandeisians, have suggested the need for a more draconian application of competition rules and the abandonment of the consumer welfare standard.[7] In my view, both schools of thoughts are misguided. While digital platforms raise important competition issues that may require intervention, the EU competition regime and standards are sufficiently flexible to address such issues.

---

6 See, e.g. G. Manne & J. Wright, "Google and the Limits of Antitrust: The Case Against the Antitrust Case Against Google," 34 (2011) *Harvard Journal of Law & Public Policy* 171.

7 For a discussion, see H. Hovenkamp, "Is Antitrust's Consumer Welfare Principle Imperiled?" (2018), Faculty Scholarship at Penn Law, 1985, available at https://scholarship.law.upenn.edu/faculty_scholarship/1985.

III. MARKET POWER, BARRIERS TO ENTRY, AND COUNTERVAILING STRATEGIES

Arguments are regularly made that market power in such markets is temporary. It is indeed easy to point out to examples of digital platforms that were displaced by more innovative competitors. For instance, social network MySpace was overtaken by Facebook, and the early search engines like Altavista and Yahoo were supplanted by Google. However, when Facebook overtook MySpace and Google unseated Yahoo and Altavista, those incumbents were much smaller in market capitalization, employees, scope of operation, user base, and every other dimension compared to today's tech giants.

Moreover, certain characteristics of digital platforms tend to make market power durable by rendering entry difficult:

- First, when services are offered for "free" (or, more correctly, without a financial counterpart), the classic trade-off between quality and price, which allows new entrants to gain market share by offering their products at a somewhat lower level of quality but for a much cheaper price (what has been labelled "disruptive innovation"), is absent.[8] Thus, in the absence of a positive price that can be undercut, entry may be made difficult, especially as it forces the new entrant to compete at the same level of quality of the incumbent. This may not be possible when, as is often the case in digital platform markets, quality depends wholly or partly on scale (see next bullet point).[9]

- Second, digital platform markets may be characterized by the presence of user and monetization "feedback loops."[10] User feedback loops arise as more users allow a platform to collect more user data which in turn allows the platform to provide better quality services, which in turn attract a larger number of users. This user feedback loop may also translate into a monetization feedback loop where the more data a platform can collect, the better it can target its ads and monetize its services. Whether the presence of such feedback loops can be overcome by smaller providers and new entrants depends on the point at which returns to additional customer information begin to diminish, as well as the extent to which a data disadvantage can be overcome by innovation. These are complex questions to which there are no clear answers.

---

8 Joseph Bower & Clayton Christensen, "Disruptive Technologies: Catching the Wave," *Harvard Business Review*, January-February 1995.

9 B. Edelman & D. Geradin, *supra* note 5..

10 See A. Lerner, "The Role of Big Data in Online Platform Competition," August 27, 2014, available at http://ssrn.com/abstract=2482780.

- Digital platforms may also be characterized by "network effects" (also called network externalities or demand-side economies of scale), which arise when the value of the platform to each user grows with the number of other people using the platform. Such network effects are observable in social networks, such as Facebook, where the attractiveness of the platform grows with the number of users. The presence of such network effects may reach a tipping point with the market turning to monopoly.[11]

While these feedback loops and network effects may provide benefits to consumers, they can also "contribute to the development and durability of platform monopolies."[12]

Thus, some digital markets indeed appear to tend towards only one or a small number of firms and this is largely due to inherent features of these markets. For instance, to be commercially successful, a new search engine would have to face the near impossible equation of having to provide a service that would at the same time (i) be free (as users would not be willing to pay more than for Google Search); (ii) offered at a level of quality equivalent to that of Google Search (as the new search engine would not be cheaper than Google Search); (iii) which in turn hinges to a large extent on the ability to have access to data and develop scale.

Competing against incumbents offering high quality services at zero price thus seems particularly challenging as customers have no incentives to switch to an alternative product whose quality will likely be inferior to start with.

This does not necessarily mean the market entry is not possible in market dominated by such incumbents.[13]

- First, with sufficient capitalization, a platform could try to overcome the presence of user and monetization loops by accepting to incur significant costs to develop a free service at scale, which it would then be able to monetize through ads. For the very large and best-funded entrants, these strategies seem to be possible, though with exceptional expense and risk. And it is not clear this strategy will succeed. For instance, Microsoft's decade-plus commitment to invest in online search, at one point leading to losses of as much as $1 billion per quarter, was not sufficient to allow it to compete on equal terms with Google.[14]

---

11 H. Shelanski, "Information, Innovation, and Competition Policy for the Internet," 6 (2013) *University of Pennsylvania Law Review* 1663, 1682.

12 *Id.* at 1684.

13 This part of the paper draws on B. Edelman & D. Geradin, *supra* note 5.

14 David Goldman, "Microsoft's Plan to Stop Bing's $1 Billion Bleeding," *CNN Money*, September 20, 2011, https://money.cnn.com/2011/09/20/technology/microsoft_bing/.

- Second, an entrant could try to offer an entirely new service that does not directly compete with any incumbent, and thus is not vulnerable to the difficulty of undercutting a free incumbent. For example, at its launch, Twitter offered a service that was quite different from Facebook. Now, only rarely does an entrant devise an entirely new type of offering, of broad interest, with potential far-reaching effects. There is also the risk that new innovative services may be acquired by incumbents. For instance, Facebook acquired Instagram, which appeared as an attractive alternative to its social network.

- Third, an entrant may find an opportunity to attract consumers when they are dissatisfied with the incumbents' service despite it being "free." For example, after Facebook faced a series of scandals including data broker Cambridge Analytica siphoning data about 87 million users, as well as Russian meddling and the spread of "fake news," some users indicated that they would leave the service.[15] However, if entry is limited to situations when incumbents face a combination of multiple problems, it will most likely be infrequent.

- Finally, an entrant may attempt to respond to the incumbent's free service, by charging a positive price and eliminating features of the incumbent's service about which consumers are dissatisfied. For example, in response to an incumbent offering free service monetized through advertising, an entrant could instead charge a subscription fee and forego advertising. Netflix's positioning vis-à-vis YouTube broadly fits this pattern. In other circumstances, an entrant may offer its customers both free and paid service, typically the former with ads and the latter without. Spotify's free and paid services fit this approach.

Even where these strategies create opportunities for entrants, there are doubts about their feasibility in the face of today's large and entrenched incumbents. When Google unseated Yahoo and Altavista, those firms were much smaller in market capitalization, employees, scope of operation, user base, and every other dimension compared today's tech giants. Any entrant seeking to oust a dominant tech firm today would face larger, better-organized, multi-product competitors that are better positioned to respond and defend their market position. The idea that market power in digital platforms is ephemerous and that no antitrust intervention is needed thus fails to convince.

---

15 Deepa Seetharaman, "Facebook Shares Tumble as Growth Outlook Darkens," *The Wall Street Journal*, July 25, 2018.

16 M. Katz & H. Shelanski, "'Schumpeterian' Competition and Antitrust Policy in High-Tech Markets," Fall/Winter 2005, *Competition*, at 47, 49.

IV. THE OVERSTATED CASE AGAINST ANTITRUST INTERVENTION: SCHUMPETERIAN COMPETITION AND THE RISK OF TYPE-II ERRORS

Concerns have been expressed that the conventional antitrust framework, which focuses on prices and output competition, may fail to capture that competitive pressure may come less from actual competitors trying to have a stab at the incumbent's market share than from rivals innovating to supplant the incumbent.[16] In other words, pursuant to Schumpeterian competition, firms compete sequentially for the market as a whole. In this context, antitrust intervention in digital markets is not only superfluous, but – because of the complexity of digital platform markets – it is also subject to type-II (over-enforcement) errors.

While these concerns may be valid, they are not sufficient to justify antitrust inaction when a dominant platform engages in exclusionary behavior. First, while it is true that in the high-tech industry competition often takes place for the market rather than in the market, this is not necessarily true. For instance, Google's vertical search engines compete with other firms' verticals, and intervention may thus be necessary when Google leverages its market power in general search to exclude downstream rivals. The same is true for third-party resellers, which compete with Amazon on its e-commerce platform. Such third-party resellers do not try to displace Amazon, but compete on the merits on its platform. Thus, while Google and Amazon may eventually be displaced by more innovative companies (subject to my observations in Section II), they should not be allowed to abuse their market power in the meantime.

Second, the risk of type-II errors should not in and of itself prevent intervention when platforms engage in exclusion. First, while digital markets are complex and competition authorities should exercise their powers with care, competition authorities regularly intervene in markets raising complex technical issues (e.g. telecommunications, financial services, etc.). Moreover, while over-enforcement may not be desirable, type-I (under-enforcement) errors should not be discounted. In fact, such errors may be particularly damaging considering that these platforms not only control access to their own products and services, but also – and this is a critical observation – to third-parties' products and services given their intermediation functions ("bottleneck monopolists").[17]

---

17 Shelanski, *supra* note 12, at 1676 ("While a typical monopolist controls its own products and services, a typical bottleneck monopolist both controls access to its own service and can affect access to some number of other products and services. Thus, a digital platform monopolist controls its own product or service as well as access to a much broader universe of products or services; it affects the decisions of a much broader universe of users").

V. VERTICAL FORECLOSURE THROUGH SELF-PREFERENCING

As illustrated by the Google Shopping decision of the European Commission, competition problems may arise when a firm that owns a dominant platform (Google Search) competes on a downstream market (comparison shopping services) with other firms that need to have access to the dominant platform to provide their services.[18] In that decision, the Commission found that Google abused its dominant position by systematically giving prominent placement to its own comparison-shopping service in its search results, while demoting rival comparison shopping services in these results. The abusive conduct identified by the Commission has been labelled as "self-preferencing" in that Google used its dominant platform to give a competitive advantage to its comparison-shopping services over rival services.

A related concern seems to have led the Commission and the Bundeskartellamt to investigate Amazon.[19] While little is known about these investigations, they seem to be focused on Amazon's dual role as a competitor, but also host, to third-party merchants, which sell goods on Amazon's e-commerce platform. Because of this dual role Amazon has access to valuable data on the availability, prices, return rates and popularity of competitors' products, which it could potentially use to stimulate its own retail activities at the expense of third-party sellers on its marketplace.

These cases raise several questions. First, is discrimination/self-preferencing a competition law issue? The Commission and the Bundeskartellamt clearly think it is, and I agree as the risk of foreclosure created by vertical integration is not new in competition law. It is, however, important for competition authorities to articulate a clear theory of harm, as well as limiting principles allowing dominant platforms to distinguish pro-competitive from anti-competitive behavior. Should, for instance, antitrust intervention be limited to cases where the platform is an "essential facility" or should it be broader? And what should be the demarcation line between a benign (or even pro-competitive) discrimination and an anticompetitive one? Or should we go further and consider that a company cannot at the same time own the platform and compete on the platform because of the presence of an inherent "conflict of interest"? These are important questions to consider going forward.

Second, what is the best way to remedy situations of anticompetitive discrimination? The remedy offered by Google in response to the Commission's *Shopping* decision seems to do little to address the concerns expressed by the vertical search engines competing with

---

18 Press Release, "Antitrust: Commission fines Google €2.42 billion for abusing dominance as search engine by giving illegal advantage to own comparison shopping service," IP/17/1784, June 27, 2017.

19 R. Toplensky & S. Shannon Bond, "EU opens probe into Amazon use of data about merchants," *Financial Times*, September 19, 2018, available at https://www.ft.com/content/a8c78888-bc0f-11e8-8274-55b72926558f; R. Toplensky, "German cartel office launches investigation into Amazon marketplace," *Financial Times*, November 29, 2018, available at https://www.ft.com/content/ed2d1980-f3ef-11e8-ae55-df4bf40f9d0d.

Google.[20] Thus, the approach of the Commission to essentially leave it to Google to offer a remedy responding to the finding of infringement was not successful. The reluctance of the Commission to adopt a precise remedy may be linked to the difficulty to define remedies in digital cases. The adoption of behavioral remedies raises a variety of issues when applied to platforms operating intermediation services not only in terms of design, but also with respect to implementation and monitoring. This is why, although they are often depicted as extreme, structural remedies may present advantages, especially when, as noted above, these platforms not only control access to their own products and services, but also to third-parties' product and services.

As will be further discussed below, one of the downsides with competition cases is that they take a long time to resolve (although the CMA may have a better record than the Commission in this respect) and remedies may come at a time where the market has already tipped in favor of a company. In addition, there may be instances where the platform and a company that may have suffered from what could be perceived as discrimination (e.g. a change in an algorithm) may be able to resolve the issue without the intervention of a competition authority. Thus, informal dispute settlement mechanisms – possibly led by independent third-parties – allowing users of the platform to voice concerns and giving the possibility to the platform to address them before the issue becomes contentious might be helpful.

VI. OTHER EXCLUSIONARY ISSUES

While vertical foreclosure has been the main concern of the European Commission, other antitrust concerns may also arise. That is the case of what I would refer to as innovation-suppressing conduct, i.e. dominant platform conduct that has the effect of making it harder for other companies to innovate. While some conducts belonging to this category may take the form of vertical foreclosure, others may not. The reason why competition authorities should focus on protecting the ability of firms to innovate is two-fold:

> - First, suggesting that competition authorities focus on innovation-suppressing conduct makes sense considering that there is a broad consensus, even among those suggesting that competition authorities should generally not intervene in digital markets (see Section III), that – in these markets – competition is based on innovation, i.e. that incumbents are eventually displaced by more innovative firms.[21]

---

20 R. Toplensky & M. Acton, "Google antitrust remedy delivers few changes for rivals," *Financial Times*, October 27, 2017, available at https://www.ft.com/content/b3779ef6-b974-11e7-8c12-5661783e5589.

21 For a good discussion of the Schumpeterian argument, see Shelanski & Katz, *supra* note 17, at 49 (explaining that "[a]t the heart of the Schumpeterian argument is the assertion that, in important instances, competition primarily occurs through cycles of innovation, rather than through static price or output competition," and that in such instances firms compete "sequentially for the market as a whole").

- Second, the risk that digital platforms engage in innovation-suppressing conduct is particularly heightened considering the large amount of information they are able to collect as part of their intermediation role. For instance, Google Search gives Google unparalleled insight into consumer and market trends and thus the ability to anticipate where competitive challenges may come from, even if such challenges may not necessarily come from direct rivals.

Without claiming to be exhaustive, I hereafter present several forms innovation-suppressing conduct can take.

A. *Appropriating a Platform User's Content*

For instance, Google has long been accused by Yelp of "scraping" content to fill its own rival site with content and reviews.[22] Google also extracts snippets from news publishers' content, which will appear in response to search queries on its SERP or on Google News. As pointed out by a leading scholar:

> [W]hen viewed from the perspective of innovation, such conduct is damaging, even absent any intellectual property violation... Specifically, scraping sends the message that as soon as a firm develops a complementary product that is superior to the platform's proprietary complement, the platform will snatch the improvements for itself. This conduct also removes the platform's incentive to continue developing its own product, thus further magnifying the harm to competition.[23]

While in the case of Yelp scraping could be seen as a form of vertical foreclosure harming a downstream competitor, innovation can also be discouraged when a platform takes advantage of the content produced by businesses that are not direct competitors (e.g. news publishers) as scraping produces the same innovation-suppressing effect.

B. *Suppressing Access to Data or Making Such Access More Difficult*

Given the role of user data as a central input to products and services in the digital economy, digital platforms' actions that prevent actual or potential rivals to obtain access to categories of data that are not replicable may produce an innovation-suppressing effect. For instance, restrictions to the portability of online advertising campaign data to

---

22 See N. Tiku, "Yelp Claims Google Broke Promise to Antitrust Regulators," *Wired*, December 9, 2017, available at https://www.wired.com/story/yelp-claims-google-broke-promise-to-antitrust-regulators/.

23 See Shelanski, *supra* note 12, at 1700.

competing online advertising platforms may be problematic as they prevent these rival platforms to build scale and improve their services.[24] Similarly, when a platform is able to gather data from the interactions between users and content produced or services offered by third-parties (e.g. online newspapers), these third-parties should obtain easy access to that data as it may be necessary to improve and monetize their services.

C. Predatory Innovation (i.e. the alteration of one or more technical elements of a product to limit or eliminate competition)[25]

While predatory innovation is still a "burgeoning" theory of harm in EU competition law, it should receive greater attention in the context of digital platforms, especially when these platforms do not limit themselves to a pure intermediation function. To the extent that a digital platform alters a product or service (e.g. by degrading interoperability or compatibility with rival products or services) specifically to interfere with the competitiveness of actual or potential competitors, it impedes innovation to the detriment of consumers.[26]

VII. EXPLOITATION

An additional antitrust concern is exploitation. There is an inherent "give-and-take" relationship between an intermediation platform and its users. For instance, in return for freely enjoying its social network service, users allow Facebook to collect and use their data to target the display ads that appear in their newsfeed. Business users are also involved in a give-and-take relationship with digital platforms. For instance, while Google's ability to respond to user queries by providing links to news stories is beneficial to Google, publishers also benefit from the traffic that is sent to them in response to such queries.

The give-and-take relationship may, however, become unbalanced when platforms acquire market power. This can lead to user exploitation, not in the traditional form of excessive pricing (as services are free), but by the platform giving less (in the form of lower quality of the rendered service, less privacy, etc.) and taking more (collecting more data, scraping content from publishers, etc.). While some forms of exploitation can be addressed by regulation, there will be instances where the Commission should step in to prevent digital platforms to engage in exploitative behavior.[27]

---

24 See Press Release, "Antitrust: Commission probes allegations of antitrust violations by Google," IP/10/1624, November 30, 2010.

25 See Thibault Schrepel, "Predatory Innovation: The Definite Need for Legal Recognition," July 2017, available at https://papers.ssrn.com/sol3/papers.cfm?abstract_id=2997586.

26 See Shelanski, *supra* note 12, at 1697.

27 The Commission's proposal for a Regulation on promoting fairness and transparency for business users of online intermediation services (Brussels, 26.4.2018 COM(2018) 238 final 2018/0112 (COD)) takes useful steps in this direction.

VIII. ENSURING COMPETITIVE ONLINE ADVERTISING MARKETS

Online content providers typically rely on two types of revenues to fund their operations: Subscription fees and/or advertising. In some cases, these operators will charge their users subscription fees. That is, for instance, the case of premium newspapers (e.g. the Financial Times) or specialized magazines (e.g. The Economist). But in most instances, advertising is the only source of revenue for online content providers, and even publishers relying on subscription fees need advertising revenues to balance their budget.

While there are different types of online advertising, publishers typically rely on display ads, i.e. visual-based advertisements (e.g. texts, images or videos) shown on their website, as a source of revenue.[28] Initially, online display advertising was no more complex than ordinary offline advertising, e.g. in print media or TV. Publishers wishing to monetize their available ad space (called "ad inventory") would engage in direct negotiations with advertisers to sell ad space at a given price. But now the sector is dominated by so-called "programmatic advertising," whereby dedicated software and complex algorithms fueled by various categories of user data (behavioral, demographic, etc.) are used to sell and purchase ad inventory within fragments of a second, avoiding "human" negotiation between publishers and advertisers.[29]

Because of its vital importance to advertisers and publishers, healthy competition in the advertising ecosystem is desirable. Yet, despite the spectacular growth of online display advertising, the picture is not entirely rosy. The ad tech sector, which comprises all the intermediaries providing ad intermediation and ad delivery services, is characterized by a high degree of opacity. Moreover, publishers and advertisers are concerned about the so-called "ad tech tax," i.e. the large and opaque fees applied by intermediaries.[30] For instance, The Guardian revealed in 2016 that "in worst case scenarios, for every pound an advertiser spends programmatically only 30 pence actually goes to the publisher," meaning that ad tech intermediaries could extract up to 70 percent of programmatic revenues.[31] Moreover, while the ad tech sector comprises a wide variety of actors, some of

---

28 As opposed to search ads, i.e. text-based ads that appear typically above the natural, so-called "organic" search results in the results page of a search engine.

29 For an excellent introduction to the programmatic revolution, see M. Sweeney, "The Colorful History of Advertising Technology in Just 63 Slides," *The Clearcode Blog*, May 12, 2015, available at https://clearcode.cc/blog/the-colorful-history-of-advertising-technology-in-just-63-slides/.

30 See for example S. Gatz, "Publishers And the Hidden 'Ad Tech Tax,'" *AdExchanger*, April 1, 2016, available at https://adexchanger.com/the-sell-sider/publishers-and-the-hidden-ad-tech-tax/; M. Sweeney, "Transparency in Ad Tech: The Problems, Fallouts and Solutions," *The Clearcode Blog*, available at https://clearcode.cc/blog/ad-tech-transparency/.

31 D. Pidgeon, "Where did the money go? Guardian buys its own ad inventory," *Mediatel Newsline*, October 4, 2016, available at https://mediatel.co.uk/newsline/2016/10/04/where-did-the-money-go-guardian-buys-its-own-ad-inventory/.

its segments appear to be dominated by a single operator (usually Google), with concerns being expressed that it may engage in both exploitative and exclusionary strategies.[32]

It is thus not surprising that competition authorities are looking closely at the competitive dynamics in online advertising. The French Competition Authority launched in 2016 a sector enquiry in the online advertising sector and in March 2018 it published its opinion, "in which it analyses a very complex market, characterized by a fragile competitive equilibrium."[33] On November 8, 2018, the Authority announced "the opening of litigation investigations on abusive data collection and processing as well as access restrictions."[34] The German Competition Authority announced on 1 February 2018 that it launches its own sector enquiry into online advertising, and released a related short paper.[35] In the UK, the Select Committee on Communications appointed by the House of Lords observed in its 2018 Report the lack of transparency in digital advertising and advised that the CMA "conduct a market study of digital advertising to investigate whether the market is working fairly for businesses and consumers."[36]

Thus, while the attention of commentators has largely focused on the competition problems created by digital platforms on the "free" side of the market, it is important to keep in mind that maintaining healthy competition in online advertising markets is critical

---

32 Google is the market leader in online display advertising, offering, *inter alia*, DoubleClick For Publishers ("DFP"), the leading ad server technology for publishers, and operating the most popular ad exchange ("Ad Exchange") where ad impressions are sold to advertisers through real-time auctions. However, it has been suggested that Google might use its strength in DFP and its informational advantage to favour its own Ad Exchange *vis-à-vis* competing ad exchanges. See G. Sloane, "WTF is Dynamic Allocation?," *Digiday*, April 14, 2016, available at https://digiday.com/media/wtf-dynamic-allocation-google-ad-auctions/ (noting that a feature of DFP "allowed Google's exchange to cherry-pick the best ad impressions as they came through the Google-owned ad server, DFP [...] Google had an informational advantage to buying the best impressions, and the informational advantage came from the fact that they own the ad server"); G. Dunaway, "Rethinking the Ad Server," *AdMonsters*, August 23, 2016, available at https://www.admonsters.com/rethinking-ad-server/. In response to industry backlash and the rise of alternative technologies, Google introduced in 2018 a new feature in DFP, apparently exposing Ad Exchange to competition from other ad exchanges. However, commentators are still concerned about the lack of transparency of Google's offer. See B. LaRue, "Last Stand for Google's 'Last Look': What's Next?," *Admonsters*, available at https://www.admonsters.com/last-stand-googles-last-look-whats-next/ (noting that Google's latest solution, called Exchange Bidding, "still comes out looking something like a black box, unified auction or no"); S. Sluis, "Google Removes Its 'Last-Look-Auction Advantage,'" *AdExchanger*, March 31, 2017 available at https://adexchanger.com/platforms/google-removes-last-look-auction-advantage/; As regards *exploitative* concerns, Google could take advantage of the existence of consecutive second-price auctions that take place within Ad Exchange and engage in arbitrage, pocketing the difference between the price charged to the advertiser and the price paid to the publisher. The ad intermediaries' possibility for arbitrage has been flagged up in specialized press articles; See R. Benes, "In programmatic, buyers sometimes don't know what type of auction they're bidding in," *Digiday*, June 30, 2017, available at https://digiday.com/marketing/ad-buyers-programmatic-auction/; R. Benes, "Ad buyer, beware: How DSPs sometimes play fast and loose," *Digiday*, March 25, 2017, available at https://digiday.com/marketing/dsp-squeeze-buyers/.

33 Opinion no. 18-A-03 of March 6, 2018 on data processing in the online advertising sector, available at http://www.autoritedelaconcurrence.fr/doc/avis18a03_en_.pdf.

34 See https://twitter.com/Adlc_/status/1060459904417316864.

35 Press release of Bundeskartellamt of January 1, 2018, "Bundeskartellamt launches sector inquiry into market conditions in online advertising sector," available at https://www.bundeskartellamt.de/SharedDocs/Meldung/EN/Pressemitteilungen/2018/01_02_2018_SU_Online_Werbung.html; Bundeskartellamt, "Competition and Consumer Protection in the Digital Economy": Online advertising, available at https://www.bundeskartellamt.de/SharedDocs/Publikation/EN/Schriftenreihe_Digitales_III.html?nn=3600108.

36 House of Lords, Select Committee on Communications, 1st Report of Session 2017-2019 "UK advertising in a digital age," April 11, 2018.

for the thousands of publishers, large and small, which offer valuable content to Internet users. But for online display advertising, many such publishers would not subsist, and the Internet would be impoverished.

IX. RECOMMENDATIONS

One of the challenges for competition authorities in the digital space is that they are subject to institutional constraints in terms or resources and procedures.

The following bullet points make several suggestions that the Commission should consider in order to address concerns that are regularly expressed about the way in which investigations are conducted in fast moving technology markets.

A. Greater Output

Although the competition issues raised by dominant platforms regularly make headlines in the press, the decisional output of the Commission, which is limited to the Google Shopping and Android decisions, has been somewhat limited so far. Decisions of competition authorities and judgments of the EU Courts are public goods as they may not only bring competition infringements to an end and provide remedies restoring competition, but they also (i) provide guidance to undertakings active in the sectors concerned, (ii) improve the knowledge pool on the competition issues created by digital platforms within the agency and in the public sphere and (iii) reduce the risk of missing important cases both in terms of harm to consumers and in terms of the opportunity these cases may offer to set important principles.

B. Faster Outcomes

While the Commission cannot rush the conduct of its investigations as it is subject to strict judicial review, the best way to increase output and restore competition in markets that are distorted by digital platforms is to increase the speed with which cases are processed. While some of the measures that could be taken may require a modification of Article 1/2003, there may be for instances merits in establishing time limits to some of the phases of the procedure. Whether a complaint should be rejected or lead to the opening of formal proceedings is a decision that should, for instance, be taken within a reasonable period of time. That is not always the case and once proceedings have been opened the investigation can last up to ten years. Thus, I would suggest the adoption of a two-stage process whereby in stage one complaints are examined within a period of one year at the end of which they should either be rejected or formal proceedings be opened and in stage two the cases for which proceedings would have been opened would be dealt with in no longer than two years. This approach would have procedural and staffing implications (with greater resources having to be channeled to the enforcement of competition rules in digital markets), but a maximum period of three years from the filing of complaint until the adoption of a decision sounds reasonable to produce an outcome in fast-moving markets.

C. Use of Interim Measures

While the Commission is yet to use its powers to impose interim measures under Article 8 of Regulation 1/2003, the digital space is probably an area where such measures could be adopted when justified. The conditions included in the current legal test for the adoption of interim measures are quite stringent, but there are considerable merits in using such measures in industries where markets can tip quickly and, unless the Commission steps in, harm to the competition process may be irreversible.

D. Need for Data Science Expertise

While the lawyers and economists who regularly compose case teams have great skills, it would be helpful to consider the recruitment of data scientists. Some authorities, such as the UK CMA have already taken steps in this direction and, unless done already, the Commission should perhaps follow suit.

E. Stimulating Debate and Research

While competition authorities are enforcement bodies, they should also seek to stimulate independent research in the field of competition policy and digital platforms. For instance, enforcement actions have allowed the Commission to acquire significant knowledge on the possible impact of certain digital platform actions on competition. Yet, many important questions remain unsolved and independent research is scarce.

FROM WEB2.0 TO WEB3.0 AND CRYPTO: IS THERE ROOM FOR THE DISTRIBUTED LEDGER TECHNOLOGY IN THE TELECOMMUNICATION AND MEDIA SECTOR?

By Gabriella Muscolo & Giovanni Pitruzzella[1]

ABSTRACT

We stand at the dawn of a new revolution led by Blockchain, which may disrupt the platform-based economy. Blockchain is developing in sectors, such as the media sector, which have been so far remarkably impacted by online giants. This contribution deals with the economic and technological basics of the phenomenon, attempting to sketch a definition of blockchain. It will then examine the expansion of the distributed ledger technology on the media and telecommunication markets and focus on the analysis of antitrust implications of blockchain. A few remarks on blockchain patentability are also added. Finally, the contribution will try to draw some conclusions on the effective relevance of blockchain in the antitrust field and on the role that policy makers and decision makers should play in the face of this new phenomenon.

I. THE DIGITAL AND DATA DRIVEN ECONOMY: FROM PLATFORMS TO BLOCKCHAIN

The Internet was developed with the idea of providing a global computer network based on valuable principles such as freedom and democracy. Indeed, this ecosystem was char-

---

1 Gabriella Muscolo is a Commissioner at the Italian Competition Authority. Giovanni Pitruzzella is Advocate General at the Court of Justice of the European Union. All views expressed in this paper are strictly personal and do not reflect the opinion of the institutions to which the authors belong. We are grateful to Alessandro Massolo, economic advisor of Commissioner Muscolo, for the insightful conversations we had on the topics considered in the present contribution and Veronica Piccolo, stagiaire at the Italian Competition Authority, for her help in the research work.

acterized by decentralized, interconnected networks which allowed peer to peer communication without the need of intermediaries.[2]

Today, the Internet is dominated by online platforms, particularly by the five most popular
U.S. tech stocks: Google, Apple, Facebook, Amazon and Microsoft ("GAFAM"), which
intermediate most of the transactions and communications among internet users every
day. Most importantly, GAFAM have become the leading collectors of Big Data and are
able to provide targeted services which strengthen their market power.

Many scholars and policymakers have fiercely debated this concentration of market power
and an increasing will of re-establishing a level playing field in the Internet has emerged.
The topic of empowering consumers, publishers, or any other users to extract value from
data in parallel platforms' ecosystem has been widely discussed: According to this tendency it seems that the new cultural zeitgeist for the next decades will be "decentralization."

The European Commission also implemented the Decode project a couple of years ago,
which is in response to people's concerns about the loss of control over their personal information on the Internet. Decode is exploring how to build a data-centric digital economy
where data that is generated and gathered by citizens, the Internet of Things ("IoT"), and
sensor networks is available for broader communal use, with appropriate privacy protections.

Furthermore, this need to decentralize the web is spreading throughout the whole industry.

For instance, Tim Berners-Lee, the inventor of the World Wide Web, has launched the
Solid project ("Social Linked Data"). The project aims to radically change the way Web
applications work today, resulting in true data ownership as well as improved privacy by
developing a platform for linked data applications that are completely decentralized and
fully under users' control, rather than controlled by other entities.

As a result, innovators, start-ups, NGOs, cooperatives, and local communities could take
advantage of that data to build apps and services that respond to their needs and those of
the wider community.[3]

In this context new technologies, such as blockchain, are emerging which offer an opportunity to eliminate the centralized control of digital platforms and, consequently, to
redesign the industry architecture in order to promote competition. On the one hand,
there is the online platform model characterized by multi-sided markets, network effects,
economies of scale which have led to winner takes all effects. On the other hand, the
blockchain model enables peer-to-peer communications and transactions among users

---

2 See Ioannis Lianos, *Blockchain Competition Gaining Competitive Advantage in the Digital Economy: Competition
Law Implications* (BRICS Competition Law center, research paper series: 1/2018) who mentions the "democratic ethos"
of the origins of Internet.

3 For further information see: https://decodeproject.eu/.

without the need of intermediaries through the tokenization of assets. This model, therefore, makes it possible to decentralize the Internet industry.

We stand at the dawn of a new revolution led by Blockchain, which may disrupt the platform-based economy. Blockchain is developing in sectors, such as the media sector, which have been so far remarkably impacted by online giants.

In the contribution that follows we will first deal with the economic and technological basics of the phenomenon, attempting to sketch a definition of blockchain. We will then examine the expansion of the distributed ledger technology on the media and telecommunication markets and focus on the analysis of antitrust implications of blockchain. A few remarks on blockchain patentability are also added. Finally, we will try to draw some conclusions on the effective relevance of blockchain in the antitrust field and on the role that policy makers and decision makers should play in the face of this new phenomenon.

II. BLOCKCHAIN: BASICS AND DEFINITION

There is no generally accepted definition of "blockchain;"[4] moreover, there are manifold types of blockchain that, nevertheless, share the same main features.

Blockchain is an infrastructure based on Distributed Ledger Technology (DLT), whose functioning has been depicted by the World Economic Forum in the following terms:

> [B]lockchain allows consumers and suppliers to connect directly, removing the need for a third party. Using cryptography to keep exchanges secure, blockchain provides a decentralized database, or "digital ledger", of transactions that everyone on the network can see. This network is essentially a chain of computers that must all approve an exchange before it can be verified and recorded.

---

4 There is a widely-held view about blockchain being a new General Purpose Technology ("GPT") as outcome of the combination of all three key characteristics: pervasiveness, improvement, and innovation spawning. The requirement of pervasiveness has to be interpreted as the susceptibility of the technology at issue to be applied in different productive sectors. In this way, it is possible to note that blockchain presents this character, given that this technology, also if originally created for the crypto-currency sector, has actually, especially in the digital economy, a very wide scope of application ranging from smart contracts to advertising. The character of improvement consists instead in the susceptibility of the technology in question to be improved over time with also a concurrent lowering of costs for its users. Blockchain is a technology whose margins for improvement are not yet well defined, but certainly noticeable considering its wide scope of application. In this way, it can contribute to significantly lower the costs that its users have to bear to carry out a large number of activities.
Finally, the requirement of innovation spawning is satisfied when a technology is able to make innovation easier by facilitating the creation of new products or processes. As noted above with regard to pervasiveness, blockchain is contributing decisively to technological innovation. Suffice it to consider that, through its application to sectors other than that for which it was originally intended, new procedures and new products have been created (on all, smart contracts) that have made it easier to carry out certain activities. See Philipp Hacker, Ioannis Lianos, Georgios Dimitropoulos, Stefan Eich, *Regulating Blockchain: Techno-Social and Legal Challenges - An Introduction,* in REGU-LATING BLOCKCHAIN. TECHNO-SOCIAL AND LEGAL CHALLENGES 3 (Philipp Hacker et al. eds., 2019), https://ssrn.com/abstract=3247150. For a more detailed knowledge on GPT see Boyan Jovanovic & Peter L. Rousseau, *General Purpose Technologies* (NBER, Working Paper No. 11093, January 2005); Ioannis Lianos, Blockchain And Competition Law: A Conceptual Guide, Lecture at Faculty of laws UCL (2018).

[…] The technology can work for almost every type of transaction involving value, including money, goods and property. Its potential uses are almost limitless: from collecting taxes to enabling migrants to send money back to family in countries where banking is difficult. Blockchain could also help to reduce fraud because every transaction would be recorded and distributed on a public ledger for anyone to see.[5]

In a nutshell, blockchain could be simply defined as a long list of records, "blocks," which are linked. Each block can contain a cryptographic hash of the previous block, a timestamp, and transaction data.[6] Therefore, a blockchain can be considered as a technology consisting in a ledger (a sort of database), which is deployed in a peer-to-peer computer network.

This kind of architecture, contrary to the client-server model, does not work via a given hierarchical organization. Indeed, the blockchain infrastructure is formed by nodes (i.e. computers, laptops, servers) which are simply the participants of the blockchain. These nodes are connected and they store and exchange data with each other.

Most importantly, new blocks can only be added by Miners which run the so-called "full nodes." This is because full nodes contain the entire history of the blockchain and can validate transactions accordingly. Thus, if one Miner leaves the network, it does not impact the system's operation[7]; that is why the technology is said to be a "distributed" ledger. Miners receive a remuneration for their activity which varies according to the value of the transaction.

The validation process depends on the type of blockchain adopted.

The main distinction occurs between public and private blockchains. The first are permissionless, in other words, access is granted to everyone who also takes part in the validation process (i.e. "distributed").[8]

Private blockchains (i.e. permissioned) are designed by a restricted group of individuals who defines both governance, rules and information access conditions. Therefore, access is not granted to all users and their validation power may be restricted as well. Hence, the validation process could be based on a "hierarchical" model.[9]

---

5 Rosamond Hutt, *All you need to know about blockchain, explained simply*, WORLD ECONOMIC FORUM, June 17, 2016, https://www.weforum.org/agenda/2016/06/blockchain-explained-simply/.

6 See ARVIND NARAYANAN, JOSEPH BONNEAU, EDWARD FELTEN, ANDREW MILLER & STEVEN GOLDFEDER, BITCOIN AND CRYPTOCURRENCY TECHNOLOGIES: A COMPREHENSIVE INTRODUCTION, 10-20 (2016).

7 Satoshi Nakamoto, *Bitcoin: A Peer-to-Peer Electronic Cash System* (White Paper, 2008), http://satoshinakamoto.me/bitcoin-draft.pdf.

8 Observatory for Blockchain & Distributed Ledger of the School of Management at *Politecnico of Milan*, speech at the Conference 'Blockchain & Distributed Ledger: verso l'Internet of Value' (Apr. 17, 2018).

9 Observatory for Blockchain & Distributed Ledger, *id*. According to professor Arvind Narayanan, the private blockchain would be nothing but a "shared database," with the only outcome of distorting the principle the technology is based on (Princeton University, Sept. 18, 2018).

Public or private blockchains can be based on a proof of work ("PoW") or proof at stake ("PoS") protocol. The first is a requirement to define an expensive computer calculation, also called mining. A reward is given to the first Miner who solves each block's problem. Network miners compete to be the first to find a solution for the mathematical problem. When using the PoS protocol, the creator of a new block is chosen in a deterministic way, depending on its wealth, also defined at stake. In the PoS system there is no block reward, so, the Miners take the transaction fees.

Blockchains are generally called by the name of their tokens. There are a wide range of tokens. The most well-known are the utility tokens. This category includes crypto currencies, such as Bitcoin, which are used for specific purposes, for instance financial speculations or buying particular goods and services. A second category of tokens is security tokens which underline real world assets like traditional stocks and bonds or other property rights. Therefore, tokens can be defined as digital assets based on blockchain which can be exchanged among parties without the need of an intermediary.

Indeed, copyright managing entities such as Soundreef use blockchain as technology copyright certification in order to fully guarantee their rights holders' music protection.[10] In addition, blockchain is used for food[11] or logistics[12] traceability.

Another important feature of blockchain is the possibility to diverge into two or more potential paths which are known as forks. These last ones have been used to add new features to a blockchain or to reverse the effects of hacking or catastrophic bugs on a blockchain.

The supply chain of blockchain can be divided in three different levels: (i) the infrastructure; (ii) the platforms; and (iii) the distributed ledger applications ("DApps").

In the upstream level, there is the infrastructure which needs cloud computing services (i.e. Amazon Web Services, Microsoft Azure, etc.) and which guarantees that participants can access blockchain simultaneously. The middle level is characterized by blockchain platforms which define the rules, such as the consensus mechanism (i.e. Ethereum, Hyperledger, etc.). The downstream level is characterized by DApps which provide services to end users (i.e. Sunfish – Ministero delle Finanze, R3-Corda etc.).

Different operators are vertically integrated within the supply chain. For example, Ripple,[13] who is renowned as crypto currency, is in reality active in each of the three above described levels.

---

10 https://soundreef.zendesk.com/hc/en-us/articles/360000531138-How-does-Soundreef-certify-your-copyright-with-the-blockchain-technology-.

11 http://www.carrefour.com/current-news/food-traceability-carrefour-a-blockchain-pioneer-in-europe-has-joined-the-ibm-food.

12 https://www.maersk.com/en/news/2018/06/29/maersk-and-ibm-introduce-tradelens-blockchain-shipping-solution.

13 https://ripple.com/.

There is a soaring tendency to band blockchain with the use of smart contracts,[14] even if these last ones were conceived far before than blockchain was, and regardless of it.[15] In particular, according to some authors, blockchain allows you to manage very complex smart contracts and can be useful when smoothing articulated processes within supply chains.[16]

From a legal point of view, a smart contract is an agreement between two or more parties that is self-executing among them when simple and certain conditions occur.
All elements of the contract, both essential and accidental, are clearly written in computer codes. In this way, following the computational identification of clauses and conditions of the contract, the executing command is automatically run without human processing.

However, smart contracts need the contribution of legal practitioners on both formation and interpretation of the contract. For instance, the automatic computational execution of commands is rigid. This could lead to a situation where some "technical" errors are perceived by the machine as obstacles to the execution of the contract.

The drafting of the contract is therefore crucial. Lawyers and advisors must carefully consider and define all the possible variables that can affect the execution of the obligation; conversely, machines lack the necessary legal reasoning and are not able, at present, to interpret a contract. This proficiency remains with the jurist.

III. THE DISTRIBUTED LEDGER TECHNOLOGY IN THE DIGITAL MEDIA SECTOR

The new digital and data-driven economy has paved the way for the proliferation of online platforms. Today, we can distinguish different categories of platforms such as e-commerce marketplaces, app stores, social media, search engines and online advertising platforms.

The media sector, as many others, has been remarkably impacted by the new digital and data-driven economy. Thus, the media value chain is now also characterized by online platforms which have created new ways for consumers to access content and they have introduced new business models which heavily depend on advertising such as social networks or search engines.[17]

In recent years, we have seen an increase in the use of online giants, such as social networks, platforms for publishers where users share, read, watch, and comment on more and more articles and videos.[18]

---

14 See for example Ethereum, a blockchain especially known for smart contracts: https://www.ethereum.org/.

15 The first theoretical rationalization of smart contracts was due to Nick Szabo, a computer scientist who coined the expression in 1997. See, Nick Szabo, *Formalizing and Securing Relationships on Public Networks*, 2/9 First Monday (Sept. 1, 1997).

16 See Mauro Bellini, Blockchain e Bitcoin, (2018).

17 Inge Graef, EU Competition Law, Data Protection and Online Platforms 13 (2016); Néstor Duch-Brown, *The Competitive Landscape of Online Platforms* (JRC Digital Economy Working Paper 2017-04).

18 Néstor Duch-Brown, *id*.

Moreover, since these platforms are considered multi sided platforms ("MSPs"),[19] the higher the number of users who join the platform, the higher the utility for advertisers to purchase advertising space.[20] Most importantly, these platforms are able to profiling their users. Therefore, they enable advertisers to deliver personalized ads to users, making the mechanism for delivering ads more efficient.

As a result, the online adverting sector has profoundly changed with a range of new activities, technologies, and stakeholders, especially due to the growth and development of "programmatic" advertising[21] and, in general, to various forms of advertising targeting Internet users in real time.[22]

More in depth, programmatic advertising functioning is similar to stock exchanges because there are computer algorithms which sell and buy media ad inventory in real time making the whole process automatic. This process involves technical and non-technical intermediation service providers for advertisers and publishers, and players specialized in supplying and analyzing data with the role of improving the performance of advertising campaigns.[23]

More specifically, there is a central platform called Ad Exchanges which facilitates the acquisition and selling of media ad inventory from multiple sources. Ad Exchanges usually interact with supply-side and demand-side platforms ("SSP" and "DSP"). SSPs are platforms focused on providing services to publishers, by managing the sale and fulfillment of publishers' advertising supply. DSPs provide services to advertisers by managing advertising campaigns of advertisers and by providing features for buying advertising placements online in real time.

However, even though there are several players at different stages of the above described process, there is a high level of concentration. In particular, online giants have occupied strategic positioning in these markets and are either integrated or participate in different stages of the process.[24]

---

19 Jean-Charles Rochet & Jean Tirole, Platform Competition in Two-Sided Markets, 1 Journal of the European Economics Association 990-1029 (2003). For an exhaustive review on multi-sided platforms and network effects see Cristiano Codagnone and Bertin Martens, Scoping the Sharing Economy: Origins, Definitions, Impact and Regulatory Issues (IPTS Digital Economy working paper 2016/01).

20 Codagnone & Martens, *Id.*

21 Programmatic media buying, marketing and advertising is the algorithmic purchase and sale of advertising space in real time. During this process, software is used to automate the buying, placement, and optimization of media inventory via a bidding system. Automating the process means that it can be done in real time and does not rely on the human touch, manual insertions and manual trading.

22 Autorité de la concurrence, *Opinion no. 18-A-03 of 6 March 2018 on data processing in the online advertising sector.* Available at http://www.autoritedelaconcurrence.fr/doc/avis18a03_en_.pdf.

23 Autorité de la concurrence, *id.*

24 Néstor Duch-Brown, *supra* note 17.

Indeed, these online giants have gained significant competitive advantages and, most importantly, they can easily monetize the attention of their users since they generate the highest volume of internet traffic and they hold the highest audiences.

Thus, different stakeholders have started to raise competition concerns and some national competition authorities are closely monitoring competition dynamics within these markets.[25]

Moreover, there is a growing literature which considers that the platform-based system is becoming inefficient, opaque, and characterized by several forms of hidden costs. First of all, this literature opinioned that the advertising online market seems overcrowded by overcompensated middlemen which are acquiring an increasing share of revenues of the online advertising market at the expenses of publishers and advertisers.[26]

Secondly, this fierce competition in getting shares from the market has incentivized certain agents to adopt fraudulent behaviors, such as malware attacks[27] or phishing,[28] which have compromised users' privacy[29] and security.[30]

Thirdly, due to the pervasiveness of advertising (in mobile apps, web pages etc.), end users are experiencing an increasing deterioration of web surfing speed and higher costs for data usage (i.e. loading ads from a remote server requires network usage, for which many users are billed by the number of bytes and too many trackers are slowing down mobiles' batteries).[31] Hence, users are protecting themselves by using ad blockers which in turn

---

25 For instance: The Italian Competition Authority has launched an inquiry on Big data (IC53); the French Competition Authority has published in cooperation with the GCA, a report on *Competition Law and Data* (May 10, 2016) at www.autoritedelaconcurrence.fr/doc/reportcompetitionlawanddatafinal.pdf, and, on the March 6, 2018, it concluded the sector specific investigation into Online advertising:
http://www.autoritedelaconcurrence.fr/user/standard.php?lang=en&id_rub=684&id_article=3133.
The Dutch Authority for Consumers and Markets (ACM) published a study into the market for online video streaming platforms, on the October 6, 2017: https://www.acm.nl/en/publications/closer-look-online-video-platforms.

26 Alexandra Bruell, *Inside the hidden costs of programmatic*, ADVERTISING AGE (Sept. 14, 2015); Jack Neff, *P&G tells digital to clean up, Lays down new rules for agencies and Ad Tech to get paid*, ADVERTISING AGE (Jan., 2017); Basic Attention Token (BAT), *Blockchain based digital advertising* (BAT white paper, Mar. 13, 2018).

27 "A malware attack is a piece of malicious software which takes over a person's computer in order to spread the bug onto other people's devices and profiles. It can also infect a computer and turn it into a botnet, which means the cyber criminal can control the computer and use it to send malware to others," Emma Barnett, *What is the difference between spam, malware and phishing?*, THE TELEGRAPH, Jan. 19, 2011.

28 "Phishing attacks are designed to steal a person's login and password details so that the cyber criminal can assume control of the victim's social network, email and online bank accounts. Seventy per cent of internet users choose the same password for almost every web service they use. This is why phishing is so effective, as the criminal, by using the same login details, can access multiple private accounts and manipulate them for their own good," Emma Barnett, *id.*

29 Mustafa Ogera, Isa Olmeza, Erinc Incia, Serkan Kücükbaya & Fatih Emekcib, *Privacy Preserving Secure Online Advertising*, 195 PROCEDIA - SOCIAL AND BEHAVIORAL SCIENCES 1840-1845 (2015); Steve Mansfield-Devine, *When advertising turns nasty*, 11/2015 NETWORK SECURITY 5-8 (November 2015).

30 Aditya K. Sood & Richard J. Enbody, *Malvertising – exploiting web advertising*, 4/2011 COMPUTER FRAUD & SECURITY 11-16 (2011).

31 Jiaping Gui, Stuart Mcilroy, Meiyappan Nagappan & William G. J. Halfond, University of Southern California, Los Angeles, CA, USA, Truth in Advertising: The Hidden Cost of Mobile Ads for Software Developers, 2015 IEEE/ACM 37th IEEE International Conference on Software Engineering (May 16-24, 2015).

reduce publisher revenues and leave the remaining ad-viewing audience even harder to target.[32]

In order to solve part of these issue, new business models have been developed based on new technologies such as blockchain also in the media sector.

In the digital media sector, too, the desire for decentralization is spreading. In particular, new models based on blockchain technology are emerging, which aim at restoring a level playing field among players within the markets. These models aim at attributing monetary value to personal data so that users get paid for receiving advertising.[33]

In this context, Brave is a web browser designed to evaluate advertising experience through the use of Basic Attention Token ("BAT") as currency, whose functioning is based on a decentralized system which, first of all, eliminates middlemen so that publishers are no longer compelled to pay. Brave allows users to browse online blocking ads, trackers, and mal-advertising. Furthermore, it seeks to promote a virtuous circle of remuneration among all the three actors in this market.

Also AdEX, a blockchain-based advertising network built on Ethereum, allows for disintermediation, i.e. direct negotiation, between publisher and advertiser. The flow of value on this side of the market (paid side) is provided by exchanging fiat currency in tokens whose sum is totally earned by the publisher who does not share anything with the intermediator, nor pay any commissions.[34]

On the other hand, privacy-focused concerns affecting the online experience in zero-price markets (related to the interface between publisher and user) is addressed by giving users the control over their preferences and advertising receipts.

In this context, Tide Foundation has engaged in getting valuable the zero-price side of the market. In brief, they have been implementing blockchain in order to foster a new economic model, attributing monetary values to personal data so that users get paid for receiving advertising.[35]

---

32 BAT, *supra* note 26.

33 Jonathan Shapiro, *Tide Foundation pitches blockchain solution to digital advertising privacy woes*, THE AUSTRALIAN FINANCIAL REVIEW (2018), https://www.afr.com/business/media-and-marketing/advertising/the-tide-turns-the-elegant-blockchain-solution-to-20180822-h14cmm.

34 See https://www.adex.network/.

35 Shapiro, *supra* note 33.

IV. COMPETITION ISSUES

A. *Competition between Blockchain and Non-Blockchain Models*

A first competitive issue refers mainly, but not exclusively, to the rivalry between the blockchain system and the online platform model. The latter being the one who has allowed the emergence of the GAFAM online giants.

From a competition law and economics perspective it would be interesting to compare these systems examining the issues of defining relevant markets, assessing market power, and alleged competitive conducts.

First of all, the online platform economy is characterized by two or multi-sided platforms which are active in several markets. Their strategy is to optimize the platform profits rather than on market profitability.[36] This has important implications when defining relevant markets because online platforms have softened the boundaries of markets.

Indeed, traditional businesses perceive highly competitive pressure from online platforms which can enter into their markets anytime. Not surprisingly part of the literature has coined this phenomenon as gatekeeping. In other words, in order to access markets, traditional businesses have to join online markets.[37]

Following this theory, it seems that online platforms have framed the digital economy by imposing a dominant industry architecture.

However, as already mentioned, recent innovations have given birth to new technologies such as blockchain which challenge this framework. Indeed, blockchain eliminates the centralized control of digital platforms and reestablishes a level playing field among players and we are witnessing the emergence of businesses specialized in complementary fields which work for the same purpose, that is to create value for the same ecosystem.

Therefore, as technology continues to evolve, we will see actors competing for strategic or architectural advantage. Thus, as some scholars[38] observed, the starting point of competition analyses will no longer be based only on defining relevant markets, but rather on strategies adopted by players in order to capture value within a certain framework. Therefore, competition law tools should be able to capture interactions among players which take place outside the relevant market.

---

36 Lianos, *supra* note 2.

37 Among others see Rupprecht Podszun, Innovation, Variety & Fair Choice – New Rules for the Digital Economy: Expert Opinion for Finanzplatz Munchen Initiative (FPMI), Sept. 22, 2018.

38 Lianos, *supra* note 2.

Second, when assessing market structures and dominance, the online platform world is characterized by economies of scale and scope and by network effects that, on the one hand, can translate into benefits for the digital consumer. However, data-driven markets can be highly contested, and on the other hand, they can favor concentration and dominance, causing the so-called winner takes all outcomes, and raising significant barriers to entry of competitors able to challenge the incumbent on the market.[39] As already observed, these market features, will lead to competing "for" the market rather than "on" the market.

On the contrary, in blockchain network effects are less pronounced. Indeed, blockchain allows for peer-to-peer interactions without involving an intermediary. Multi-homing is incentivized because users keep control on their data and can easily switch to other blockchains. Tokenization facilitates the exchange of assets not just on the platform but among different platforms of different ecosystems since it is easy to convert assets.

Moreover, the fork feature provides a credible exit option for users. In addition, blockchain's protocols are based on consensus, thus, in order to gain market power an economic actor needs to bias the whole system.

However, in private blockchains decisions on the governance are made by a restricted group of agents which could lead to competition issues stemming from excessive concentration of power in few hands. Likewise, mining activities could be concentrated in few Miners which increase their market power at the expense of an effective functioning of blockchains.

All in all, market power of a blockchain can be assessed by considering the number of participants, recorded transactions, and hashing power.

Thirdly, online platforms have already been under scrutiny of competition authorities for anticompetitive behaviors such as abuse of dominant positions, horizontal and vertical restrictions, and merger control.[40]

---

39 Michael L. Katz & Carl Shapiro, *Systems Competition and Network Effects*, 8/2 THE JOURNAL OF ECONOMIC PERSPECTIVES 105 (1994).

40 Abuse of dominant position cases: Press Release, *Bundeskartellamt, Bundeskartellamt prohibits Facebook from combining user data from different sources* (Feb. 7, 2019), available at https://www.bundeskartellamt.de/SharedDocs/Meldung/EN/Pressemitteilungen/2019/07_02_2019_Facebook.html;jsessionid=97544D2BEC89D4CF6E4583F9C366D-CA5.2_cid378. European Commission, *Google Android* – Case 40099, 18/07/2018; European Commission, *Google Search (AdSense)* – Case 40411, 14/07/2016; European Commission, *Google Search (Shopping)* – Case AT.39740, 27/06/2017; *PeopleBrowsr, Inc. v. Twitter, Inc.*, United States District Court Nothern District of California, No. C-12-6120 EMC (N.D. Cal. Mar. 6, 2013). Merger cases: European Commission, *Google/Doubleclick* Case M.4731, 11/03/2008; European Commission, *Microsoft/Yahoo* – Case M. 5727, 18/02/2010; European Commission, *Facebook/Whatsapp* – Case M.7217, 3/10/2014; European Commission, *Microsoft/LinkedIn* – Case M.8124, 6/12/2016; European Commission, *Apple/Shazam* – Case M.8788, 6/09/2018. Horizontal or vertical resctrictions: CMA, Online sales of posters and frames Case 50223, 12 August 2016, available at https://www.gov.uk/cma-cases/online-sales-of-discretionary-consumer-products; U.S. v. *Daniel William Aston and Trod Limited*, DoJ, d/b/a Buy 4 Less, d/b/a BUy For Less, d/b/a Buy-For-Less-Online, August 27, 2015, available at https://www.justice.gov/atr/case/us-v-daniel-william-aston-and-trod-limited.

In the next section we will explore the possible competition issues that may occur within blockchain ecosystems. Although blockchain has not yet raised competition concerns in practice, it should be worth highlighting some implications when applying competition law. In particular, when examining anticompetitive conducts in the context of blockchain the first issue is whether the activity under scrutiny can be qualified as economic, and thus the entity exercising it is an undertaking.[41] A blockchain can indeed be specialized in public activities such as providing a public registry.

Furthermore, determining who is liable in blockchain ecosystems is complex due to the distributed nature of this technology. For instance, when assessing collusive behaviors, public enforcers should adopt a case by case approach in order to determine who is liable: whether it be the agents who defined the governance of the blockchain or the miners who validated the transactions. Indeed, the latter could be considered mere agents of a principal, the blockchain, and, hence, they may benefit from immunity.

Also, liability may pose issues with regards to sanctions. Public enforcers either will have to sanction single individuals or the core developers. And, considering that these sectors, as online platforms ones, are rapidly changing, remedies should be forward-looking.

B. Competition into Blockchains

Concerns related to competition in the blockchain systems are different but not fully explored. The immaturity of the theoretical debate is determined both by the lack of knowledge of the structure and functioning of this technology, and by the fact that the ability to apply blockchain to dynamic markets has only recently been undertaken.

Nonetheless, the theoretical speculations of experts about competitive concerns[42] were directed not so much towards public blockchain as towards the private blockchain.

First of all, blockchain may facilitate the risk of collusion.[43] Indeed, blockchain is characterized by transparency: every participant of the blockchain has access to the transaction records. Most importantly, blockchain strengthens the stability of cartels by allowing an easier monitoring of cartel members' behavior and by providing tools for sanctioning possible deviations (i.e. automatic sanctions through smart contracts). Moreover, blockchain can be characterized by oligopolistic structures, such as Mining activities, wherein transparency could facilitate tacit coordination.[44]

---

41 Lianos, *supra* note 2.

42 Thibault Schrepel, *Is blockchain the death of antitrust law?, The blockchain antitrust paradox*, 3 Geo. L. Tech. Rev. (forthcoming), available at https://papers.ssrn.com/sol3/papers.cfm?abstract_id=3193576. See also Lianos, *supra* note 2.

43 Thibault Schrepel, *Collusion By Blockchain And Smart Contracts* (Jan. 14, 2019), available at https://papers.ssrn.com/sol3/papers.cfm?abstract_id=3315182.

44 OECD Secretariat, *Blockchain Technology and Competition Policy*, DAF/COMP/WD(2018)47.

Second, as already underlined, players could be incentivized to acquire competitive advantage and, thus, market power, by vertically integrating. Therefore, there may be vertical foreclosure strategies such as exclusive deals aiming at excluding fierce competitors such as mavericks, refusals to deal, predatory pricing strategies or possible exploitative practices such as excessive pricing.

Third, merger control regulations should take into account mergers between certain operators such as Miners. Indeed, an excessive concentration of power on this type of player may soften competition among blockchains or even lead to collective dominance abuses.

Moreover, the question arises as to whether access may be an essential factor in competing on the market in the event that a group of stakeholders acting as gatekeepers may implement a private blockchain.[45]

A concern similar to that of "(F)RAND" encumbered SEPs' owner (i.e. Standard Essential Patents), whose refusal to access might be qualified as exclusionary abuse.[46]

Nevertheless, those conclusions ought to be better analyzed under the rationale established by the European Court of Justice throughout time, whose orientation has been consolidated since the *Magill* case.[47]

> First, the peer-to-peer network is close to purely decentralized, since anybody can run a Bitcoin node, and the entry barrier is fairly low. [...] Second, Bitcoin mining [...] requires a high capital cost. As a result, the Bitcoin mining ecosystem has a high degree of centralization or concentration of power. [...] Third, Bitcoin nodes run updates to the software, which has a bearing on how and what the rules of the system change. [...] most nodes run the reference implementation, and its developers are trusted by the community and have a lot of power.[48]

---

45 Observatory for Blockchain & Distributed Ledger, *supra* note 8.

46 Schrepel, *supra* note 42.

47 *Radio Telefis Eireann (RTE) and Independent Television Publications Ltd (ITP) v. Commission of the European Communities*, joined cases C-241/91 P and C-242/91 P (E.C.R. 1995 I-00743). The case Magill is known as the leading case on application of Essential Facilities Doctrine to Intellectual Property, steadily referred to in subsequent judgements *Oscar Bronner GmbH Co KG v. Mediaprint Zeitungs-und Zeitschriftenverlag GmbH & Co. KG*, Case C-7/97 (E.C.R. I-7791, 1998); *IMS Health GmbH & Co. OHG v. NDC Health GmbH & Co. KG.*, Case C-418/01 (E.C.R. I-05039, 2004). Those principles find concrete application to cases connected with standards: *Motorola - Enforcement of GPRS standard essential patents*, Case AT.39985 (OJ C 344, 2.10.2014); *Samsung - Enforcement of GPRS Standard Essential Patents*, Case AT.39939 (OJ C 350, 4.10.2014); *Huawei Technologies Co. Ltd v. ZTE Corp. &. ZTE Deutschland GmbH*, C-170/13 (OJ C 302, 14.9.2015).

48 NARAYANAN ET AL. 28, *supra* note 6.

V. BLOCKCHAIN AND INTELLECTUAL PROPERTY: A FEW REMARKS

When Satoshi Nakamoto released his White Paper on Bitcoin, in 2008, he did not claim any IP protection. He introduced Bitcoin as an open source technology, freely accessible by the whole community. Since then, blockchain has started to become a limitless working space, where everyone interested could contribute to updating this platform. In this context, some practitioners opined that any attempt to protect blockchain as back end, i.e. the "foundational technology" was incompatible with the diffusion and deployment of blockchain.[49] Nonetheless, patentability seems not completely precluded.

Indeed, blockchain can be separated in two distinct segments. The first is the lowest layer of abstraction which, in computer science, describes the fundamental structure of one software. In the case at stake, this structure is undeniably open source. The second is the high layer, which may intersect the patentability area to the extent that it involves a sharp and valuable improvement. Thus, improvements such as cross-communication between different blockchains are worthy to be patented.[50]

Both China[51] and the United States have so far been the leading countries in terms of blockchain-based patent applications. Most of the applicants have been firms active into the financial and banking sectors.[52] Particularly, their patents have been focused on improving payment systems and tools for security and/or encryption.

However, this trend is set to spread in many other different countries as well as Europe. Hence, patentability of blockchain-based technologies is becoming a sensitive issue.

In the United States, 35 U.S. Code §101 provides that "Whoever invents or discovers any new and useful process, machine, manufacture, or composition of matter, or any new and useful improvement thereof, may obtain a patent therefor, subject to the conditions

---

49 Mirko Boehm, Open Invention Network, Germany, IP landscape of blockchain, EPO one-day conference on Patenting Blockchain, Hague (Dec. 4, 2018). Benjamin Bai, Ant Financial Services Group/Alipay, China, IP landscape of blockchain, EPO one-day conference on Patenting Blockchain, Hague (Dec. 4, 2018).

50 Benjamin Bai, *id.*

51 Wang Xinyi, Communication Invention Exam. Dept., CNIPA, How does CNIPA deal with Blockchain, speech at the Conference of European Patent Office on Patenting Blockchain, (Dec. 4, 2018).

52 Laura Noonan, *China leads blockchain patent applications*, Financial Time, Mar. 25, 2018. It is not surprising that Fintech is recording the highest rate of bottom-up pressure towards innovations.

and requirements of this title." Therefore, the sole novelty and usefulness of internet-implemented applications is reputed worthy of patent protection.[53]

However, regardless of legal standards, it is very challenging to address patent eligibility in light of the U.S. Supreme Court's case law, which has proven to be a more severe approach. According to *Mayo*,[54] monopolization of abstract concepts, through the grant of a patent, may tend to hinder innovation, rather than promote it, for the reason that "they are the basic tools of scientific and technological work."[55]

In particular, business methods, software patents as well as generic computer-implemented technologies are basically ascribed within abstract idea that, together with laws of nature and physical phenomena,[56] come under one of the three exceptions to patent eligibility which, nonetheless, are still worthy of patent-eligibility only when they fulfill the further concept of inventive step. In this regard, the Supreme Court has constantly pointed out how the inventive concept is met only when "*additional features*" occur.

These further factors are considered necessary in order to avoid monopolization of basilar scientific or technological thoughts and, on the other hand, to encourage the creation of "novel and useful structure"[57] by granting patent protection solely to their practical applications.[58] A process or product which is claimed to be based on *abstract ideas* must be regarded in its entirety as not being a bare trivial and obvious application, but rather a particular and useful implementation of that principle, assessed on a case-by-case basis.

---

53 Which may, for instance, include "1. applications that use the block-chain technology over the internet, such as applications for financial data such as cryptocurrencies, public records, identification, private records, attestation, tangible and intangible assets, remittance, securities transactions, loyalty points, electronic coupon, smart contracts, escrow transactions, and third-party arbitration; 2. improvements in the architecture of one or more of the following individual technologies that collectively form the blockchain technology implemented over the internet, such as: asymmetric encryption, hash functions, Merkle trees, key-value database, peer-to-peer (P2P) communication protocol, and proof of work; 3. improvements in methods executed by the aforementioned individual technologies, such as: (a) a method of sharing transactions and blocks as executed using the P2P communication protocol, (b) a process of validating transactions and achieving distributed consensus, which use the block-chain concepts of proof of work, proof of stake, and decentralized consensus, (c) a method of efficiently packaging transactions into blocks, using the concept of Merkle trees, (d) a method of performing hashing of at least one of blocks and transactions, and a method of obfuscating public keys, (e) a method of searching previous transactions to prevent double-spends, which uses the concept of key-value database, and (f) a method of signing transactions, which can use the technologies of digital signatures based on public and private keys, asymmetric encryption, and elliptic curve cryptography; and 4. computing systems or devices, computer program products, and articles of manufacture that are used by the end customer to execute the internet-implemented applications that implement the block-chain technology." Gurneet Singh, *Are Internet-Implemented Applications of Block-Chain Technology Patent-Eligible in the United States?*, 17 CHI.-KENT J. INTELL. PROP. 358 (2018).

54 *Mayo Collaborative Services v. Prometheus Laboratories Inc.*, 566 U.S., 132 S. Ct. 1289 (2012).

55 *Gottschalk v. Benson*, 409 U. S. 63, 67 (1972).

56 See *ex multis, Bilski v. Kappos*, 561 U.S. 593, 601 (2010) which reaffirms that these three exceptions already settled by the case law (abstract ideas, laws of nature and physical phenomena) are *per se* ineligible.

57 *Mackay Radio & Telegraph Co. v. Radio Corp. Of America*, 306 U.S 86 (1939).

58 See *ex multis, Mackay Radio & Telegraph Co. v. Radio Corp. Of America*, 306 U.S 86 (1939); *Diamond v. Diehr*, 450 U.S. 175, 185 (1981).

Returning to the internet-implemented technologies, the Supreme Court in the Alice v. CLS Bank decision[59] adopted the same framework above described, according to which an abstract idea, which barely requires implementation by a computer, fails to be considered a patent-eligible invention. In particular, the Supreme Court stated that, in order to be patent eligible, those abstract ideas should fulfill an additional criterion such as the capability of enhancing the substantial practical applications other than those strictly connected with its physical machine.[60]

By the same token, Article 52(2) of the European Patent Convention ("EPC")[61] prescribes that presentations of information (i.e. database[62]), pure algorithm methods or methods for mental acts and programs for computers are not per se patent-eligible. Besides, the technological inventions generally obtain patent protection across Europe only when they are novel, involve an inventive step and are susceptible to industrial application.[63]

Nevertheless, the practice has broadly overcome these issues.[64]

The European Patent Office (EPO) has indeed shown a proper inclination aimed at considering those creations within the computer-implemented inventions[65] worthy of protection, by virtue of the keynote technical character,[66] i.e. the capability of the invention under examination to generate a technical effect that would exceed *"the 'normal' physical interactions between the program (software) and the computer (hardware) on which it is run."*[67] Thus, blockchain may obtain patent protection[68] under the condition that

---

59 *Alice Corporation Pty. Ltd. v. CLS Bank International Et Al.*, 573 U. S., 134 S. Ct. 2347 (2014). The claims was related to the patent ineligibility of a computer-implemented scheme for mitigating "settlement risk."

60 Antonio M. DiNizo Jr., *From Alice to Bob: The Patent Eligibility of Blockchain in a Post-CLS Bank World*, 9 JOTLI 21 (2018).

61 Convention on the Grant of European Patents (European Patent Convention) of 5 October 1973 as revised by the Act revising Article 63 EPC of 17 December 1991 and the Act revising the EPC of 29 November 2000. See also article 45 of the Italian Code of Industrial Property.

62 Article 3 of the Directive 96/9/EC of the European Parliament and of the Council of 11 March 1996 on the legal protection of databases (Official Journal of European Communities L77/20, 27 March 1996) grants database the copyright protection when it constitutes the author's own intellectual creation. But, in this context, to determine whether blockchain has or not a database nature may narrowly help to unravel the tangle of its protection. In fact, even strong improvements of the blockchain's foundational architecture – notably updated on an open source basis - cannot be worth protection under the European patent law nor copyright law.

63 Article 52(1) EPC.

64 "Traditionally, improvements in CPU processing speed, a decrease in energy consumption or memory usage for a particular device, and/or progress in information encryption have been considered as providing a technical solution to a technical problem having technical effects and, thus, eligible for patentability," Lianos 36, *supra* note 2.

65 The Guidelines for Examination underline that, by definition, a computer-implemented invention involves "the use of a computer, computer network or other programmable apparatus, where one or more features are realised wholly or partly by means of a computer program" (Part F – Chapter IV - 9).

66 Koen Lievens, Patent examination director, Head of CII guidelines workgroup, EPO, Examining Blockchain Inventions based on our established CII practice, speech at the Conference of European Patent Office on Patenting Blockchain, (Dec. 4, 2018).

67 Guidelines for Examination (Part G - Chapter II - 3.6).

68 *Supra* Lianos 36, *supra* note 2.

it would involve technical implementations.[69] Once the obstacle of patent-eligibility is overcome, when it comes to novelty[70] and inventive step,[71] the European Patent Office tends to adopt the so-called problem-solution approach.[72]

There is no specific issue related to the problem-solution approach involving blockchain applications. The European Patent Office rather seeks to extend to the blockchain-related inventions the same assessment of the inventive step adopted for computer-implemented inventions.

All these inventions share the same mix of technical and non-technical features so that, in light of the EPO case law,[73] a more rigorous approach[74] should be required in order

---

69 See Marieke Flament, Managing Director, and Claire Wells, Director of Legal & Business Affairs, Circle, Blockchain Technology and Fields of Application, speech at the Conference of European Patent Office on Patenting Blockchain, (Dec. 4, 2018).

70 Article 54 EPC foresees "(1) An invention shall be considered to be new if it does not form part of the state of the art. (2) The state of the art shall be held to comprise everything made available to the public by means of a written or oral description, by use, or in any other way, before the date of filing of the European patent application. [...]."

71 Article 56 EPC foresees that the requirement of the inventive step is met when it is not obvious to a person skilled in the art, having regard to the state of the art.

72 Guidelines for Examination (Part G - Chapter VII – 5.4). The Board of Appeal, when addressing problem and solution approach, bases its decision on Article 42 (Content of the description), which foresees "(1)The description shall: (a) specify the technical field to which the invention relates; (b)indicate the background art which, as far as is known to the applicant, can be regarded as useful to understand the invention, draw up the European search report and examine the European patent application, and, preferably, cite the documents reflecting such art; (c)disclose the invention, as claimed, in such terms that the technical problem, even if not expressly stated as such, and its solution can be understood, and state any advantageous effects of the invention with reference to the background art; (d)briefly describe the figures in the drawings, if any; (e)describe in detail at least one way of carrying out the invention claimed, using examples where appropriate and referring to the drawings, if any; (f)indicate explicitly, when it is not obvious from the description or nature of the invention, the way in which the invention is industrially applicable. (2) The description shall be presented in the manner and order specified in paragraph 1, unless, owing to the nature of the invention, a different presentation would afford a better understanding or be more concise," See Enlarged Board of Appeal (G 0001/03, Apr. 8, 2004) and (G 0002/03, Apr. 8, 2004); Board of Appeal (T 1/80, Apr. 6, 1981), (T 20/81, Feb. 10, 1982); (T 24/81, Oct. 13, 1983), (T 248/85, Jan. 21, 1986). For an in-depth analysis of problem-solution approach see, *inter alia*, Jochen Pagenberg, *The evaluation of the inventive step in the European Patent System: more objective standard needed*, 9 IIC 1 (1978); Mario Franzosi, *Non-obviousness*, 6 JWPI 2 (2003); MARIO CISNEROS, PATENTABILITY REQUIREMENTS FOR NANOTECHNOLOGICAL INVENTIONS: AN APPROACH FROM THE EUROPEAN PATENT CONVENTION PERSPECTIVE 45-48, (2008).

73 See *ex multis* Board of Appeal (T 641/00, Sept. 26, 2002), according to which "An invention consisting of a mixture of technical and non-technical features and having technical character as a whole is to be assessed with respect to the requirement of inventive step by taking account of all those features which contribute to said technical character whereas features making no such contribution cannot support the presence of inventive step."

74 The Guidelines for Examination (Part G.VII–5.4) specifically list the steps which outline the application of the problem-solution approach to mixed-type inventions "(i) The features which contribute to the technical character of the invention are determined on the basis of the technical effects achieved in the context of the invention. (ii) A suitable starting point in the prior art is selected as the closest prior art with a focus on the features contributing to the technical character of the invention identified in step (i). (iii) The differences from the closest prior art are identified. The technical effect(s) of these differences, in the context of the claim as a whole, is(are) determined in order to identify from these differences the features which make a technical contribution and those which do not. (*a*) If there are no differences (not even a non-technical difference), an objection under Art. 54 is raised. (*b*) If the differences do not make any technical contribution, an objection under Art. 56 is raised. The reasoning for the objection is that the subject-matter of a claim cannot be inventive if there is no technical contribution to the prior art. (*c*) If the differences include features making a technical contribution, the following applies: The objective technical problem is formulated on the basis of the technical effect(s) achieved by these features. In addition, if the differences include features making no technical contribution, these features, or any non-technical effect achieved by the invention, may be used in the formulation of the objective technical problem as part of what is "given" to the skilled person, in particular as a constraint that has to be met. – If the claimed technical solution to the objective technical problem is obvious to the person skilled in the art, an objection under Art. 56 is raised."

to avoid that the inventive step would be recognized on the basis of characteristics not supporting the technical character and which is hardly likely to solve the objective technical problem. Going beyond a purely speculative reasoning, if we look at the examination procedure, many inventions have been filed[75] but a very little number of patents have been granted or intended by the European Patent Office.[76] One of these, for example, is EP3257191 (*Registry And Automated Management Method For Blockchain-Enforced Smart Contracts*), a blockchain-based patent granted in 2018, which claims:

> 1. A computer-implemented method of controlling the visibility and/or performance of a contract, the method comprising the steps:
> (a) storing a contract on or in a computer-based repository;
> (b) broadcasting a transaction to a blockchain, the transaction comprising:
> > i) at least one unspent output (UTXO); and
> > ii) metadata comprising an identifier indicative of the location where the contract is stored;
> (c) interpreting the contract as open or valid until the unspent output (UTXO) is spent on the blockchain; and
> (d) renewing or rolling the contract on by:
> generating a new key using data relating to a previous key associated with the contract; generating a script comprising the new key, the location of the contract and a hash of the contract; and paying an amount of currency to the script.[77]

Therefore, even though there is no evident reason to exclude, by default, blockchain-related applications from patent protection, the legal answer should be given with mitigation. On the one hand, it is admissible to restrict the subject-matter that can be patented in order to avoiding monopolization of abstract ideas or situations which may lead to an arbitrary usage of certain creations, which do not deserve protection or can even endanger scientific and technological advancement.

Indeed, both scholars and practitioners agree on the need to apply suitable filters, in order to avoid the unjustified proliferation of patent applications for old products, components or processes based on blockchain, implementing some kind of evergreening.

Even in China, which is the country with the highest growth rate in blockchain-related patent applications, the CNIPA (China National Intellectual Property Administration)

---

75 Sorting by "blockchain," the European Patent Register currently finds 335 items. See https://register.epo.org/smart-Search?searchMode=smart&query=blockchain&dir=asc&sort=publicationNoColumn.

76 See patents EP3257191 (Registry And Automated Management Method For Blockchain-Enforced Smart Contracts); EP3125489 (Mitigating Blockchain Attack) ; EP3387785/86 (Computer-Implemented Systems And Methods To Enable Complex Functionality On A Blockchain While Preserving Security-Based Restrictions On Script Size And Opcode Limits).

77 Patent specifications of EP 3 257 191, p. 26, available at https://data.epo.org/publication-server/pdf-document?pn=3257191&ki=B1&cc=EP&pd=20180411.

applies some requirements that must be fulfilled including the achievement of solutions to a technical problem, restrictions on rules and methods for mental activities, and lastly, novelty, inventiveness, and practical applicability.[78]

On the other hand, the adaptability of these requirements to new technologies, which varies from country to country, has a serious impact on innovation blueprints, and, eventually, may jeopardize the economic development.

In this context, we cannot simply theorize blockchain applications as the subject matter of intellectual property rights, but there is also a growing awareness to employing blockchain as means for safeguarding IPRs contents, exploiting the potential of secure, tamperproof, permanent, public, and borderless distributed ledgers in order to record titles and intellectual properties and, by virtue of smart contracts, to exercise the related rights.

A first step towards the upward IPR enforcement may consist in developing novel management systems exploiting a distributed "ledger" model – insofar it is both open and transparent – to record and track IPRs. For instance, one suggested application of timestamping is:

> to prove prior knowledge of some idea. Suppose we wanted to prove that some invention we filed a patent on was actually in our heads much earlier. We could do this by publishing the hash of a design document or schematic when we first thought of the invention – without revealing to anybody what the idea is. Later on, when the patent is filed or the idea publicized, we can publish the original documents and information, so that anybody can confirm that we must have known the idea earlier, when we published the commitment to it.[79]

Afterwards, this makes possible to deploy the timely business projects in order to exploit IPRs through transaction, licensing or distribution of digital contents so as to streamline royalty payments and remuneration of authors even through smart contracts, encouraging a more privacy-compliant advertisement through encryption, and enable a more undeviating distribution system that would hinder piracy.[80]

The implementation of blockchain technology may require in some circumstances the development of standards. On the one hand, standards foster interoperability among technologies, on the other it may impose costs, generate lock in effects or even enable hold-up issues in cases where essential IPRs are not declared prior to the setting of standards.[81] As far as the penchant for filing blockchain patents is on the rise worldwide, one

78 Wang Xinyi, *supra* note 51.

79 NARAYANAN ET AL. 214, *supra* note 6.

80 See Deloitte, Blockchain @ Media: A new Game Changer for the Media Industry?, (Report, 2017).

81 Lianos, *supra* note 2. See also European Commission, Decision of 9 December 9, 2009 in Case COMP/38.636—*Rambus*, OJ 2010/C 30/09.

last question as per those standard-implemented, relates to such patents attracting patent trolls,[82] which are "companies that obtain the rights to one or more patents in order to profit by means of licensing and litigation, rather than by producing their own goods and services."[83]

It is widely acknowledge that new industrial sectors, which give raise to promising new technologies[84], are heavily exposed to patent thickets[85] and, to the extent that legal and technical fragmentation tower above them, these industries also attract Non Practicing Entities ("NPEs") whose goal is not "acquiring or maintaining a competitive advantage in the market of the commodity or service covered by the patent, but simply to obtain money."[86] Nonetheless, the very same blockchain application, namely timestamping, has been suggested as that which can provide a solution to patent trolling.[87]

VI. CONCLUSIONS

Due to the very recent emergence of the debate on implications of blockchain for competition law and its enforcement, in particular in the media sector, drawing conclusions on this topic results mainly in raising a number of questions.

The first open issue is about blockchain really raising peculiar points for competition law, different from those related to centralized platforms, deeply examined by the economic and legal literature in the last decade. The considerations developed above seem to show that this may be the case.

Moving to the next question-of which such specificities may be, however, also on account of the multiple and not yet completely outlined features of the phenomenon, they should still be clearly identified and analyzed.

One point of reference for such analysis could certainly be the decentralization and disintermediation mechanisms characterizing the DLT.

---

82 ROBIN JACOB, *Patent Trolls in Europe - Does Patent Law Require New Barriers?*, in IP AND OTHER THINGS, A COLLECTION OF ESSAYS AND SPEECHES (R. Jacob, 2015).

83 https://en.oxforddictionaries.com/definition/patent_troll retrieved 21.01.2019.

84 Birgit Clark, *Blockchain and IP Law: A Match made in Crypto Heaven?*, WIPO MAGAZINE, February 2018, https://www.wipo.int/wipo_magazine/en/2018/01/article_0005.html.

85 Expression coined by Carl Shapiro, *Navigating the patent thicket: cross licenses, patent pools, and standard setting*, in *Innovation policy and the economy*, 1 MIT Press 119-150 (2001). The most mentioned metaphor ascribed at Shapiro is that of the "pyramid" for describing cumulative innovation that occurs in the current key industries, such as computer software, Internet, nanotechnology, etc.

86 Mario Franzosi, *SEP, NPE, PAE, Trolls and Huawei v. ZTE*, in THE INTERPLAY BETWEEN COMPETITION LAW AND INTELLECTUAL PROPERTY: AN INTERNATIONAL PERSPECTIVE 209 (Gabriella Muscolo, Marina Tavassi eds., 2019).

87 Felix Hamborg, Moustafa Elmaghraby, Corinna Breitinger & Bela Gipp, *Automated Generation of Timestamped Patent Abstracts at Scale to Outsmart Patent-Trolls*, Report on the 2nd Joint Workshop on Bibliometric-enhanced Information Retrieval and Natural Language Processing for Digital Libraries (BIRNDL 2017); Jean-Maxime Rivière, *Blockchain technology and IP – investigating benefits and acceptance in governments and legislations*, 3/1 JUNIOR MANAGEMENT SCIENCE 1-15 (2018).

Several additional questions are raised in relation to blockchain patentability and a few among them — such as the standardization or the patent trolls — are interconnected with antitrust issues.

Once again, we should wonder if these questions are really new if compared to those already debated in the IP and Competition law field with reference to other, better known, technologies.

A conclusive remark is on the dilemma already faced by policy makers with regard to platforms: If there is room for regulation of blockchain in the future, what could be the best approach? That of the *ex post*, case by case, by means of enforcement – public or private, by decision makers, or the *ex ante* one, resulting in more general regulation, by the legislator and/or the regulators in the strictest sense?

For the time being, the novelty of the phenomenon and its as yet unclear implications for competition, as well as IP Law, suggest a more cautious and flexible approach, better guaranteed by law enforcement agencies.

DAILY NEWSPAPERS AND ANTITRUST: AS RELEVANT AND CRUCIAL TO OUR DEMOCRACY AS EVER

By Thomas J. Horton[1]

ABSTRACT

Daily newspapers today are under siege. The future viability of traditional daily newspapers is being questioned due to the rise of Internet information sources, as well as the current political attacks on the press. This article argues that those predicting "doom and gloom" for the daily newspaper industry are short-sighted, given the continued popularity of high-quality investigative journalism and ever-present need for accountability reporting in our democracy. With many readers consuming daily newspapers' content through their innovative online platforms, the competition of the Internet has increased the quality of newspaper journalism, after a period of declining quality due to aggressive consolidation in the print industry. Discussing the 1970 Newspaper Preservation Act ("NPA"), which was supposed to protect editorial diversity by allowing horizontal economic consolidations, the author observes that it actually led to lower quality journalism and less competitive newspapers. The author argues that the NPA should be repealed, and aggressive competition encouraged between newspapers at both the local and national geographic levels through the rigorous enforcement of the antitrust laws. Newspapers should continue to be analyzed as a distinct product market by antitrust enforcers, and further horizontal mergers and consolidations discouraged, and, if necessary, rejected.

I. INTRODUCTION

Local and national daily newspapers seem to be under siege. Newspapers today face a growing and loud cacophony of short-sighted and dangerous political attacks against their journalistic integrity. On top of that, many naysayers believe the growth of the Internet is turning newspapers into dinosaurs whose extinction is just around the corner.

---

1 Professor of Law and Heidepriem Trial Advocacy Fellow, the University of South Dakota School of Law, and Member of the Advisory Boards of the American Antitrust Institute and The Capital Forum. The author wishes to thank Robert Lande and Spencer Weber Waller for their helpful comments and insights; and Kristin Derenge, Julia Wessel, and Emily Posthumus for their assiduous assistance.

This article argues that the current political attacks on newspapers and the many questions about their economic futures are misguided and short-sighted. Politically, newspapers have always been crucial to the health of our democracy, and they remain so today. Economically, the "gloom and doom" scenarios some commentators paint for newspapers' sustainable futures miss the point that newspapers are not only surviving, but starting to thrive again in the age of the Internet.

As a starting point, this article discusses how newspaper reporters, editors, and publishers are fighting back against the misguided political attacks against them. Newspapers have played a key role throughout our nation's history in protecting and preserving our democratic roots and values, and they are determined to continue doing so in the coming years.

Next, the author discusses how newspapers today are building and growing their own unique Internet sites. Through their appealing Internet sites, newspapers are building strong relationships with readers who turn to their favorite newspapers for both local and national news, as well as high-quality editorial and investigative journalism. Advertisers are flocking to such sites, as they offer highly-targeted and individually-focused access to highly desirable demographic groups of readers.

Ultimately, this article rejects the "doom and gloom" scenarios for newspapers' futures. Instead, the author argues that promoting aggressive horizontal newspaper competition is the best way to ensure the future of local and national newspapers, as keystone protectors of America's democracy. The article discusses the Newspaper Preservation Act of 1970 ("NPA") to show the importance of aggressive horizontal newspaper competition. The NPA was supposed to protect editorial diversity through economic consolidation. However, it actually harmed newspapers' long-term health. Instead of aggressively competing, consolidated newspapers were more than happy to continue living off an economic bonanza of monopoly profits while dangerously cutting the quality of their journalism.

Ironically, the Internet has forced newspapers to wake up and start improving their quality again, in order to stay competitive. Such competition is responsible for the bright future newspapers are beginning to see once again. The author therefore argues that the NPA should be repealed, and aggressive competition encouraged between newspapers at both the local and national levels. Newspapers should continue to be seen as a distinct product market by antitrust enforcers, and further horizontal mergers and consolidations discouraged, and, if necessary, rejected.

---

2   See Michal S. Gal & Daniel L. Rubinfeld, *The Hidden Costs of Free Goods: Implications for Antitrust Enforcement*, 80 Antitr. L. J. 521, 545 (2016)(discussing how "newspapers play a unique role in the democratic process and guarding the rule of law"); Sheila S. Coronel, *The Pivotal Role of Free Media in Building a Healthy Democracy*, Tadias Mag. (op.ed. Oct. 21, 2014)("Since the 17th century, the role of the press as Fourth Estate and as a forum for public discussion and debate has been recognized. Today..., the notion of the media as watchdog, as guardian of the public interest, and as a conduit between governors and the governed remains deeply ingrained."); John W. Whitehead, *Why Local Newspapers are the Basis of Democracy*, The Blog, Huffington Post (May 25, 2011)("Local newspapers are the clarion call of democracy").

II. THE IMPORTANCE OF LOCAL AND NATIONAL NEWSPA-PERS TO OUR DEMOCRACY

Throughout our nation's history, newspapers have played a key role in preserving and protecting America's democratic roots and values.[2] By continually watching over those in power, and daily reporting their words and deeds, newspapers serve as powerful guardians of the public interest. Americans have always recognized the importance of free newspapers in holding government officials accountable and responsible for their actions. America's second President, John Adams, observed that "none of the means of information are more sacred, or have been cherished with more tenderness and care by the settlers of America, than the Press."[3]

Newspapers have become a critical part of our nation's "Fourth Estate," seen by many as "a co-equal branch of our government that provides the check[s] and balance[s] without which [our] government[ ] cannot be effective."[4] High school history students learn about Benjamin Franklin, "[t]he pioneer of printing and publishing in America."[5] Franklin developed and grew his newspaper, the *Pennsylvania Gazette*, into a hugely successful publication "with the largest circulation in the colonies."[6] Newspapers "became a political force in the campaign for American independence,"[7] and were eulogized by French

---

3 John Adams, *V. A Dissertation on the Canon and the Feudal Law, No. 3*, FOUNDERS ONLINE, NATIONAL ARCHIVES, (Sept. 30, 1765), https://founders.archives.gov/documents/Adams/06-01-02-0052-0006. Thomas Jefferson added that "[o]ur liberty depends on the freedom of the press, and that cannot be limited without being lost." Thomas Jefferson, *From Thomas Jefferson to James Currie, 28 January 1786*, FOUNDERS ONLINE, NATIONAL ARCHIVES, (Jan. 28. 1786), http://founders.archives.gov/documents/Jefferson/01-09-02-0209. George Washington similarly noted: "If Men are to be precluded from offering their sentiments on a matter, which may involve the most serious and alarming consequences, that can invite the consideration of Mankind, reason is of no use to us -- the freedom of Speech may be taken away – and, dumb & silent we may be led, like sheep, to the Slaughter." George Washington, *From George Washington to Officers of the Army, 15 March 1783*, FOUNDERS ONLINE, NATIONAL ARCHIVES, (Mar. 15, 1783), http://founders.archives.gov/documents/Washington/99-01-02-10840.

4 Coronel, *supra* note 2, at 4. Professor Coronel adds:

> Contemporary democratic theory appreciates the media's role in ensuring governments are held accountable. . . the notion of media as watch dog and not merely a passive recorder of events is widely accepted. Governments, it is argued, cannot be held accountable if citizens are ill informed about the actions of officials and institutions. The watchdog press is guardian of the public interest, warning citizens against those who are doing them harm.

Id. See also Stephen Holmes, *Liberal Constraints on Private Power?*, in DEMOCRACY AND THE MASS MEDIA, 21-65 (Judith Lichtenberg ed., 1991)(discussing America's founders' agreements with French political philosopher Montesquieu's belief that publicity was the cure for abuses of power – leading to their recognition of the importance of the press in making government officials aware of the public's discontents, and allowing governments to act accordingly); Jonathan Rauch, *Put the damn paper out: Why the newsroom is a bedrock of American democracy*, BROOKINGS (June 29, 2018), https:www.brookings.edu/blog/fixgov/2018/06/29/put-the-damn-paper-out (describing American newspapers and their newsrooms as "one of the most important institutions of American life"). See also Whitehead, *supra* note 2, at 2 (describing newspapers' newsrooms as "the watchdog power of the media").

5 Benjamin Franklin, in ADVERTISING HALL OF FAME, available at http://advertisinghall.org/members/member_bio.php?memid=632.

6 *Id.*

7 See *Newspapers of Colonial America Webinar Deck*, ACCESSIBLE ARCHIVES INC. (2018), https://www.accessible-archives.com/collections/newspapers-colonial-america/ (last visited Sep 18, 2018). In fact by the mid-1760s, there were 24 weekly newspapers in America's 13 colonies. See Alison Olson, *The Zenger Case Revisited: Satire, Sedition and Political Debate in Eighteenth Century America*, 35(3) EARLY AMERICAN LITERATURE 223-245.

historian Alexis de Tocqueville, who proclaimed that "[t]he power of the [American] periodical press is second only to that of the people."[8]

America's founders understood the importance of newspapers in creating and buttressing the "competitive 'marketplace of ideas'" necessary to a flourishing democracy.[9] Through the First Amendment to our Constitution, the founders "established what has become an insurance policy for the continued health of our republic: A free press."[10] Our Constitution's First Amendment ensures that our newspapers can catalyze and promote vigorous debates and public criticism without a fear of governmental censorship. Ben Franklin, for example, noted that "[i]f all printers were determined not to print anything till they were sure it would offend nobody, there would be very little printed."[11]

The First Amendment "rests on the assumption that the widest possible dissemination of information from diverse and antagonistic sources is essential to the welfare of the public, [and] that a free press is a condition of a free society."[12] Newspapers allow a diverse and cacophonous array of voices to compete for attention, and thereby help ensure a well-informed citizenry. As Thomas Jefferson famously observed in 1787: "Were it left to me

---

8 ALEXIS DE TOCQUEVILLE, DEMOCRACY IN AMERICA (Harvy Mansfield & Delba Winthrop trans. & eds., 2000).

9 See Maurice E. Stucke & Allen P. Grunes, *Toward a Better Competition Policy for the Media: The Challenge of Developing Antitrust Policies that Support the Media Section's Unique Role in Our Democracy*, 42 CONN. L. REV. 101, 105 (2009). Stucke and Grunes describe "the marketplace of ideas [a]s '[a] sphere in which intangible values . . . compete for acceptance." *Id.* at 105, fn. 11, citing WEBSTER'S THIRD NEW INTERNATIONAL DICTIONARY 1383 (1986); See also *Abrams v. United States*, 250 U.S. 616, 630 (1919) (Holmes, J., dissenting)("[T]he ultimate good desired is better reached by free trade in ideas. . . the best test of truth is the power of the thought to get itself accepted in the competition of the market. . . .").

10 Dan Rather & Elliot Kirschner, *Why a Free Press Matters*, THE ATLANTIC (Aug. 16, 2018), available at https://www.theatlantic.com/politics/archive/2018/08/why-a-free-press-matters/567676/. Rather and Kirschner further applaud "the wisdom of our Founders, who conceived the First Amendment as a check on tyranny. *Id.* at 10. "The Founding Fathers believed newspapers to be so important to the development of the young country that they facilitated the creation of a robust distribution network. They provided newspapers with subsidized postal rates that were far below the actual costs of fielding, feeding, and caring for that day's distribution technology: (horses)." Steven Waldman & the Working Group on Information Needs of Communities, *The Information Needs of Communities: The changing media landscape in a broadband age*, FCC Rpt. 34 (July 2011), available at www.fcc.gov/infoneedsreport.

11 *Quotes*, YOUR DICTIONARY, http://quotes.yourdictionary.com/author/benjamin-franklin/553628#t_censorship (last visited Sep 16, 2018). Franklin additionally wrote in *The Pennsylvania Gazette*: "Freedom of speech is a principal pillar in a free government; when this support is taken away, the constitution is dissolved, and tyranny is erected on its ruins." *Quotes*, YOUR DICTIONARY, http://quotes.yourdictionary.com/author/quote/586722 (last visited Sep 16, 2018) (*quoting Benjamin Franklin, On Freedom of Speech and the Press*, Pennsylvania Gazette, Nov. 17, 1737). Justice Oliver Wendell Holmes similarly observed: "If there is any principle of the Constitution that more imperatively calls for attachment than any other it is the principle of free thought – not free thought for those who agree with us but freedom for the thought that we hate." *Oliver Wendell Holmes, Jr. Quotes*, BrainyQuote, https://www.brainyquote.com/quotes/oliver_wendell_holmes_jr_125145 (last visited Sep 16, 2018). Finally, President Franklin D. Roosevelt added: "Freedom of conscience, of education, or speech, and of assembly are among the very fundamentals of democracy and all of them would be nullified should freedom of the press ever be successfully challenged." The Newnan Times-Herald, *Freedom of the press is never your enemy*, THE NEWNAN TIMES-HERALD, (Aug. 15, 2018, 6:52 AM), http://times-herald.com/news/2018/08/freedom-of-the-press-is-never-your-enemy.

12 *Associated Press v. United States*, 326 U.S. 1, 20 (1945). Justice Black added: "Freedom to publish means freedom for all, and not for some." *Id.* See also *United States v. Associated Press*, 52 F. Supp. 362, 372 (S.D.N.Y. 1943), aff'd, 326 U.S. 1 (1945)(Hand, L. J.)(The First Amendment "presupposes that right conclusions are more likely to be gathered out of a multitude of tongues, than through any kind of authoritative selection."); See also Maurice E. Stucke & Allen P. Grunes, *Antitrust and the Marketplace of Ideas*, 69 ANTITR. L. J. 249, 252 (2001)(arguing that "an important purpose of the First Amendment is to preserve an uninhibited marketplace of ideas in which truth ultimately will prevail. . . .").

to decide whether we should have a government without newspapers, or newspapers without a government, I should not hesitate a moment to prefer the latter."[13]

In addition to serving as effective vehicles for bolstering the "marketplace of ideas," newspapers historically have helped drive and propel investigative journalism at both the local and national levels. For example, the deep investigative "muckraking" publications in the Progressive Era "were able. . . , not merely to name the malpractices in American business and politics, but to name the *malpractitioners* and their specific misdeeds, and to proclaim the facts to the entire country."[14] As famous muckraking publisher S. S. McLure aptly observed in 1905: "public disgrace" awaited evildoers, and "there is no punishment so terrible as public disclosure of evildoing."[15]

Digitalization and the growth of the Internet have not lessened the keystone importance of newspapers to our democracy. Much of today's high-quality investigative reporting continues to be found in local and national newspapers. For example, a July 2011 Federal Communications Commission study on "[t]he changing media landscape in the broadband age" noted that "[n]ewspapers tend[ ] to do the majority of accountability reporting." The Report continued:

Because of the size of their staffs, the mobility of their reporters, and the many column inches they [can] dedicate to news, they [can] devote more time and resources to labor-

---

13 Letter from Thomas Jefferson to Edward Carrington (Jan. 16, 1787), available at http://press-pubs.uchicago.edu/founders/documents/amendI_speeches8.html). Fourteen years later, as he was assuming the Presidency, Jefferson further wrote: "[I]n every country where man is free to think and to speak, differences of opinion will arise from differences of perception, and the imperfection of reason; but these differences when permitted, as in this happy country, to purify themselves by free discussion, are but passing clouds overspreading our land transiently and leaving our horizon more bright and serene." Letter of Thomas Jefferson to Benjamin Waring, 1801, in 10 THE WRITINGS OF THOMAS JEFFERSON 235 (Memorial Ed. 1904).

14 The term "muckraking" had its origins in a series of speeches by President Theodore Roosevelt in 1906, in which "[h]e recalled 'the Man with the Muck-Rake' in John Bunyan's Pilgrim's Progress, while seeking to restrain aggressive Progressive-era journalists." MICHAEL MCGERR, A FIERCE DISCONTENT: THE RISE AND FALL OF THE PROGRESSIVE MOVEMENT IN AMERICA, 175-176 (2003); RICHARD HOFSTADTER, AGE OF REFORM, 188 (1955). Hofstadter added: "It now became possible for any literate citizen to know what barkeeps, district attorneys, ward leaders, prostitutes, police-court magistrates, reporters, and corporation lawyers had always come to know in the course of their business." *Id.* See also *id.* at 186-214. Ultimately, according to Hofstadter, the muckrakers "confirmed, if they did not create, a fresh mode of criticism that grew out of journalistic observation." *Id.* at 198. For an excellent discussion of muckraking's history, see *Id.* at 186-214. Hofstadter observes:

> to an extraordinary degree the work of the Progressive Movement rested upon its journalism. The fundamental critical achievement of American Progressivism was the business of exposure, and journalism was the chief occupational source of its creative writers. It is hardly an exaggeration to say that the Progressive mind was characteristically a journalistic mind, and that its characteristic contribution was that of the socially responsible reporter-reformer.

Id. at 186. Hofstadter went on to add that "[w]hat was new in muckraking in the Progressive Era was neither its ideas nor its existence, but its reach – its nationwide character and its capacity to draw nationwide attention, the presence of mass muckraking media with national circulations, and huge resources for the research that went into exposure." *Id.* at 187. Ultimately, according to Hofstadter, the muckrakers "confirmed, if they did not create, a fresh mode of criticism that grew out of journalistic observation." *Id.* at 198.
Going back further to before the American Revolution of 1776, New York's then-Governor brought John Peter Zenger to trial on criminal charges of libel after he published satirical attacks against the Governor. Recognizing the importance of a free investigative press in 1734, the jury acquitted Zenger. See Olson, *supra* note 7, at 223.

15 HOFSTADTER, AGE OF REFORM, *supra* note 14, at 212, quoting S.S. McLure, XXVI MCLURE'S 223 (December 1905).

and-time-intensive projects, sustain ongoing beat reporting, and offer more in-depth explanation and analysis of complex issues.[16]

Professors Michael Gal & Dan Rubinfeld similarly laud "the role of investigative journalism and analysis of current events [in newspapers] based on a high level of professionalism and knowledge that are not always available in other sources."[17] In 2013, Professor Robert H. Lande and the current author reported that newspapers and other traditional media continue to garner the bulk of prestigious journalism awards for investigative reporting despite ongoing expense and newsroom resource reductions.[18]

Healthy daily newspapers nurture and support our current diverse and growing media ecosystem by continuously publishing up to the minute stories and reporting. For example, daily newspapers continue to provide much of the original cutting-edge reporting of local and national information that helps enable other media, such as television, to provide their own unique reporting and analyses.[19] As noted by journalism professors Damian Radcliffe and Christopher Ali, "[t]he volume and value of local reporting originating from [news]papers remains incredibly important to the wider news ecosystem. . . ."[20] Radcliffe and Ali estimate that between 45 percent and 85 percent "of all original reporting is done by [a] newspaper and then picked up by other media."[21] Pulitzer Prize winning journalism Professor Alex Jones similarly estimates that newspapers account for about 85 percent of all accountability within a media ecosystem.[22] Consequently, "[n]ewspapers remain an integral part of the local media ecosystem."[23]

---

16 2011 FCC RPT., *supra* note 10, at 242.

17 Gal & Rubinfeld, *supra* note 2, at fn. 87. The authors add: "Newspapers thus still play an important role in a democracy, creating a basis for checks and balances in many areas of our lives, including governmental, consumer, and cultural spheres. This was recently exemplified by the role some newspapers played in the social uprising against crony capitalism." *Id.* For a study of the continuing excellence of investigative journalism of newspapers and other more traditional "old media," see Thomas J. Horton & Robert E. Lande, *Should the Internet Exempt the Media Sector from the Antitrust Laws?*, 65 FLA. L. REV. 1521, 1553-55 (2013).

18 Horton & Lande, *supra* note 18, at 1553-55.

19 See, e.g. Damian Radcliffe & Christopher Ali, *Local News in a Digital World: Small Market Newspapers in the Digital Age*, TOW CENTER FOR DIGITAL JOURNALISM, COLUMBIA JOURNALISM SCHOOL (Fall 2017) at 66-67.

20 *Id.* at 66. The authors add that many media professionals they interviewed were "surprisingly optimistic about the future of local news and newspapers." *Id.* A key reason is that "in many cases, the work local journalists produce is seldom replicated elsewhere." *Id.*

21 *Id.* at 66. Journalists Dan Rather and Elliot Kirschner similarly note that local daily newspapers have always been "the engines that powered much of American journalism, as great local reporting would bubble up to the national newspapers and television. Local newspapers also provided a check on local and state governments, reporting on mayors, city councils, school boards, and statehouses. Rather & Kirschner, *supra* note 10, at 9.

22 Christopher Ali & Damian Radcliffe, *Small-market newspapers in the digital age*, COLUMBIA JOURNALISM REVIEW (Nov. 15, 2017), https://www.cjr.org/tow_center_reports/local-small-market-newspapers-study.php/. Professors Ali and Radcliffe question Professor Jones' methodology, but recognize that a 2010 study by the Pew Research Center in Baltimore "did discover that newspapers accounted for nearly half (forty-eight percent) of the original reporting in [Baltimore] during the time period covered. Taken at face value, this suggests that the bulk of stories covered by television and cable news find their origins in newspaper reporting." Radcliffe & Ali, *supra* note 20, at 15.

23 Radcliffe & Ali, *supra* note 20, at 15.

National and local daily newspapers ultimately are keystone media contributors and competitors whose long-term health is critical to our local and national media ecosystems, and ultimately our democracy.[24] For example, in 2015, R.K. Nielsen argued that newspapers "serve as 'keystone media' by existing as 'the primary providers of a specific and important kind of information and enable other media's coverage.'"[25] Given the historic and current importance of healthy newspapers and their editorial and investigative reporting to our democracy, we should do everything in our power to promote their future economic sustainability. Unfortunately, as set forth in Section II below, newspapers today are facing unprecedented short-sighted political threats and attacks, as well as serious questions about their economic futures.

III. CURRENT POLITICAL AND ECONOMIC THREATS TO LOCAL AND NATIONAL NEWSPAPERS

Despite the keystone importance of local and national daily newspapers to America's democratic and communal health and prosperity, "the institution of a free press in America is presently in a state of crisis greater than . . . perhaps in any moment in this nation's history."[26] The severe cutbacks in reporters and editors experienced by local and national daily newspapers since 2000, have been well-documented.[27] As an example, Professors Radcliffe and Ali reported in 2017, that "[t]he newspaper industry's statistics over the past decade do not make for pretty reading."[28] Piling on, the 2017 Pew Report "described an industry in decline, with subscriptions retreating . . . , and advertising revenue dropping on newspapers. . .[coupled with]a notable reduction in newsroom employees. . . ."[29]

---

24 In biology and ecology, a "keystone species" is a "species, such as the sea otter, that affects the survival and abundance of many other species in the [ecological] community in which it lives. Its removal or addition results in a relatively significant shift in the composition of the community and sometimes even in the physical structure of the environment." EDWARD O. WILSON, THE DIVERSITY OF LIFE 401 (1992).

25 Radcliffe & Ali, *supra* note 20, at 16, *quoting* R.K. Nielsen, *Local Newspapers as Keystone Media*, in THE DECLINE OF NEWSPAPERS AND THE RISE OF DIGITAL MEDIA (R. Nielsen ed., 2015).

26 Rather & Kirschner, *supra* note 10, at 2. Rather and Kirschner add:
> The winds of instability howl from many directions: a sustained attack on press freedom from those in political power, crumbling business models, rapidly changing technologies, and some self-inflicted wounds. This is a test, not only for those of us who work in journalism, but also for the nation as a whole.
Id.

27 See, e.g. 2011 FCC REP., *supra* note 10, at 34 (discussing the "severe cutbacks" newspapers across the country have experienced); Mark Jurkowitz, *What the Digital News Boom Means for Consumers*, PEW RESEARCH CENTER'S JOURNALISM & MEDIA (Mar. 26, 2014), http://www.journalism.org/2014/03/26/what-the-digital-news-boom-means-for-consumers/ ("Alarm bells about the decline in local reporting have been ringing for some time"); Lauren Rich Fine, *Bad Public Relations or is This a Real Crisis?* DUKE CONF. ON NONPROFIT MEDIA (May 4-5, 2009)(Newspapers are suffering financially and many question their fate"); and Rather & Kirschner, *supra* note 10, at 9 (discussing "the decimation that has come to local newspapers").

28 Radcliffe & Ali, *supra* note 20, at 16.

29 Radcliffe & Ali, *supra* note 20, at 16, quoting Jesse Holcomb, Amy Mitchell & Rachel Weisel, *State of the News Media 2016*, PEW RESEARCH CENTER (2016), available at http://assets.pewresearch.org/wp-content/uploads/sites/13/2016/06/3013308/state-of-the-news-media-report-2016-final.pdf. See also Rather & Kirschner, *supra* note 10, at 9 ("The deep cuts to newsrooms in print and electronic media have resulted in far fewer reporters waking up each morning deciding what story they will chase. There [also] is less investigative reporting and international coverage.").

As a result of such severe cutbacks at local and daily newspapers, civic and media leaders have grown alarmed.[30] Media experts have increasingly voiced concerns that continuing newspaper cutbacks could have a potential "seismic effect on our democracy."[31]

Adding to the economic stresses facing local and national daily newspapers, our nation's President has begun unleashing unprecedented attacks against daily newspapers and other mainstream media. For example, the President and others have questioned newspapers' and other forms of media's objectivity and integrity, and labeled them as purveyors of supposedly "fake news" and "the enemy of the people."[32]

The President's incessant attacks have created "a dangerous political moment" in our history.[33] "President Trump and his supporters' ongoing assault on the media is harmful to both journalism's pursuit of truth and community-based information, and to democracy itself."[34] As noted by the *Long Beach Post* on August 16, 2018, "In happier times it didn't need to be

---

30 See, e.g. 2011 FCC Rpt., *supra* note 10, at 8 ("That sense of the vital link between informed citizens and a healthy democracy is why civic and media leaders grew alarmed a few years ago when the digital revolution began undercutting traditional media business models, leading to massive layoffs of journalists at newspapers. . . ").

31 Rather & Kirschner, supra note 10, at 8. In an interview with former beat reporter turned author and television writer David Simon, Bill Moyers brought up the dangers of a society without strong newspapers:

    Q. (Moyers): You recently told The Guardian in London, 'Oh to be a state or local official in America' – without newspapers – it's got to be one of the great dreams in the history of American corruption?

    A. (Simon): Well, I was being a little hyperbolic.

    Q. (Moyers): But it's happening?

    A. (Simon): Yes, it absolutely is. . .[major] institutions are no longer being covered by beat reporters who are looking for the systemic. . . . I was being a little flippant with The Guardian, but what I was saying was, you know, until they figure out a new model, there's going to be a wave of corruption.

Bill Moyers, *Interview with David Simon*, in Bill Moyers Journal: The Conversation Continues, 75, 83-84 (2011).

32 See, e.g. Jaclyn Peiser, *The New York Times Joins Effort to Combat Trump's Anti-Press Rhetoric*, N.Y. Times (Aug. 14, 2018), https://www.nytimes.com/2018/08/14/business/media/trump-news-media-editorials.html. Ms. Peiser wrote:

    At a recent rally in Pennsylvania, Mr. Trump pointed to the group of journalists covering the event, saying they 'only make up stories' and called them 'fake, fake disgusting news.' On Twitter, he has revived an old phrase – 'the enemy of the people'—to describe 'much of the media' and 'the Fake News Media.'

Id. See also Editorial, *Journalists Are Not the Enemy*, Boston Globe (Aug. 16, 2018), http://apps.bostonglobe.com/opinion/graphics/2018/08/freepress/ ("Today in the United States we have a president who has created a mantra that members of the media who do not blatantly support the policies of the current U.S. administration are the 'enemy of the people' and 'the enemy of the American people.'"). See also Mike Snider, *Trump invokes 'fake news' at press conference*, USA Today (Jan. 11, 2017 6:17 PM), https://www.usatoday.com/story/money/2017/01/11/trump-tackles-fake-news-press-conference/96438764/.

33 Rather & Kirschner, *supra* note 10, at 2. See also Editorial, *President Trump, we are not the nation's enemy*, Mercury News & E. Bay Times (Aug. 16, 2018), https://www.mercurynews.com/2018/08/15/editorial-president-trump-we-are-not-the-nations-enemy/. The editorial observed:

    We are not the enemy

    It is shocking that in this country, built on the foundation of a free press, we would ever have to say that. But we live in shocking times. And we are under attack – from our President. He has called us 'the enemy of the American people.' He disparages our work as 'fake news.' At his rallies, he verbally abuses us. Not surprisingly, some of his supporters have taken it to the next step, threatening violence.

Id.

34 Editorial, *'Enemy of the people' rhetoric damaging*, Freeman, S.D. Courier (Aug. 16, 2018), https://www.freemansd.com/article/editorial%C2%A0%E2%80%98enemy-people%E2%80%99-rhetoric-damaging. The editorial continued: "Rhetoric diminishing that process [of free community conversation] – regardless of where it comes from – should concern every one of us, whether in Freeman, or Sioux Falls, or St. Louis or New York." *Id.* at 3.

said that a free press is essential to democracy. Now, sadly, it does."[35] Quite simply, America's historic belief in our First Amendment and the need for a free press is under siege. "This is a test, not only for those of us who work in journalism, but also for the nation as a whole."[36]

Thankfully, our national and local daily newspapers have not taken such misguided and dangerous attacks lying down. On August 16, 2018, more than 350 national and local daily newspapers published editorials promoting and defending our Constitution's First Amendment's freedom of the press, and the need to "[k]eep[] the public informed."[37] The words of the *Whitman-Hanson Express* and the *Plympton-Halifax Express* in Hanson, Massachusetts express the feelings of newspaper publishers, editors, and reporters throughout the United States: "We work together. . . in our unflinching support of the First Amendment and its guarantee of a free press, as the best protection of our basic freedoms and status as a democratic republic. That's why it is our First Amendment."[38] The *Omaha World News* in Omaha, Nebraska, similarly observed: "History has demonstrated, time and again, the importance of journalism in shining a light on government and explaining key issues confronting communities and our nation."[39]

Foreign newspapers have joined in to support America's newspapers. For example, *The Guardian*, in London, United Kingdom, stated:

> Press freedom was not invented in the United States, but there are few nations
> in which the importance of an independent press has been so closely woven
> into its long history. This great American tradition of respect for truth and
> truth-telling is now under threat.[40]

---

35 Tim Grobaty, *The media as 'your enemy' is perhaps Trump's biggest lie*, LONG BEACH POST (Aug. 16, 2018), https://lbpost.com/commentary/the-media-are-your-enemy-is-perhaps-trumps-biggest-lie/. See also Editorial, *The Core Principles of Journalism*, THE ANNISTON STAR (Aug. 16, 2018), https://www.annistonstar.com/opinion/editorials/editorial-the-core-principles-of-journalism ("Trump's favored 'enemy of the people' pejorative has been used for centuries by autocrats in Rome, in Nazi Germany and in the Soviet Union to condemn minority groups or those seen as hostile to their rule. When Trump uses it, he aligns himself with some of history's worst human beings").

36 Rather & Kirschner, *supra* note 10, at 2. The authors add:
The most immediate threat comes from the dangerous political moment in which we find ourselves. We have seen individual journalists and some of our best press institutions singled out for attack by the highest of elected officials for reporting truths that the powerful world would rather remain hidden; for pointing out lies as lies; and for questioning motivations that deserved scrutiny.
Id. at 1-2. See also Editorial, *A Free Press Needs You*, N.Y. TIMES (Aug. 15, 2018), https://www.nytimes.com/interactive/2018/08/15/opinion/editorials/free-press-local-journalism-news-donald-trump.html (". . .calling journalists the 'enemy of the people' is dangerous, period. These attacks on the press are particularly threatening to journalists in nations with a less secure rule of law and to smaller publications in the United States, already buffeted by the industry's economic crisis"). *Id.* at 2.

37 Editorial, Terri Lynn Oldham House, *We are not your enemy*, THE PAGOSA SPRINGS SUN (Aug. 16, 2018), http://www.pagosasun.com/we-are-not-your-enemy/, reprinted in part in *A Free Press Needs You*, *supra* note 37, at 2. See also Editorial, MERCURY NEWS & E. BAY TIMES, *supra* note 34, at 2 (". . . we believe in the foundational premise behind the First Amendment – that our nation is stronger if it is informed").

38 Editorial, THE WHITMAN-HANSON EXP. & THE HAMPTON-HALIFAX EXP., *reprinted in part* in N.Y. TIMES, Aug. 15, 2018, *supra* note 37.

39 Editorial, OMAHA WORLD-HERALD, *Omaha World-Herald remains committed to our community and state*, (Aug. 14, 2018), https://www.omaha.com/opinion/editorial-omaha-world-herald-remains-committed-to-our-community-and/article_91f21698-3c63-589f-9392-926cf44732c6.html, reprinted in part in N.Y. TIMES, Aug. 15, 2018, *supra* note 37.

40 Editorial, THE GUARDIAN, *reprinted in part in* N.Y. TIMES, Aug. 15, 2018, *supra* note 37, at 14.

In the midst of the loud and vicious attacks upon their integrity, national and local daily newspapers also must deal with the popularity of the Internet. Numerous commentators have published articles discussing the threat to newspapers from the Internet and the new digital age. Rather and Kirschner, for example, have noted:

> The technological challenges to a sustainable business model for journalism have only grown since the early years of this [twenty-first] century. . . . We have seen how online advertising has proven elusive and disappointing, and efforts such as paywalls have not proven generally effective, as consumers can readily find news online for free. Newspapers in particular suffered. . . most importantly, our evolving media landscape has made it more difficult for television news networks and newspapers to have the resources to employ editors and reporters.[41]

Undoubtedly, "[d]igital disruption has transformed the media landscape over the past decade. As a result, the business models for most newspapers are very different than they were ten years ago."[42]

There is little doubt that continuously cutting newsroom and editorial staffs could lead to further reductions in newspaper quality, which could precipitate "a classic death spiral . . . ."[43] Fortunately, more and more, the newspaper industry is beginning "to change the 'doom and gloom' narrative that surrounds it, at both the national and local levels."[44]

IV. LOCAL AND NATIONAL NEWSPAPERS' CURRENT HEALTH AND FUTURE ECONOMIC VIABILITY IN THE DIGITAL AGE

Rather than succumbing to the powerful and threatening forces of the Internet, both local and national daily newspapers are steadily leveraging and transforming their high-quality publishing with attractive and compelling synergistic Internet sites. One key reason behind newspapers' increasing digital success is that readers continue to hunger for the high-quality local and national news and investigative journalism that local and

---

41 Rather & Kirschner, *supra* note 10, at 8. The authors additionally lament "the decimation that has come to local newspapers." *Id.* at 9.

42 Radcliffe & Ali, *supra* note 20, at 79. See also Horton & Lande, *supra* note 18, at 1543 (discussing how "[n]ewspaper publishers lament declining circulation and readership. . . .").

43 Philip Meyer & Yuan Zhang, *Anatomy of a Death Spiral: Newspapers and Their Credibility*, Remarks at the Media Mgmt. & Econ. Div., Assoc. for Education in Journalism and Mass. Comm., Miami Beach, Fla., Aug. 10, 2002. The authors add that if newspaper owners and managers "continue to regard quality as mere cost, [then] the self-reinforcing loop of the death spiral will continue." *Id.* at 9. See also Wolf Richter, *Here's why billionaires keep buying newspapers despite them being in a death spiral*, Bus. Insider (Feb. 21, 2018), https://www.businessinsider.com/why-billionaires-keep-buying-newspapers-despite-them-being-in-death-spiral-2018-2; and Moyers, *supra* note 32, at 84 (discussing how newspaper publishers allowed their reportorial and editorial quality to diminish while making huge profits – leading to substantial losses in readership).

44 Radcliffe & Ali, *supra* note 20, at Exec. Summary 5.

national newspapers continue to provide.[45] Through their constantly updated Internet sites, newspapers are carving out keystone niches for themselves, as the premium digital purveyors of high-quality daily news and investigative reporting. Readers continue to be attracted to newspapers' high-quality local and investigative reporting.[46] "Far from being nearly-extinct dinosaurs, the traditional media players – TV stations and newspapers – have emerged as the largest providers of local news online."[47]

Newspapers, in both digital and published forms, continue to appeal to readers as an excellent source for one-stop information and reporting shopping. "Newspapers are relatively distinct because they save readers the transaction costs of finding, sifting through, and assessing the quality of a huge number of Internet sites."[48] For example, by perusing a local newspaper's Internet site, a reader can catch up on all of the local business, politics, sports, and entertainment news of the day. Similarly, a national newspaper's readers can follow all of the breaking national and international news, as well as the opinions of the newspaper's bloggers on a single site. Furthermore, the ability to constantly update

---

45 See, e.g. Horton & Lande, *supra* note 18, at 1538. We observed:

   . . . there usually is no single Internet equivalent containing anything even close to the content of a traditional newspaper – with the notable exceptions of newspapers' own online sites. Newspapers are relatively distinct because they save readers the transaction costs of finding, sifting through, and assessing the quality of a huge number of Internet sites. The finding and assembling of distinct types of information in one place is crucial for readers. So is sifting through the cacophony of an almost infinite number of sources of information, many of which are duplicative or may be unreliable. A newspaper's sifting and 'certification' function is as important as its news-generation and aggregation function.

   Id.

46 See, e.g. Radcliffe & Ali, *supra* note 20, at 4 (discussing how local newspapers have "experienced notable resilience thanks in part to exclusive content not offered elsewhere, the dynamics of ultra-local advertising markets, and an ability to leverage a physical closeness to their audiences"). *Id.* at 68 (discussing how "[i]t is unique content which is most likely to ensure the continued prosperity and existence of local newspapers"); Laura Wansley, *Big Newspapers are Booming: Washington Post to Add 60 Newsroom Jobs,* (NPR Broadcast Dec. 27, 2016)(discussing how the Washington Post was "now a profitable and growing company" whose "online traffic had increased nearly 50% in the past year, and new subscriptions [had] grown by 75%, more than doubling digital subscription income"; and further observing surging subscriptions at the *New York Times* and "record growth in subscriptions at the *Los Angeles Times* and the *Wall Street Journal*"); Michael Bartel, *Despite subscription surges for largest U.S. newspapers, circulation and revenue fall for industry overall,* Pew Research Center (June 1, 2017)(discussing how following the 2016 "presidential election, some major U.S. newspapers reported a sharp jump in digital subscriptions"); Horton & Lande, *supra* note 18, at 1541 (discussing how newspapers' "online readership is soaring"); *Id.* at 1551 (discussing how "the high-quality journalistic reporting and editing of the traditional media generally continues to serve crucial democratic and societal functions that have not been displaced by the Internet"); Matthew Gentzkow, *Trading Dollars for Dollars: The Price of Attention Online and Offline,* 104(5) Amer. Econ. Rev. 481, 482 (2014)(discussing how "[c]ontrary to most popular accounts, the growth of the Internet has not obviously caused a large decline in newspaper readership"); 2011 FCC Rpt., *supra* note 10, at 12-13 ("In most communities, the number one online local news source is the local newspaper, an indication that despite their financial problems, newspaper newsrooms are still adept at providing local news."); and *id.* at 55 (". . . from a traffic perspective, newspapers have come to dominate the Internet on the local level").

47 2011 Fcc Rpt., *supra* note 10, at 6. See also *id.* at 55 (discussing how the websites of "legacy news organizations – mainly major newspapers and cable television stations – dominate online news space in both traffic and loyalty;" and how a Pew Research Study of "local news sources in three cities – Toledo, Richmond, and Seattle – came to the same conclusion. In each city, the number one online source for news was the website of the city's long-standing newspaper."); See also Horton & Lande, *supra* note 18, at 1541 ("The crucial issue facing local daily newspapers is not competing with the Internet, but 'finding ways to make more money from a growing online audience that generally reads the paper for free'"); quoting Suzanne M. Kirchoff, Cong. Research Serv., R40700, The U.S. Newspaper Industry in Transition 10 (2009).

48 Horton & Lande, *supra* note 18, at 1538. The authors further note that "[t]he one-stop shopping convenience of a local daily newspaper cannot be minimized. . . A local daily newspaper's bundle of sifted and sorted news and features often provides a welcome sense of order in a world of 'complexity. . . run[ ] amok.'" *Id.* at 1538-39, quoting Jeffrey Kruger, Simplexity, Why Simple Things Become Complex (and How Complex Things Can Be Made Simple) 231 (2008).

its content on an Internet site greatly increases a newspaper's ability to satisfy its readers' desires to read the most up-to-date breaking news and stories.

"Newspaper publishers like Dean Singleton of MediaNews Group have long recognized that local daily newspapers typically offer the best available and most easily accessed one-stop shopping of high-quality content, including news, comics, sports, op-eds, entertainment and features."[49] Quite simply, "[t]he one-stop shopping convenience of a local daily newspaper [whether in print or online] cannot be minimized."[50]

Local daily newspapers have "experienced notable resilience thanks in part to exclusive content not offered elsewhere, the dynamics of ultra-local advertising markets, and an ability to leverage a physical closeness to their audience."[51] Moreover, readers can trust their local newspapers because of the "goodwill and trust," which many of them have "earned through decades of thorough investigative reporting and serious journalism that has uncovered government corruption and waste, and offered an inside scoop on local sports and civic interests."[52]

Despite the "gloom and doom" scenarios we hear on a daily basis, local and daily newspapers continue to add substantial value to Americans' lives through their ongoing investigative watchdog roles, their community-building and solutions-oriented functions, and their overall integral importance in supporting local media ecosystems.[53] Perhaps most surprisingly, readers younger than fifty years old are increasingly beginning to pay more attention to online newspapers. For example, a February 17, 2017 *Pew Research Report* showed that for election news covering the 2016 presidential election, three national newspapers – *The New York Times*, the *Washington Post*, and the *Wall Street Journal* – "attracted more readers younger than 50 and older as regular readers."[54] "This reinforces findings that when asked about reading, watching, or listening to news, younger Americans are more likely than their elders to prefer reading it. . . though they overwhelmingly prefer to do this reading online.'"[55]

---

49 Horton & Lande, *supra* note 18, at 1540.

50 *Id.* at 1538.

51 Radcliffe & Ali, *supra* note 20, at Executive Summary 4. Radcliffe and Ali further argue that "[s]mall-market newspapers – by being bold, engaging, and offering content and information of value to their communities – can continue to be a monument to the past, present, and future of the areas they serve. . . If all news is local, than this sector will continue to matter for a long time to come." *Id.* at 80.

52 Horton & Lande, *supra* note 18, at 1534. See also Paul Farhi, *A Bright Future for Newspapers*, Am. Journalism Rev., June/July 2005, at 58 ("Newspapers big and small have spent millions of dollars over the years reminding people what they do. This has created a vast but hard-to-measure reservoir of good will for newspapers. . . .").

53 See Radcliffe & Ali, *supra* note 20, at 13-16.

54 Michael Barth, *For election news, young people turned to some national papers more than their elders*, Pew Research Rpt. (Feb. 17, 2017).

55 *Id.*

In terms of future potential revenue generation, "attracting these younger, digital readers may help grow digital advertising revenue and even subscriptions."[56] On top of this, since "the Internet allows more efficient targeting of ads, revenue per hour is higher in online newspapers than in print newspapers."[57] Advertisers place a high value on online newspaper advertising because "online newspapers attract [ ] higher-income and more educated readers of a particular value to advertisers, [and] online newspapers [are] able to target ads [based on] . . . detailed information of reader characteristics."[58] In short, advertisers today value ads in digital newspapers substantially higher than ads for the Internet as a whole.[59]

Adding these developments together reveals that the future of high-quality local and national daily newspapers is much brighter than media naysayers often predict. In addition to the increasing success of such national daily newspapers as the *New York Times*, the *Washington Post*, the *Wall Street Journal*, and *USA Today*, local newspapers increasingly are exploiting local niches and finding ways to both survive and thrive in the new digital era.[60] Consequently, this author predicts a vibrant and profitable future for local and daily newspapers based on their increasing ability to leverage and exploit, rather than fear, the Internet.

V. APPLYING AMERICA'S ANTITRUST LAWS TO NEWSPAPERS IN AN INCREASINGLY DIGITAL WORLD

Given all the potential competition local and national newspapers face on the Internet, do America's antitrust laws really have any meaningful relevance for newspapers today? To answer this question, it is important to focus on the crucial implications for our democracy that local and daily newspapers continue to play in our increasingly digital world. As previously discussed, newspapers continue to provide the keystone foundations for the diverse and healthy media ecosystem necessary to protect our democracy in these troubled times.

---

56 *Id.* at 2.

57 Gentzkow, *supra* note 47, at 481; *Id.* at 485.

58 *Id.* at 485.

59 See *id.*; and Horton & Lande, *supra* note 18, at 1531 ("Advertisers have long understood the importance of media quality and diversity. Since higher quality generally induces more readers or viewers to spend time reading a newspaper...it increases demand among advertisers"); quoting Charles J. Romeo & Aran Canes, *A Theory of Quality Competition in Joint Operating Agreements*, 57 ANTITRUST BULL. 367, 400 (2012).

60 See Barth, *supra* note 55 (stating large newspapers have enjoyed a surge of young readership); See, e.g. 2011 FCC Rpt., *supra* note 10, at 42 (discussing how "many smaller newspapers [are] going very well due to their unique marketing position"); Radcliffe & Ali, *supra* note 20, at 4 (discussing the "notable resilience" of local newspapers and their continuing willingness "to explore opportunities to broaden their revenue and income base"); and Joe Mahon, *News flash: Small-market papers prosper*, FEDERAL RESERVE BANK OF MINNEAPOLIS (Jan. 1, 2007), https://www.minneapolisfed.org/publications/fedgazette/news-flash-smallmarket-papers-prosper (discussing the success of small local newspaper based on substantial market penetration).

The most important competitive elements newspapers provide today include "quality, variety, perspective, [easy one-stop shopping access], and editorial independence. In fact, for [newspapers], the choice of non-price competition is even more important than price competition or competition in terms of potential savings in the costs of generating news."[61] Consequently, this author continues to believe, as Professor Lande and he concluded in 2013, that "courts should continue to find that newspapers often constitute their own relevant markets for antitrust, and that the rise of online media should not effectively immunize [newspapers] from the antitrust laws."[62]

America needs great newspapers and the "aggressive, thorough, intelligent [community] coverage and revelatory accountability reporting" they can uniquely provide.[63] The Internet has actually provided a valuable new forum for local and national newspapers to spread their high-quality investigative and reportorial contents. Therefore, we must continue to vigorously protect, promote, and, encourage the keystone roles that local and daily newspapers play in providing high-quality local and national journalism in a world of steadily and often dangerously increasing media consolidation and concentration. Protection of high-quality print and online journalism is vital to protect the free exchange of ideas and political accountability in our democracy.

This author refuses to buy into the 'doom and gloom' opinion that the Internet has somehow turned our local and national daily newspapers into nearly-extinct dinosaurs. Ironically, one of the biggest problems newspapers faced, as the Internet gained prominence, was that they had been spoiled by decades of bloated monopoly profits. For example, in the "late 1990s, after years of circulation declines, the [newspaper] industry's average cash flow margins were 29%, according to newspaper analyst Lauren Rich Fine."[64] In the early 2000s, newspapers continued exploiting their monopoly and oligopoly market positions by "squeeze[ing] higher profits out of newspapers."[65] Despite their alleged troubling competi-

---

61 Horton & Lande, *supra* note 18, at 1558.

62 *Id.* As we additionally urged in 2013, "a failure to recognize the crucial role that non-price competition plays in defining distinct media sectors would be a prescription for disaster for the future of our democracy." *Id.*

63 LEONARD DOWNIE JR. & ROBERT G. KAISER, THE NEWS ABOUT THE NEWS: AMERICAN JOURNALISM IN PERIL 108 (2002).

64 2011 FCC RPT., *supra* note 10, at 36. The FCC Report added:
    As competition disappeared, surviving newspapers raised ad rates. Between 1965 and 1975, ad rates rose 67%. . . ; but between 1975 and 1990, as more newspapers became monopolies, rates skyrocketed 253% (compared with 141% for general consumer prices).
Id.

65 *Id.* The 2011 FCC Report further noted that ". . . responding in part to Wall Street investors, . . . the papers themselves began to shrink in physical size (many used smaller pages and ran fewer pages) and in editorial scope."
Id.

tive positions, the newspaper "industry reported operating margins averaging 19.3%. That's double the average among Fortune 500 companies."[66]

Instead of looking to increase their competitiveness, it "became clear that many [news-paper] buyers were financing consolidation and growth by taking on huge amounts of debt."[67] Professor James Hamilton of Duke University calculated that "[i]f in 2008, the newspaper industry had accepted a 9% cash margin instead of taking 13%, it could have generated enough additional cash to avoid virtually all the layoffs that occurred around the period."[68] In short, newspapers had allowed themselves in the early 2000s, to be spoiled by decades of "wild profitability."[69] As observed by James O'Shea, the former managing editor of the *Chicago Tribune* and past editor-in-chief of the *Los Angeles Times*, the newspaper industry was not forced into a so-called "death spiral" because of forces unleashed by declining circulations and the migration of readers to the Internet . . . [Instead], "[t]he lack of investment, the greed, incompetence, corruption, hypocrisy, and downright arrogance of people who put their interests ahead of the public's are respon-sible for the state of the newspaper industry today."[70]

Ironically, the newspaper industry's reduced competitiveness was buttressed by the 1970 Newspaper Preservation Act.[71] In order to hopefully spur editorial and reportorial com-petition among daily newspapers, the NPA allowed competing newspapers to enter into joint operating arrangements ("JOAs") with the approval of the United States Attorney General.[72] Under the NPA, newspaper JOAs were allowed to jointly set their prices and divide their markets without fearing the Sherman Act.[73]

Although the NPA's supporters claimed that the Act would generate increased efficiencies and consumer welfare, several commentators expressed concerns about the Act's effect on the long-term competitiveness of newspapers. For example, in 1971, Professor John H. Carlson of the Indiana University School of Law concluded that "[t]he NPA [would]

66 *Id.* at 38 (quoting Pew Research Center: Journalism and Media Staff, *Last Call at the ASNE Saloon*, Pew Research Cen-ter (Apr. 26, 2006), http://www.journalism.org/2006/04/26/last-call-at-the-asne-saloon/). The FCC reported that Mr. Carroll, the editor of the *Lexington (KY) Herald-Leader, the Baltimore Sun, and the Los Angeles Times* "became convinced that owners were sacrificing the long-term health of their newspapers for a short-term gain." 2011 FCC Rpt., *supra* note 10, at 38.

67 2011 FCC Rpt., *supra* note 10, at 38

68 2011 FCC Rpt., *supra* note 10, at 270-71, citing James Hamilton, *Newspapers: News Investment*, in Pew, State of the News Media 2010, http://stateofthemedia.org/2010/newspapers-summary-investment/. See also Lauren Rich Fine, *supra* note 28. Ms. Fine observed that although newspaper margins peaked in the late 1990s at 29 percent, in 2008, "the average was [still] 13% with fairly sizeable returns." *Id.*

69 2011 FCC Rpt., *supra* note 10, at 56.

70 James O'Shea, The Deal From Hell: How Moguls and Wall Street Plundered American Newspapers 11-12 (2011).

71 15 U.S.C. § 1801, et seq. (1970).

72 15 U.S.C. § 1803

73 15 U.S.C. § 1, et seq. (1890).

not serve the public's interest in an independent and competitive press."[74] Similarly, John Patkus warned in 1984, that the NPA was failing "to achieve the stated goal of Congress to maintain competing voices in the press."[75]

Unfortunately, the history of the newspaper industry since 1970 supports the prescient concerns of such critics. Rather than using the NPA to generate efficiencies that could spur higher quality, the newspaper industry was more than happy to enjoy monopoly profits while cutting quality and variety. Not unexpectedly, cities like "Seattle and Denver suffered significant negative declines in civic engagement when they lost one of their daily newspapers."[76] Analyzing a simulated consolidation of two newspapers in the Minneapolis market that was blocked by the Department of Justice, Ying Fan concluded in 2013, that:

> [I]f the merger had occurred, both newspapers would have decreased the news content quality, the local news ration, and the content variety. These changes in the newspaper characteristics would have been accompanied by a rise in both newspapers' subscription price. Overall, circulation would have declined, and the local news content per household would have decreased.[77]

Fan therefore concluded that newspaper mergers do not enhance consumer welfare, but instead enhance "publisher surplus."[78] The Federal Communications Commission

---

74 John H. Carlson, *Newspaper Preservation Act: A Critique*, 46 IND. L. J. 392, 411 (1971). Professor Carlson added:
There is no demonstrable need for exempting joint newspaper operating arrangements from the antitrust laws since there has been no showing that a significant number of newspapers would fail without the exemption. Moreover, this Act will insure the effective monopolization of the newspaper business in the twenty-two cities where newspapers are participating in joint operations. This monopolization is likely to effectively cripple the growth of small newspapers and prevent the successful establishment of new competing dailies in these communities. To the extent that new joint operating arrangements are entered into in accordance with this Act, any possible increase in newspaper competition will be retarded. This Act, therefore, may raise the issue of possible infringement upon the first amendment freedom of the press. The public's interest in having access to independent and competing sources of news would be better served by application of the antitrust laws.
Id. at 411-12 (citations omitted).

75 Note, *The Newspaper Preservation Act: Why It Fails to Preserve Newspapers*, 17 AKRON L. REV. 435, 452. Mr. Patkus further opined that the NPA was "a failure of strategy since the choice of JOAs as the method of saving newspapers is unsound. JOAs, in practice, foster monopolies and chains, not independent voices." *Id.* As an example justifying Mr. Patkus's fear of the potential loss of independent voices, on May 7, 2004, the *Charleston (WV) Gazette's* owner, the Gazette Company, decided to purchase and shut down the *Charleston Daily Mail.* The U.S. Department of Justice's Antitrust Division later sued to rescind the transaction under § 7 of the Clayton Act (15 U.S.C. § 18 (2006) and the Sherman Act (15 U.S.C. §§ 1-2 (1890). The United States alleged that immediately after acquiring its competitor, the Gazette Company immediately began implementing a plan to weaken the *Daily Mail* "to the point where it would fail and could be eliminated as a competitor to the *Charleston Gazette.*" See Complaint at 2-3, *United States v. Daily Gazette Co.*, 567 F. Supp. 2d 859 (S.D. W. Va. 2008). For a detailed discussion of the case, see Horton & Lande, *supra* note 18, at 1522-1525. By way of disclosure, author Horton was the lead trial lawyer for the United States in the case. The case ultimately settled before trial. Final Judgment, *U.S. v. Daily Gazette Co.*, 2010 WL 11586679 (S.D.W.Va.).

76 Radcliffe & Ali, *supra* note 20, at EXECUTIVE SUMMARY 14, quoting Lee Shaker, *Dead Newspapers and Citizens' Civic Engagement*, 1.0 POLITICAL COMMS. 144 (2014) http://www.tandfonline.com/doi/abs/10.1080/10584609.2012.762817.

77 Ying Fan, *Ownership Consolidation and Product Characteristics: A Study of the U.S. Daily Newspaper Market*, 103 AM. ECON. REV. 1598, 1599 (August 2013).

78 *Id.* at 1599. For an excellent discussion of declines in newspaper editorial and reportorial quality, as a result of severe cost-cutting to enhance publisher profits, see 2011 FCC RPT., *supra* note 10, at 43-55.

("FCC") similarly concluded in 2011, that in addition to reducing a diversity of meaningful reporting, newspaper concentration increases "Wall Street pressure to focus on short-term profits over long-term goals."[79]

As a result of such studies and the promise of enhanced newspaper competition through newspapers' own unique Internet sites, this author concludes that the answer to newspapers' current profitability issues ironically is more, not less, direct competition. This author therefore agrees with the FCC's 2011 conclusions that newspaper innovation and diversification, rather than consolidation and NPA-antitrust immunity, can help America create the best local and national daily newspapers we have ever had.[80] Quite simply, the rise of the Internet should not immunize newspapers, or other media, from the antitrust laws.[81]

VI. CONCLUSION

From the American colonies' earliest years to today, local and national daily newspapers have been crucial to the health and growth of our American democracy. Shockingly, however, newspapers, along with other media, have found themselves as the targets of short-sighted, misguided, and dangerous political attacks. At the same time, newspapers are fighting to stay relevant and economically sustainable in the age of the Internet.

All of this would seem to bolster the many "gloom and doom" naysayers, who seek to portray newspapers as outdated and nearly-extinct dinosaurs. Fortunately, however, both local and national daily newspapers increasingly have discovered creative and effective ways to leverage and maximize their own Internet sites, instead of succumbing to the Internet's ubiquitous presence. Consumers, including a growing number of younger readers, are showing their appreciation for newspapers, as the premier source of high-quality one-stop local and national news reporting and investigative and editorial journalism. As a result, newspapers continue to serve as keystone media whose health bolsters and ensures vigorous media competition of all types.

---

79 2011 FCC Rpt., *supra* note 10, at 270; and *id.* at 11-12 (discussing a 2009 Columbia Journalism School study on the loss of newspaper competition in major cities across the country, including Baltimore, Philadelphia, and Raleigh-Durham, North Carolina; along with a diminution in "the number of reporters covering essential beats").

80 2011 FCC Rpt., *supra* note 10, at 10. Indeed, "[i]n most communities, the number one online local news source is the newspaper, an indication that despite their financial problems, newspapers are still adept at providing news." *Id.* at 11-12.

81 See Horton & Lande, *supra* note 18, at 1558.

The history of newspapers shows that the 1970 Newspaper Preservation Act, which ostensibly was designed to promote competition while effectively limiting it, has been an abysmal failure. Instead of increasing competition, the NPA allowed newspapers to continue to bolster and maximize their monopolistic positions while cutting innovations and quality. Instead of creating better and more competitive newspapers, the NPA allowed rampant consolidation and dangerous cuts in quality.

Based on the history of newspapers since the passage of the NPA, the best way to promote and secure newspapers' economic futures is not through lax antitrust laws and regulations, or enforcement that limits aggressive competition. More – not less – head-to-head competition between local and daily newspapers is the better answer.

In conclusion, going forward, antitrust enforcers should recognize local and daily newspapers as distinct product markets (within their respective geographic markets) for purposes of antitrust enforcement – especially in the area of merger enforcement. At the same time, the ironically named NPA, which has done far more to harm the long-term health of newspapers than the growth of the Internet, should be immediately repealed. Instead of seeking to shelter newspapers from aggressive competition, newspapers should be encouraged to continue vigorously building their keystone media niches. As our nation's founders would surely recognize if they were with us today, nothing less than the future of our democracy is at stake.[82]

---

82 See also DOWNIE & KAISER, *supra* note 66, at 266 (arguing that "[t]he fate of good journalism in the new century will be a leading indicator of the health of American society"). Joseph Pulitzer's thoughts are enshrined on a plaque at the Columbia University Journalism School in New York, which was founded with his bequest in 1912: "Our republic and its press will rise or fall together. An able, disinterested, public-spirited press, with trained intelligence to know the right and courage to do it, can preserve that public virtue without which popular government is a sham and a mocking."

NEWSPAPER MERGER CONTROL: THE LONG-TERM COSTS OF A SHORTSIGHTED APPROACH

By Craig Pouncey & Veronica Roberts[1]

ABSTRACT

Newspapers of record play a critical role in holding a democracy's leaders to account and in ensuring that scrutiny is given to the processes and institutions of our society. Those same newspapers are seeing the advertising revenues on which they depend to play this role drastically eroded by competition from on-line media which play no such role. Whilst this function should not render newspapers immune from a full and proper assessment of their merger activities, transactions which are subject to review must, at the least, be reviewed in a proper market context, with full consideration given to the intense pressures they face. This is not currently happening with sufficient predictability, with the result that desirable market consolidation has been hampered. This article looks at the history of newspaper merger regulation in the UK and tries to identify ways in which this situation might be improved.

I. INTRODUCTION

When merger control was first introduced in the UK in 1965, newspaper mergers were singled out for the strictest regulatory treatment. Unlike mergers in all other sectors, newspaper mergers (of a particular size) were subject to mandatory notification to the Secretary of State ("SoS") and assessed against a special public interest test. At a time when newspapers were the primary source of news and opinion in the country, this treatment was justified by a very real concern that an increasing concentration of newspaper ownership in too few hands could potentially stifle the free expression of opinion and argument, and distort the accurate presentation of news.

1   Craig Pouncey and Veronica Roberts are partners at Herbert Smith Freehills, Brussels and London respectively. Both have advised newspaper companies on a number of merger reviews. They would like to thank Alex White, associate at Herbert Smith Freehills London, for all his assistance with this article.

Over half a century later, the way that news is produced, consumed, and shared has radically changed, with many of the changes driven by technological transformation. Now, TV and an entirely new form of media – the internet – which only existed in the realms of science fiction in the 1960s, are the most popular sources of news, with the latter increasingly dominating today's media landscape. In the last decade alone, online news consumption has experienced exponential growth. Within the space of three years (2013 to 2016) online consumption of national news rose from a third of the UK population to over half and that figure has continued to grow higher since.[2] Many of these advances, however, have come at the cost of traditional printed newspapers. Whereas newspaper circulation has experienced a gradual decline over the past several decades, in recent years this decline has gone into overdrive with an exodus of readers, and with them advertisers, primarily to online sources of news.[3]

Newspaper groups have sought to respond to these changes by embracing the digital era, and many have experienced growing online readerships. However, with the challenge of achieving step-by-step growth in advertisers they have generally been unable to make up for losses in print revenues and ultimately to break even. Hardest hit has been the local and regional press: Historically most reliant on classified advertising, they have been heavily outcompeted by online giants and specialist portals.[4] Newspaper groups have therefore had to retreat increasingly into survival mode: Making staff cuts, closing titles (the period between 2012 and 2016 saw a net reduction of 26 local and regional newspapers alone) – or seeking to consolidate.[5]

Despite these dramatic and noticeable changes, the merger control regulatory regime has been remarkably slow to keep up (as compared to the previous mandatory one). A significant change did occur at the turn of the century, at which point newspaper mergers

---

2   CMA, 21st Century Fox, Inc and Sky Plc: A report on the anticipated acquisition by 21st Century Fox, Inc of Sky Plc, May 1, 2018 (*Fox/Sky CMA review*), para. 52; Ofcom News Consumption in the UK: 2018, available at: https://www.ofcom.org.uk/__data/assets/pdf_file/0024/116529/news-consumption-2018.pdf.

3   Between 1990 and 2011, circulation of national daily titles fell 37 percent and local and regional titles more than 40 percent (see Rt Hon Lord Justice Leveson, *The Leveson Inquiry: An Inquiry into the Culture, Practices and Ethics of the Press*, November 2010 (*Leveson Inquiry*), page 94). Between 2010 and 2016, national daily circulation fell a further 37 percent (Ofcom, News consumption in the UK: 2016, June 29, 2017). Regional dailies have seen accelerated year-on-year decreases, by 12.5 percent in 2016 alone (Press Gazette, "UK regional dailies lose print sales by average of 12.5 per cent: Wigan Post and The National are biggest fallers," February 23, 2017, http://www.pressgazette.co.uk/uk-regional-dailies-lose-print-sales-by-average-of-12-5-per-cent-wigan-post-and-the-national-are-biggest-fallers/).

4   Aware of their impact, Google and Facebook have in fact recently sought to restore some of the balance by setting up initiatives to support local journalism. See Google "Building a stronger future for journalism," available at https://newsinitiative.withgoogle.com/, and The Guardian, "Facebook gives £4.5m to fund 80 local newspaper jobs in UK," November 19, 2018, available at https://www.theguardian.com/technology/2018/nov/19/facebook-gives-45m-to-fund-80-local-newspaper-jobs-in-uk-media.

5   Ofcom, *Public interest test for the proposed acquisition of Sky plc by 21st Century Fox, Inc, Ofcom's report to the Secretary of State*, 20 June 2017 (*Fox/Sky Ofcom review*), para. 5.14; At the time of writing, the most recent manifestation of these difficulties has been the collapse of Johnston Press (publisher of The Scotsman, The Yorkshire Post, and around 200 other regional and local titles), taken over by its bondholders via a pre-pack administration deal in November 2018, see Financial Times, "Johnston Press agrees administration deal with lenders," November 17, 2018, available at https://www.ft.com/content/a54afd66-e9eb-11e8-a34c-663b3f553b35.

joined all other mergers to be subject to a voluntary notification regime and an exclusively competition-based substantive test. However, the application of that test has raised new problems, chiefly a heavy reluctance by the UK competition authorities to accept that the fortunes of printed newspapers and online media are in any way linked. Indeed, to this day, astonishingly, the UK competition authority has refused to accept that print and on-line news media compete to a significant enough extent to belong in the same economic market. In addition, while newspaper mergers are now subject to voluntary notification, the SoS has nonetheless retained a power to intervene on similar public interest grounds as under the 1965 regime. While this public interest regime has also been extended to TV and radio transactions, online–only media enterprises are not caught. It is also the case that the public interest test is still being operated so that a sufficient plurality of views is assessed only in respect of "newspaper markets" – in isolation to all other types of media.

As a result, newspaper groups have found themselves confronted by unusually high bar-riers to their attempts to keep titles open and remain viable businesses through merging and consolidating. In some cases, closing titles has been the only reasonable option com-pared to the costs and uncertainties of a merger review process.

These issues with the regulatory regime for newspapers are coming more and more sharp-ly into focus in recent years. Indeed, with online competition said to threaten the closure of hundreds of newspaper titles in the short term, while also presenting new dangers in terms of the proliferation of inaccurate and misleading news, the UK Government has recently launched a public inquiry into what Theresa May has described a veritable "danger to democracy."[6] In this wider context, UK merger control may even find itself partly responsible for threatening exactly what it was originally set up to protect: quality journalism and the free expression of opinion.

This article sets out to provide a critical look at the UK newspaper merger control regime. Section II provides a brief historical overview of how the regime works; Section III exam-ines a number of key UK newspaper merger decisions over the last decade; and Section IV concludes with some suggestions on the way forward.

---

6   The Irish Times, "UK government to review future of British newspapers," February 6, 2018, available at https://www.irishtimes.com/business/media-and-marketing/uk-government-to-review-future-of-british-newspapers-1.3382664. The "Cairncross" review is intended to look into the financial sustainability of newsrooms, regional papers and high-quality journalism in the face of the digital media challenge, with a particular focus on the local and regional press, given their "core social importance in highlighting and addressing local issues, bringing communities together, and holding local government and public service providers to account"; see UK Government, "Call for evidence on sus-tainable high-quality journalism in the UK," June 28, 2018, available at: https://www.gov.uk/government/consultations/call-for-evidence-on-sustainable-high-quality-journalism-in-the-uk; In particular, polling has revealed almost half of British adults (47 percent) believe that the quality of news available has declined in the last five years (Government Press Release, "Cairncross seeks views on threats to press," September 3, 2018, available at https://www.gov.uk/govern-ment/news/cairncross-seeks-views-on-threats-to-press).

II. UK NEWSPAPER MERGER CONTROL REGIME IN HISTORICAL PERSPECTIVE

Ever since merger control was first introduced in the UK, newspaper mergers were singled out for special treatment. Under the Monopolies and Mergers Act 1965 (and as further augmented by the Fair Trading Act 1973) the regime applicable to non-newspaper mergers was subject to voluntary notification. Where such mergers were voluntarily notified, or called-in by the Director General of Fair Trading, they were subject to a preliminary review before the Secretary of State for Trade and Industry (as then was) who would then decide whether to refer the merger for a further in-depth review. Such mergers were also assessed on the basis of a broad public interest test that made reference to various factors (including, among others, the maintenance and promotion of competition).[7]

By contrast, newspaper mergers of a particular size (where the total daily paid-for circulation of the newspapers concerned would be 500,000 or more) were subject to mandatory prior consent from the SoS. In such cases, before deciding on the merger, the SoS was obliged to refer the proposed acquisition for an in-depth review (by the Monopolies and Mergers Commission, as then was), bypassing any preliminary assessment stage. These mergers were also assessed against a more narrowly construed public interest that made specific reference to "the need for accurate presentation of news and free expression of opinion."[8]

In many ways the special treatment of newspaper mergers at the time made some sense. Newspapers were still the primary source of news and opinion. At a time when newspaper titles were increasingly being consolidated under the arms of so-called corporate newspaper chains, there was a real risk, as the earlier Shawcross Royal Commission identified, that increasing concentration in too few hands could stifle the expression of opinion and argument and distort the presentation of news.[9]

The special newspaper regime remained in place for the following three decades. There were some exceptions to the prior consent rule, namely where the newspaper being purchased was not economic as a going concern or had de *minimis* circulation (although the de *minimis* threshold was very low at less than 50,000 copies).[10] Nevertheless, towards the end of the century, the regime often resulted in a large number of (usually) regional newspaper mergers being considered in detail by the competition authority, in most cases only to be cleared with limited or no remedies.

---

7 Fair Trading Act 1973, section 84.

8 *Ibid.* section 59(3). On how the newspaper public interest test was applied in practice see Livingston D, *Competition Law and Practice*, (Pearson Professional Limited, 1995), pages 870-884.

9 *Royal Commission on the Press 1961 – 1962, Final Report* (Cmnd 1811). The Royal Commission, chaired by Lord Shawcross, presaged the introduction of newspaper merger regime under the Monopolies and Mergers Act 1965.

10 Free sheets were deemed to have nil circulation and therefore could also benefit from the de *minimis* exception.

By the turn of the century, the entire merger control regime was modernized. Under the Enterprise Act 2002, non-newspaper mergers became subject to an exclusively competition-based test. The SoS's role in the process was also removed, except for a residual power to intervene on national security grounds, or under further public interest grounds specified through statutory instrument. Furthermore, and following considerable agitation from local newspaper groups concerning the hurdles of the newspaper regime, newspaper mergers were finally treated like any other merger: subject to an exclusively competition-based test and voluntary notification under the Enterprise Act.[11]

One exception would remain, however. The Communications Act 2003 set out further public interest grounds under which the SoS could intervene, including special grounds for newspaper mergers.[12] These were the "need for accurate presentation of news and free expression of opinion in newspapers" (mirroring the language of the old regime), and the need for "sufficient plurality of views in newspapers in each market for newspapers in the UK or a part of the UK."[13] Public interest grounds, including in respect of a plurality of views, were also added for TV and radio mergers. What is notable, however, is that the approach to plurality in such mergers is much wider. Whereas in newspaper mergers plurality is to be assessed by reference to specific newspaper markets, for radio or TV mergers, plurality is assessed by reference to "media enterprises," defined to include both TV and radio broadcasters, as well as newspapers (to the extent a TV/radio merger also involves newspaper interests).[14]

While the Communications Act did much to streamline the former special newspaper merger regime, new problems soon arose with the application of a strictly competition-based test to newspaper mergers. These lay chiefly in the reluctance of the competition authority in practice to take fully into account actual and impending competition from other media – particularly online media – in its competitive assessment of newspaper mergers, especially transactions involving local and regional newspapers that were being hardest hit by such competition.

This came to a head in 2009, when the Government intervened as part of its Digital Britain Report, and asked the Office of Fair Trading (OFT) to reconsider its overall approach to local media mergers.[15] The OFT responded somewhat robustly, however, in defense

---

11 Under the Enterprise Act, a merger becomes notifiable where the UK turnover of the acquired company exceeds £70 million or the transaction results in a market share of 25 percent or more. Where either threshold is met, the parties may decide to notify or run the risk of being called-in by the competition authority for review up to four months post-completion.

12 Note that the power of the Secretary of State to intervene on any specified public interest ground only arises where the parties meet the standard jurisdictional tests under the Enterprise Act or where just one of the parties has a 25 percent or more share of a market in a substantial part of the UK.

13 Enterprise Act 2002, sections 58(2A)-(2B).

14 Enterprise Act 2002 sections 58(2C)(a) and section 58A. Other public interest grounds relating to media enterprises concern the need for high quality broadcasting and a commitment to broadcasting standards (section 58(2C)(b)-(c)).

15 Now the Competition and Markets Authority or CMA; BERR/DCMS, Digital Britain: The Interim Report, January 2009.

of its approach. While acknowledging that the local and regional press was "facing very significant structural and cyclical challenges to its traditional business model," in its view the merger regime was "evidence-based" and therefore "already capable of reflecting market developments," as well as being "flexible" enough to take into account efficiencies and any failing-firm arguments.[16] The OFT did however relinquish some ground: It recommended the greater involvement of the Office for Communications ("Ofcom") in local media mergers so that the OFT could draw on its more extensive sectoral knowledge. Ofcom would not have any decision-making power, but at the OFT's request could provide a Local Media Assessment ("LMA") to the OFT in any local media merger raising prima facie competition issues, to offer its views in particular on potential competitive constraints and consumer benefits arising from a transaction.

III. REVIEW OF RECENT NEWSPAPER MERGERS

How flexible and responsive to market developments has the UK's newspaper merger regime subsequently proved to be? This is the question considered in the sections that follow below in which we review the key newspaper merger decisions up to the present day.[17]

Kent Messenger Limited/Northcliffe Media Limited (2011).[18] The first case under the OFT's revised regime was its phase one review of Kent Messenger Limited ("KML")'s proposed acquisition of seven local weekly titles in Kent from Northcliffe Media Limited.

In accordance with its established approach at phase one, the OFT began by seeking to determine the narrowest plausible frame of reference against which to assess the merger. This largely resulted in the OFT sticking to the approach adopted in prior cases without significant opposition raised from the merger parties. In particular, it determined that free and paid-for local weekly titles belonged to the same frame of reference, whereas regional and national newspapers fell outside of it.[19] In terms of the geographic frame of reference, it defined this to be the so-called JICREG areas in which the parties overlapped significantly.[20]

---

16 OFT, *Review of the local and regional media merger regime: final report*, June 2009.

17 Merger reviews that we do not analyze are those which, due to an absence of competition concerns, do not contain any meaningful market definition or competitive analyses, including one regional merger (*Trinity Mirror plc's acquisition of the regional newspaper titles of Guardian Media Company plc*, May 24, 2010), and two national mergers (*Completed acquisition by Northern & Shell Network Limited of CLTUFA Holdings*, November 19, 2010, and *Anticipated acquisition by Nikkei Inc. of The Financial Times Group*, November 16, 2015).

18 OFT, *Anticipated acquisition of seven local weekly newspaper titles by Kent Messenger Limited from Northcliffe Media Limited*, October 18, 2011 (*KML/Northcliffe*).

19 *Ibid*. paras. 24 and 29-33.

20 The Joint Industry Committee for Regional Media Research ("JICREG") is an industry body that collates data on its paying members' publications. JICREG areas are formed of groups of local contiguous postcode areas in which newspapers circulate, deemed useful for advertising purposes. The threshold of significance adopted by the OFT in this case was where the parties had at least 50 percent of the circulation in a given area with an increment of at least 10 percent (*KML/Northcliffe*, para. 42).

Where most debate focused, however, as might have been expected from the *Digital Britain Report*, was whether print and non-print media should be included in the same product frame of reference.

The parties argued strongly that non-print media should be included on the basis of their internal documents, examples of switching, and independent reports indicating that on-line advertising had increased at the expense of local newspaper advertising.   Ofcom's LMA was also supportive of the parties' arguments. Ofcom considered that other sources of media may be regarded as substitutes, with the constraint posed by online media only likely to become even stronger in the future.[21]

The OFT was of a different view. It accepted that the evidence of the parties as well as third parties supported the existence of "some constraint" from non-print media, but it did not find the evidence "sufficiently compelling."[22] Third party responses did not "fully support" the parties' submissions, and the examples of switching, "though directionally helpful – were not sufficient in number or detail." On a cautious basis the OFT therefore refused to widen the frame of reference beyond the supply of printed local weekly news-papers and advertising space (but accepted taking into account non-print constraints to the extent applicable in the competitive assessment).

On the basis of this frame of reference, the merger would result in a monopoly in six JICREG areas of significant overlap in Kent. The parties would also be each other's clos-est competitors, and the OFT considered that the alternatives, including those outside of the frame of reference, would not pose a sufficiently close constraint. The OFT therefore concluded that the merger gave rise to a realistic prospect of a substantial lessening of competition ("SLC").

The parties had sought to resist this conclusion by other means, including that the rel-evant counterfactual should take into account the likelihood that, but for the merger, a number of the parties' titles might close. The parties also sought to argue that any SLC would be outweighed by efficiencies. Again, Ofcom's LMA showed some support for the parties' arguments. It considered that there was a certain foreseeability that some of the titles may exit in the future. It also acknowledged that the "merger may provide the op-portunity to rationalize costs, maintain quality and investment, and provide a sounder commercial base from which to address long-term structural change."[23]

But the OFT was not persuaded. It was "unable to merely consider that the wider struc-tural challenges facing the market, in and of themselves, indicate with a sufficient degree

---

21 Ofcom, *Proposed acquisition by Kent Messenger Group of seven newspaper titles from Northcliffe Media Local Media Assessment* (*KML/Northcliffe LMA*), para. 4.30.

22 *KML/Northcliffe*, paras. 34-47.

23 *KML/Northcliffe LMA*, para. 5.55.

of certainty that any of the specific titles will exit the market."[24] If the parties wished to amend the relevant counterfactual, they would need to provide specific evidence supported by financial and/or strategic plans that exit would be imminent, which they had not. As for efficiencies, the parties' evidence was not sufficiently compelling that they would outweigh the SLC, having regard in particular to the fact that, in accordance with its decisional practice, "efficiencies will almost never justify a merger to monopoly."[25]

The OFT therefore ultimately decided to refer the merger to the Competition Commission for an in-depth phase two review.[26] Within one month of the OFT's referral decision, Northcliffe announced the closure of two of its titles affected by the transaction, and soon after KML announced it was abandoning the proposed acquisition. According to KML, "[t]he costs and time required for a full Competition Commission review would be completely unreasonable for a business of our size and a deal of this scale."[27]

For yet another time, following the *Digital Britain Report*, the OFT's approach was criticized – this time by the 2012 *Leveson Inquiry*, which recommended the Government to "look urgently as [to] what action it might be able [to] take to help safeguard the ongoing viability of this much valued and important part of the British press."[28]

Northcliffe Media Limited/Topper Newspapers Limited (2012).[29] No formal steps were taken by the Government following the Leveson Inquiry's criticism of the *KML/Northcliffe* review: However, in the next newspaper merger review, the OFT's approach was noticeably more sympathetic.

This case concerned Northcliffe's proposed acquisition of Topper Newspapers, in which the OFT had to assess the overlap between Topper Newspaper's free weekly local factsheet, *The Topper*, with Northcliffe's paid-for daily newspaper, *The Nottingham Post*.[30] As for defining the relevant frame of reference, the OFT followed prior decisional practice in accepting that daily and weekly titles, as well as all advertising categories, were part of the same frame of reference (which ultimately played into Topper and Northcliffe being found to have near monopoly shares of supply).[31]

As with *KML/Northcliffe*, however, most attention fell on whether non-print media could be included in the frame of reference. Northcliffe provided a range of evidence to seek to

---

24 *KML/Northcliffe*, para. 17.

25 *Ibid.* para. 125.

26 *Ibid.* para. 139.

27 The Guardian, "Newspaper group withdraws takeover bid because of referral," October 18, 2011, available at https://www.theguardian.com/media/greenslade/2011/oct/18/local-newspapers-mediabusiness.

28 *Leveson Inquiry*, page 152.

29 OFT, *Anticipated acquisition by Northcliffe Media Limited of Topper Newspapers Limited*, June 1, 2012.

30 Both parties also had online versions of their papers although The Topper was only available in pdf format.

31 *KML/Northcliffe*, paras. 30-35.

substantiate this. This included evidence showing how the internet had made significant incursions in all key advertising categories, especially given the ability of online alternatives to offer targeted searches, including by location. Northcliffe also provided details of the competitive set in each advertising category in the Nottingham area, evidence on switching, internal market research on lapsed readers, and a comparative yield analysis (to show that advertising yields had declined just as much in areas where the parties' titles competed, compared to areas where they did not). In fact, the OFT decided not to request an LMA from Ofcom, primarily because Northcliffe said it was happy to provide its own views and evidence on competitive constraints and relevant customer benefits directly to the OFT.

In response the OFT readily acknowledged at the outset of its decision that "total advertising allocated to local and regional newspapers has declined since around 2005, worsening significantly since 2007, attributed partly by the rapid expansion of the internet and other means of advertising."[32] However, the OFT still ultimately concluded that Northcliffe's evidence was not sufficiently "substantiated and persuasive" to support widening the market definition.[33] In particular, in assessing the evidence put forward, the OFT said it had been unable to "isolate such an effect [competition from online] from broader cyclical and structural factors such as the recession or a permanent 'one-way' shift to greater use of the internet."[34] Market research on lapsed readers did not prove that alternate media channels were the primary cause of reductions in purchasing. Views from readers and advertisers were mixed. Some saw online as a substitute, but others had a strong preference for print local newspapers because either their target audience consisted of regular readers of local newspapers who could not be reached equally effectively online, or to complement advertising placed in other advertising channels.[35]

Proceeding on the basis of a frame of reference excluding alternate media, the OFT found that the merger would result in a near monopoly in 10 JICREG areas of significant overlap.[36] Yet – and in marked contrast to its approach in *KML/Northcliffe* – the OFT was ultimately persuaded, given the limited competition between the parties' titles as well as the competitive constraint posed by alternate media, that the merger did not give rise to a realistic prospect of an SLC. In particular, the OFT considered that alternative media primarily provided a demand-side constraint. Evidence from advertisers indicated that they tended to prioritize spend on alternate media. The two-sided nature of the market also introduced a feedback mechanism that was likely to accentuate demand-side constraints.[37]

---

32 *Ibid.* para. 7.

33 *Ibid.* para. 36.1.

34 *Ibid.* para. 36.3.

35 *Ibid.* para. 37.

36 *Ibid.* para. 82.

37 *Ibid.* paras. 10 and 124.

This worked as follows: If Northcliffe were to raise prices/restrict output for certain advertising categories, those advertisers with alternate options would switch at least a proportion of their spend to alternative media. This would mean that the costs of production would need to be met by a smaller group of advertisers or by readers. Advertisers with alternative advertising options would not likely tolerate such increases. Further, were Northcliffe to raise the cover price of the title, circulation would likely fall resulting in its fixed costs having to be met by the remaining readers or by advertisers. Such increases in cover prices also appeared unlikely, given evidence of a consistent fall in circulation even in the absence of significant price increases. Declining circulation would also make it harder for Northcliffe to raise revenue from advertisers.

The OFT in fact went as far as to say – and somewhat in contradiction with its market definition – that "from a demand-side, there does appear to be a degree to which…local newspapers and other media may be considered substitutes."[38] Overall, the OFT had sufficient comfort to clear the transaction without referral for an in-depth review.

Daily Mail General Holdings Limited/the trustees of the Iliffe Settlement/Trinity Mirror plc (2013).[39] A year later came the OFT's review of a completed joint venture combining the local and regional newspapers of Northcliffe (then owned by Daily Mail & General Holdings, DMGH) and Iliffe (then owned by Yattendon). DMGH would have at least material influence over the JV, and Trinity Mirror also had a stake, which potentially gave it material influence over the joint venture as well.

Oddly, the OFT's analysis proceeded almost as if *Northcliffe/Topper* had never occurred. It gave short shrift to the appropriate frame of reference. As for the inclusion of non-print media in particular, it referred to prior decisions that had defined print and non-print media separately. As to evidence of switching provided by the parties, the OFT went no further than to say that it "may" indicate that alternate media provides some constraint, but that the evidence was not sufficient to support widening the frame of reference.[40]

The OFT then proceeded to embark on a highly detailed competitive assessment of the transaction. Following an approach adopted in earlier decisions, it sought to identify JICREG areas of significant overlap between the parties by applying four filters. In particular, the OFT first considered JICREG areas where: (1) the parties' combined share of total circulation exceeded 50 percent; and (2) where there was also an increment of at least 10 percent. The OFT then applied two further filters to consider in further detail the overlapping titles identified by the first two filters. In particular, it looked at: (3) all JICREG areas

---

38 *Ibid.* para. 119.

39 OFT, *Completed joint venture between Daily Mail General Holdings Limited, the trustees of the Iliffe Settlement and Trinity Mirror plc*, June 28, 2013 (*Local World JV*).

40 *Ibid.* para. 62.

that were core to both of the parties' titles concerned (defined as those areas that accounted for at least 30 percent of the circulation of the titles concerned); and (4) JICREG areas where both titles had a household penetration of at least 10 percent.[41]

None of the JICREG areas of overlap between the Northcliffe and Iliffe titles met all four filters. Not satisfied with this result, the OFT then adopted a number of sensitivity analyses, including modifying the second filter to look at overlap areas where the increment was just 2 percent and dis-applying the third and fourth filters entirely. This resulted in eight JICREG areas of overlap between the Northcliffe and Iliffe titles. The OFT then proceeded to make a more detailed qualitative examination of the closeness of competition between the parties in each of these areas.[42]

Ultimately, in light of that detailed assessment, including taking into account views from customers and competitors, the OFT concluded that the merger would not result in a SLC. Curiously, however, not once did the OFT take constraints from non-print media into account in the assessment. At the very end of the decision it in fact excuses this on the basis that its detailed assessment had been able to exclude concerns without having to consider such constraints.[43] Yet, surely, if it had built non-print constraints into its analysis from the start, instead of ignoring them, it could have avoided or at least reduced the burden of its detailed assessment in the first place?[44]

It is also the case that the OFT's assessment almost entirely ignored Ofcom's LMA, which again had been much more open to considering non-print constraints and wider market developments. In particular Ofcom acknowledged that local newspapers are only one source of news, with TV and radio both in fact being more frequently used, while consumers were increasingly turning to online sources of local media. While Ofcom acknowledged that it might be difficult to reach a definitive view on whether other platforms were substitutes or complements, Ofcom went on to note that the fact that local newspaper consumption was declining suggested that there was substitution, and moreover that "as use of online and mobile for local content increases, the constraint is likely to become ever stronger."[45]

---

41 *Ibid.* paras. 77-79.

42 *Ibid.* paras 80-109.

43 *Ibid.* para. 143.

44 The OFT also adopted a similar filter analysis to overlaps between Northcliffe/Iliffe and Trinity Mirror's titles, see paras. 110-118. Its approach was less detailed, however, as it was focused on examining whether Trinity Mirror's 20 percent stake in the joint venture would give it an incentive to raise prices or reduce circulation for any of its titles in areas of significant overlap, and ultimately found that it would not. Notably, when Trinity Mirror later acquired all of the shares in the Local World JV in 2015 (see The Guardian, "Trinity Mirror confirms £220m Local World deal," October 28, 2015, available at https://www.theguardian.com/media/2015/oct/28/trinity-mirror-local-world-deal), the transaction was not called-in by the CMA for the purposes of conducting a more detailed review of these overlaps – an apparent nod to a loosening of the CMA's highly cautious approach.

45 Ofcom, *Local World: Local Media Assessment,* April 11, 2013, paras. 4.50-4.53.

Fox/Sky **(2017/2018).** In *Fox/Sky* the parties did not have any horizontal newspaper overlap, but principally overlapped in the supply of TV channels in the UK as well as a number of EU Member States, and ultimately required clearance by the EU Commission on competition grounds (which was received at phase one).[46] However, the transaction was also subject to a public interest intervention by the UK's SoS, and was ultimately cleared, following a phase two review, subject to the divestment of Sky News to a third party.[47] Both the EU Commission's decision and the UK public interest reviews include interesting analysis for the discussion at hand.

As for the Commission's decision, of particular note are its findings on market definition in relation to newspapers (which were necessary for the purposes of assessing certain newspaper and TV bundling concerns to which the transaction gave rise). Firstly, on the advertising side, the Commission ultimately followed precedent in defining newspaper and TV advertising as belonging to separate markets. But the Commission left open how newspaper advertising should be further defined. In this regard, while the market investigation suggested that advertising in local and national newspapers, and in daily and non-daily newspapers, each belonged to distinct markets, it was, notably, not conclusive as to substitutability of advertising in print newspapers and online news services.[48]

On the newspaper publishing side, the Commission ultimately left the market definition open. However, notably, the market investigation was inconclusive as to whether local and national papers, and daily and non-daily newspapers, belonged to distinct markets.[49] As for the distinction between print and online, a majority of respondents to the market investigation had confirmed that printed newspapers had lost readership or audience to free and paid-for online editions, and all respondents said that readers consider internet news portals featuring editorial content on their website and/or online news aggregators and/or informal online sources (such as blogs) to be alternatives to online editions of newspapers.[50]

As for the UK public interest intervention, the SoS's concerns primarily arose from the fact that Fox's largest shareholder, the Murdoch Family Trust, was also the largest shareholder of News Corp, which had substantial UK newspaper interests (being the publisher of The Times and The Sun, plus their Sunday editions and associated websites) as well as radio interests. If the transaction would give the Murdoch Family Trust indirect material influence over Sky, and in particular, over Sky News TV channel, there was a concern that it would result in

---

46 Case M.8354 *Fox/Sky*, Commission decision of April 7, 2017 (*Fox/Sky EU Commission decision*).

47 *Fox/Sky Ofcom review* and *Fox/Sky CMA review*, see also Department for Digital, Culture, Media & Sport and The Rt Hon Matt Hancock MP, *Oral statement to Parliament*, June 5, 2018.

48 *Fox/Sky EU Commission decision*, footnote 70.

49 *Ibid.* para. 132.

50 *Ibid.* paras. 129-130.

insufficient plurality in the number of persons in control of "media enterprises" (TV, radio, and newspaper)[51] in the UK within the meaning of section 58(2C)(a) of the Enterprise Act.[52]

While plurality involves a quite different analysis compared to a competition assessment, nonetheless, the CMA's plurality review provides a pertinent discussion on the wider market context and market developments.[53] In particular, despite the fact that the statutory scheme restricted the analysis of plurality to TV, radio and newspaper media, the CMA decided to take into account online media, on the basis that the internet has become "one of the main platforms for the delivery of content."[54] Thereafter, the CMA proceeded to undergo a highly detailed assessment of how news is consumed across all four platforms. The CMA noted, in particular, the relative importance of each platform (notably finding that printed newspapers were the least popular source of national news); the impact of the rapid and significant growth in online news and its disruptive effect on newspaper business models; and how the internet has increasingly blurred the boundaries between traditional platforms.[55]

Completed acquisition by Reach Plc (formerly Trinity Mirror plc) of certain assets of Northern & Shell Media Group Limited (2018).[56] Finally, we come to the completed acquisition by Reach of the Northern & Shell business. This case was called-in by the CMA on competition grounds, but notably is the first case in which the SoS has intervened on the specified newspaper public interest grounds under the Enterprise Act. However, in our view it is doubtful that this case merited review at all, either on competition or public interest grounds.

As for the CMA's competition assessment, attention focused on the overlap in the parties' national newspapers (Reach's Daily Mirror and Sunday Mirror and Northern & Shell's the Daily Express and Daily Star (and their Sunday editions), among others). As for the frame of reference, the CMA ultimately adopted a cautious approach. As the parties overlapped only in the supply of national newspapers, the CMA did not consider whether local/regional and national titles should form part of the same frame of reference.[57] It also defined separate frames of reference for national newspaper publishing and advertising.[58]

---

51 As the transaction would potentially combine TV, radio and newspaper interests, in accordance with the statutory scheme "media enterprises" for the purposes of the assessment were defined to include all three media platforms.

52 The intervention also considered whether there would continue to be a genuine commitment to broadcasting standards by the parties post-transaction, under section 58(2C)(c) of the Enterprise Act.

53 With the principal difference being that plurality concerns can arise at much lower levels of concentration than in the context of a competition assessment, see *Fox/Sky CMA review*, para. 6.72.

54 *Fox/Sky CMA review*, para. 6.12.

55 *Ibid.* sections 9 and 10.

56 Ofcom, *Public interest test for the acquisition by Trinity Mirror plc of publishing assets of Northern & Shell Media Group Limited*, May 31, 2018 (*Reach./Northern & Shell Ofcom review*), and CMA, *Completed acquisition by Reach Plc of certain assets of Northern & Shell Media Group Limited, Decision on relevant merger situation and substantial lessening of competition*, 20 June 2018 (*Reach./Northern & Shell CMA review*).

57 *Reach/Northern & Shell CMA review*, para. 32.

58 *Ibid.* para. 27.

As to whether online news and advertising should be included in these frames of reference, the CMA's decision is at least welcome in not following the cursory approach to online constraints of its *Iliffe* decision. Instead, it recognized, based on responses to its market investigation, "the significant constraint on print advertising from other channels," and that online was "likely" to be a constraint on the publishing side of the market.[59] It also acknowledged the "structural decline in circulation of printed newspapers."[60] Ultimately the CMA decided to exclude online news and advertising from the print frames of reference, but did take them into account as constraints in the competitive assessment.[61]

Even on the basis of a narrow frame of reference for printed national newspaper publishing and advertising, however, the parties' combined shares of supply were under 30 percent.[62] Only by looking more narrowly at "national popular tabloids" were the parties' shares higher, yet "national popular tabloids" were not formally part of the CMA's frame of reference (and indeed ran counter to prior decisions, which had always found that popular tabloids, mid-market, and quality national newspapers formed part of a chain of substitution).[63] There were also clear differences in the readership, content and tone of the parties' titles such that ultimately the CMA's market analysis proved that there was indeed "very limited competitive interaction between the parties' newspapers."[64] All this does seem to beg the question why the CMA called-in the merger in the first place.

As for the public interest assessment, the SoS had decided to intervene on the basis of both newspaper public interest grounds, i.e. a sufficient plurality of views in each newspaper market, and the need for free expression of opinion in newspapers. Ofcom found, however, that there were absolutely no grounds for concerns under either.[65]

As for the free expression of opinion ground, Ofcom said that as Reach's major shareholders were all large financial institutions, there would be no concerns that a shareholder would act so as to change the editorial position of the newspapers. Moreover, provided an editor retains the ability to determine a paper's position without interference from the

---

59 *Ibid.* paras. 40, 35, and 83.

60 *Ibid.* para. 22

61 *Ibid.* para. 46.

62 *Ibid.* Tables 1 and 2.

63 *Ibid.* para. 30.

64 *Ibid.* para. 84.

65 Part of the motivation for the SoS's intervention it transpires was that on the eve of completion of the transaction, the editor of the Daily Express retired and the editor of the Daily Star resigned, and both were replaced by former Daily Mirror and Sunday Mirror editors. The SoS had concerns that this may have been relevant to the impact of the merger on the freedom of the editors to operate without interference from their proprietor (see *Letter from DCMS to Trinity Mirror and Northern & Shell*, April 23, 2018 (Redacted)). However, Ofcom did not consider this to be problematic given that the departures had nothing to do with the board or shareholders of Reach plc, and the new appointments had been the decision solely of the Editor in Chief (*Reach/Northern & Shell Ofcom review*, para. 5.15-5.18).

proprietor, Ofcom said that concerns about a possible change in editorial approach post-transaction were "simply not relevant."[66]

As for plurality, Ofcom in fact said it had "concerns that a narrow assessment of plurality in print newspapers no longer reflects the reality of the way the public gets their news," but nonetheless felt compelled to do so because it was the basis for the SoS's formal intervention notice.[67] On the basis of this narrow assessment, Ofcom said that no concerns would arise because Reach was not intending to close any titles, and post-transaction there would be still a broad range of political perspectives among printed newspapers.

Notably, Ofcom also decided to give its assessment of plurality on the basis that it considered appropriate, i.e. across all media platforms. Indeed, it said in its view, "newspapers sit within a wider news market, in which a range of sources are available and consumed."[68] It pointed to the fact that an increasing proportion is captured by online players, whereas newspaper readership has declined considerably. Further, while newspapers' digital readers were growing, Ofcom said there had been no step-by-step growth in advertisers, leaving the newspaper industry in a continued period of uncertainty.[69] In light of this wider context, Ofcom in fact welcomed the merger as a means to support the longer-term viability of newspapers and their websites: "[C]onsolidation of print publishers may offer a way to support the continued availability of newspaper titles. Given the crucial role newspapers continue to play in public debate, representing a range of opinions, efforts to support their continued viability are important."[70]

IV. CONCLUSIONS AND WAY FORWARD

Returning now back to the initial question posed at the beginning of section III: How flexible and responsive to market developments have the UK competition authorities proved to be in their review of newspaper mergers over the past decade? Perhaps most notable is that while the OFT/CMA has consistently acknowledged the structural issues facing the newspaper industry, it has done little if anything to formally take this into account in the competitive assessment of newspaper mergers. In particular, the stringency of the evidential standard applied has consistently prevented future market developments, which are inherently harder to measure but nevertheless obvious in this case, from being accorded any weight. This is particularly unfortunate at a time when the EU Commission has recently urged competition authorities, in the context of examining

---

66 *Reach/Northern & Shell Ofcom review*, para. 2.21.

67 *Ibid.* para. 1.7.

68 *Ibid.* page 15.

69 *Ibid.* para. 1.4. Between 2011 and 2017, for every £1 newspapers lost in print revenues, newspapers had gained only 15 pence in digital revenues (in real terms).

70 *Ibid.* para. 1.4.

digital markets, to move away from a purely "static, short-term" approach and to more fully embrace a "dynamic perspective" taking into account "longer-term effects, potential effects, and counterfactual effects."[71]

The closure of titles following *KML/Northcliffe* provides a clear example of the UK competition authority getting it wrong in practice. While it is possible to discern from the subsequent cases more weight gradually being given to online, it is nonetheless concerning to see cases in which online constraints have been given no attention in the competitive assessment (*Iliffe*), and cases being called-in on competition and plurality grounds despite not raising serious prima facie concerns under either (*Trinity Mirror/Northern & Shell*). Most concerning overall is the fact that the CMA has still not formally set a precedent and included online as part of the frame of reference.

Overall, such an overly cautious approach may well have had a chilling effect on newspaper merger activity in the UK, which in our view is particularly concerning when, as Ofcom at least has acknowledged, consolidation may offer a way to support the survival of newspapers, and ultimately the very crucial role they play in public debate and as part of a democratic society.

In our view, long overdue is a far more pragmatic and dynamic approach that formally places more weight on both current and reasonably foreseeable structural market developments. A greater role given to Ofcom, or greater weight formally being given to its LMAs, may also help in this respect. The statutory public interests grounds in our view are also much in need of revision – it no longer makes sense for such grounds to focus exclusively on a newspaper market to the exclusion of all other media. Finally, we also query whether ultimately the regime may need to borrow something from the old regime, namely to put in place a de *minimis* threshold, e.g. circulation of geographically overlapping titles of a certain minimum threshold – below which a newspaper would fall outside UK merger control rules completely.

---

71 Johannes Laitenberger, Director-General for Competition, European Commission, speech: "EU competition law in innovation and digital markets: fairness and the consumer welfare perspective," October 10, 2017, http://ec.europa.eu/competition/speeches/text/sp2017_15_en.pdf.

JOINT SELLING OF SPORTS MEDIA RIGHTS

By Krzysztof Kuik & Gianluca Monte[1]

ABSTRACT

The article explores the application of EU competition rules to joint selling of media rights for sports events, notably football. It covers the first decisions taken by the Commission in this field (UEFA in 2003, Bundesliga in 2005 and Premier League in 2006) as well as of the decision-making practice of national competition authorities (NCAs) in the following years and up to date. The article examines in particular the way in which, on the basis of the Commission precedents, NCAs have dealt with issues such as (i) Restrictive clauses in agreements between sports bodies and media operators providing for tacit or preferential renewals; (ii) Agreements or practices concerning combined or conditional offers for several rights packages; (iii) Duration of exclusive contracts; (iv) Imposition of the "no-single-buyer" rule; and (v) Possible abuses of broadcasters when acquiring and sub-licensing football media rights. The article also highlights new developments and new challenges, including the emergence of new online platforms and the growth of e-sports.

I. INTRODUCTION

While the combined value of media rights in the largest European markets is still half of the U.S. sports rights, it has experienced a huge increase over the past two decades.[2] Sports media rights are a must-have content for broadcasters, for the high audiences they are able to attract and the corresponding significant advertising and subscription revenues

---

1 Head of Unit and Case Handler, respectively, Unit COMP.C2 (Antitrust: Media), Directorate General for Competition, European Commission. The information and views set out in this article are those of the authors and do not necessarily reflect the official opinion of the European Commission.

2 See slide 6 of the presentation made by Anna Chanduvi at the meeting of the Intergovernmental Group of Experts on Competition Law and Policy organized by UNCTAD in Geneva on July 12, 2018: https://unctad.org/meetings/en/Presentation/ciclp17th_p_%20UNCTAD_AUDVIS_ACH_en.pdf; Comprehensive figures for all sports and countries are to our knowledge not available but these two examples show that the growth in revenues generated by the sale of media rights has been impressive from the mid-1990s to nowadays: the Deloitte Football Money League, tracking the revenues of the top 20 football clubs in Europe (https://www2.deloitte.com/uk/en/pages/sports-business-group/articles/deloitte-football-money-league.html#), notes that when the report was first established in 1996/1997, the top clubs' combined revenue was EUR 1.2 billion, growing to EUR 7.9 billion for the 2016/2017 season – a 6.5 increase in total revenues over 20 years, with the sale of media rights accounting for 45 percent of the total (or EUR 3.55 billion); the value of broadcast revenues for the summer Olympic games grew from USD 898 million in 1996 (Atlanta) to USD 2.86 billion in 2016 (Rio), a threefold increase (see the International Olympic Committee's Marketing Fact File, 2018 Edition, page 24: https://stillmed.olympic.org/media/Document%20Library/OlympicOrg/Documents/IOC-Marketing-and-Broadcasting-General-Files/Olympic-Marketing-Fact-File-2018.pdf#_ga=2.56210795.1179052556.1540216026-1392264689.1540216026).

generated, as well as for the capacity of sport to develop the brand image of broadcasters.[3] Sports also have important societal implications.[4]

Public authorities around the world have followed different approaches when enforcing antitrust rules in the area of licensing, frequently referred to as a sale, of sports media rights. When examining the two largest markets at global level, namely the U.S. and Europe, this difference is striking: in the U.S., market players are generally free to negotiate long-term agreements; whereas in Europe, as discussed in the following paragraphs, competition authorities have intervened to limit the duration of contracts and impose other remedies.[5] Moreover, legislative measures have been introduced either at the EU or national level to regulate the sale of TV rights for major sports events.

II. HISTORICAL BACKGROUND

In the past, the economic value of sports rights for broadcasters was considered as limited because national markets in Europe were dominated by a single, public service broadcaster and scarcity of spectrum limited competition and access to consumers. However, towards the end of the Twentieth century, Europe underwent liberalisation of the media markets and fundamental technological changes. These trends, combined with the emergence of pay-TV broadcasters, increased broadcaster demand for highly popular sports events and led to a significant increase in the value of sport rights.[6]

In the 1990s, when football rights started to increase their value in parallel with the growth of pay-TV operators across Europe, national competitions authorities ("NCAs") in various EU countries were confronted with the issue of compatibility of joint selling of rights with competition rules. They generally found that joint selling represented a horizontal restriction of competition and that clubs selling their rights together or under the umbrella of the national federation were acting as a cartel.[7] Certain Member States adopted legislative measures to safeguard the possibility for national leagues or federations to continue selling the rights on behalf of their clubs. For instance, in Germany, after the Federal Supreme Court upheld the NCA's decision prohibiting clubs from jointly selling

---

3 *UEFA Champions League* (Case AT.37398), Commission decision of 23.07.2003, recitals 64-76.

4 As reflected by the inclusion of sport as one of the areas of EU competence when the Treaty on the Functioning of the EU ("TFEU") entered into force: according to Article 165 TFEU, EU action in the field of sport is aimed at contributing to the promotion of European sporting issues and developing the European dimension in sport, while taking into account, among others, sports' social and educational function.

5 By way of example, the duration of the ongoing NFL and NBA agreements with their main broadcasters is 9 years (https://www.wsj.com/articles/SB10001424052970204026804577098774037075832 and http://www.nba.com/2014/news/10/06/nba-media-deal-disney-turner-sports/).

6 Claude Jeanrenaud & Stefan Késenne, The Economics of Sport and the Media, (Edward Elgar, Cheltenham 2006) 1-4.

7 The decisions of NCAs (or other administrative bodies) and courts concerning collective selling of rights in The Netherlands, UK and Germany are listed in the 1998 Commission document, "Broadcasting of Sports events and Competition law," (http://ec.europa.eu/competition/publications/cpn/cpn19982.pdf, pages 24-25). Another decision was issued by the Italian Competition Authority in 1999 (Autorità Garante della Concorrenza e del Mercato, Annual Report 1999, pages 24-25).

their rights for the home matches of the European competitions, the Parliament amended the competition law in 1998 to explicitly exempt collective selling from the scope of application of German antitrust rules.

The European Commission has closely monitored these developments and recognised in its decisions that certain sports events and/or competitions represented premium content for broadcasters and as such they were a key driver for competition in the media market, notably with regard to pay-TV.[8] Among the premium sport events that attract viewers and generate a high demand from broadcasters, national, and international football club competitions, namely the first division national league championships and the European club competitions organized by UEFA, have played a prominent role.[9]

Concerning national top football leagues and the UEFA club competitions (the Champions League and the Europa League), joint selling of rights is nowadays a common practice throughout Europe.[10]

III. THE COMMISSION DECISION-MAKING PRACTICE

In three decisions taken in the early 2000s: UEFA Champions League in 2003, Bundesliga in 2005, and Premier League in 2006, the Commission developed a number of (non-exhaustive) remedies and established the conditions under which it considered that joint selling, in the specific circumstances of each respective case, would be permissible under Article 101 TFEU.[11]

In the three decisions, the Commission found that joint selling agreements are caught by the prohibition of Article 101(1) TFEU as they lead to competition restrictions that are unlikely to occur in the absence of the agreements. The Commission recognised, how-

---

8 See for example *Bertelsmann/Kirch/Premiere* (Case IV/M.993), Commission decision of 27.02.1999, recital 34; *TPS* (Case IV/36.237) Commission decision of 03.03.1999, recital 34; British Interactive Broadcasting/Open (Case IV/36.539) Commission decision of 15.091999, recital 28; *Newscorp/Telepiù* (Case COMP/M.2876), Commission decision of 02.04.2003, recital 54; *CVC/SLEC* (Case M.4066), Commission decision of 20.03.2006, recital 29.

9 National team competitions in football, such as the UEFA Euro championship or the FIFA World Cup are also very popular with the public. However, the rights to these events are sold under different conditions: in many European countries the major national team competitions organized by UEFA and FIFA are included in the list of events of major importance for society which cannot be broadcast only on pay-TV operators by virtue of the provision laid down in Article 14(1) of the Audiovisual Media Services Directive. The bidding process and the licensing of rights for these events differ from the sale of rights to national/European club competitions. The national lists of major events established by EU countries on the basis of Article 14(1) of the Audiovisual Media Services Directive are available on the Commission website: https://ec.europa.eu/digital-single-market/en/avmsd-list-major-events.

10 Spain, the last major country where football clubs could sell their rights individually, adopted a law in 2015, entering into force in 2016, which made joint selling compulsory for the top division championships as well as for the national cup (Royal Decree 5/2015 of 30 April 2015, available at https://boe.es/boe/dias/2015/05/01/pdfs/BOE-A-2015-4780.pdf).

11 For a detailed analysis of the three decisions, see the article by Torben Toft, "Football: joint selling of media rights," published in the Competition Policy Newsletter nr 3 – Autumn 2003 (http://ec.europa.eu/competition/publications/cpn/2003_3_47.pdf) and the Media chapter by Krzysztof Kuik & Anthony Dawes in Faull & Nikpay: the EU Law of Competition, Oxford University Press 2014, page 1726, paragraphs 14.63-14.69.

ever, that joint selling may create substantial efficiency gains as a result of which it can meet the conditions for an exemption under Article 101(3) TFEU.

In the UEFA Champions League decision, the Commission for the first time accepted joint selling of football media rights and established the principles for a pro-competitive rights sale. The rights were to be sold in several packages thus allowing more than one broadcaster per territory to acquire such rights, clubs were allowed to sell certain live rights for their matches in case such rights remained unsold as part of the UEFA's auction and the appropriate duration of the exclusive licensing deals was fixed at three football seasons.

While a number of restrictions were still present in the amended joint selling arrangements, the Commission considered that the efficiencies generated by joint selling were sufficient to benefit from an exemption under Article 101(3) TFEU. [12]

In the two subsequent decisions on joint selling of rights for football (Bundesliga and Premier League), the Commission identified similar competition concerns as those presented in the UEFA Champions League decision. In both cases, commitments were offered to address these concerns by amending the original joint selling arrangements. Those commitments were made legally binding by the Commission under Article 9(1) of Regulation 1/2003. The commitments included, inter alia, the unbundling of rights into separate packages for TV and mobile platforms, the possibility for individual clubs to exploit unsold rights and the exploitation of deferred highlights rights. The procedure for the licensing of rights had to be public, transparent and fair. The duration of exclusive rights contracts could not exceed three football seasons. In addition, in view of the specific circumstances of the Premier League case and the UK's market situation at the time when the decision was taken, the Premier League committed not to allow one single purchaser to acquire all the live rights packages (the so-called "no single buyer" rule).

IV. ACTION AT NATIONAL LEVEL

The Commission has considered that the UEFA Champions League, Premier League and Bundesliga decisions can serve as a model for NCAs, faced with the sale of national rights on a regular basis.[13] This is because, on the one hand, following the entry into force

---

12 Clubs could not compete for the sale of most live rights and broadcasters were faced with one single point of sale fixing the price for the whole competition; In particular, the Commission identified the following three positive aspects of the joint selling scheme proposed by UEFA: (i) the creation of a single point of sale reduced transaction costs for sports bodies and broadcasters; (ii) the branding of the output helped the product receive wider media recognition and distribution; and (iii) the creation of a league product allowed programming to be planned in advance without having broadcasters negotiate with individual clubs who, on the basis of the knock-out nature of the competition, may exit the league before its final stages.

13 According to the EU contribution to the OECD Global Forum on Competition: "Competition issues in television and broadcasting" organized in 2013, between 2004 and 2010 approximately 30 decisions were taken by NCAs in this field (see http://www.oecd.org/officialdocuments/publicdisplaydocumentpdf/?cote=DAF/COMP/GF/WD(2013)52&docLanguage=En, page 3).

of Regulation 1/2003, NCAs are empowered to directly apply EU antitrust provisions (Articles 101 and 102 TFEU) and, on the other hand, undertakings can no longer apply for individual exemptions before the Commission. Rather, they have to self-assess the compatibility of their agreements and practices with EU competition law. The Commission ensures coherence in the enforcement of EU antitrust rules through its coordination role in the European Competition Network ("ECN"), gathering all NCAs.

Therefore, antitrust enforcement in the field of joint selling of media rights since the Premier League decision has taken place essentially at the national level. NCAs have followed the principles developed by the Commission, adapting them as appropriate to the national context or to technological and market developments, in coordination with the Commission in the framework of the ECN procedures.

The vast majority of NCAs decisions concern the joint selling of media rights for football competitions, confirming the prominent role of football as a sport that attracts viewers and its must-have nature for broadcasters.[14] Most of the decisions concern the application of Article 101 TFEU, although in some cases NCAs have identified possible infringements of Article 102. Prohibition decisions are rare, and most of the national cases were concluded through commitments.

Among the issues covered, NCAs have been closely scrutinising the transparent, objective and non-discriminatory conditions for the bidding process. In particular, NCAs have examined, and often found, restrictive clauses in agreements between sports bodies and media operators providing for tacit or preferential renewals, giving the historic/incumbent operator the possibility to match the highest offer made by other bidders.[15]

---

14 Four exceptions being (i) the decision of the French NCA (later upheld by the Paris Court of Appeal) to suspend the agreement concluded in January 2014 between the national rugby league (*Ligue National de Rugby*, LNR) and pay-TV broadcaster Canal Plus (*Autorité de la concurrence*, Case 14-MC-01, July 30, 2014); (ii) the investigation launched by the Swiss NCA into a possible abuse of dominance by cable operator UPC for the broadcasting of matches of the national ice hockey league (https://www.weko.admin.ch/weko/fr/home/actualites/communiques-de-presse/nsb-news.msg-id-66876.html); (iii) the decision of the Belgian NCA of November 5, 2015 on cyclocross events organised by Superprestige; and (iv) the decision by the Austrian NCA concerning the agreement between the public broadcaster ORF and the national ski federation for the broadcast of the Austrian Ski World Cup events (Case 26 Kt 42/06, Österreichischer Rundfunk und Fernsehen – Österreichischer Schiverband, decision of February 18, 2008).

15 Noteworthy, the E-commerce sector inquiry carried out by the Commission between 2015 and 2017 identified the presence of such clauses in agreements between sports right holders (as well as other owners of copyright-protected content) and digital service providers (see in particular sections 7.4 and 7.5, pages 269-273 of the Staff Working Document accompanying the Final Report, available at http://ec.europa.eu/competition/antitrust/sector_inquiries_e_commerce.html). See, for example, the following decisions: (i) decision No. 2005-I/0-40 of 29 July 2005 of the Belgian NCA (later upheld by the Brussels Court of Appeal) in the case concerning the sale of the rights for the first division football league (Jupiler Pro League); (ii) decision of the Danish NCA at the Council meeting on 31 October 2007, Journal nr. 4/0120-0204-0052/TUK/MIK, concerning the joint selling of rights offered by the Danish Football Association (DBU) and the Danish League Association (DIV); (iii) decision of the Italian NCA (AGCM) concerning the sale of the rights of the first division national football league, A362 – Diritti Calcistici, nr. 15632 of 28 June 2006, Bollettino 26/2006; (iv) decision of the Polish NCA on the sale of rights by the Polish Football League, Canal+/Polski Związek Piłki Nożnej, n° DOK-49/06 of 29 May 2006, (v) decision of the Finnish NCA of 27 November 2008 in case TV4 AB / C More Group AB (decision nr 579/81/2008); (vi) decisions of the Romanian NCA of 19 April 2011 (decision 13/2011) and of 10 August 2012 (decision 44/2012) on the Romanian Football Federation; and (vii) decision of the Portuguese NCA of 1 June 2015 in case PRC/2013/02 (Controlinveste Media, SGPS, S.A. and others).

In line with the Commission's decisions establishing the general principle that rights must be sold in different packages, the attention of the NCAs has turned to agreements or practices concerning combined or conditional offers for several rights packages and/or the significance of packages put to the auction.[16] In some countries, joint selling of football rights is regulated and legislative measures have been adopted to define the composition of the packages.[17] This has not prevented NCAs from taking action in case the design of auction has been giving rise to competition concerns.[18]

A number of NCAs addressed the issue of the duration of exclusive contracts. While the Commission considered the maximum duration as limited to three seasons, the NCAs have been accepting longer durations in view of the specificity of the national media markets, in particular to give new entrants the opportunity to recoup their initial investment or to ensure the long-term development of new sports.[19]

---

16 See the decision of the Danish NCA at the Council meeting on October 31, 2007, Journal nr. 4/0120-0204-0052/TUK/MIK, concerning the joint selling of rights offered by the Danish Football Association (DBU) and the Danish League Association (DIV), where it is stipulates at paragraph 4.1 that bids must relate to one individual package and may not be conditional on the acquisition of other packages or rights.

17 See for instance the French Code du Sport, Article R-333-3, Article 8 of the Italian law regulating collective selling of rights for football (Decreto Legislativo 9 gennaio 2008, n. 9) and Article 4 of the Spanish Royal Decree 5/2015 of May 1, 2015 on the exploitation of TV rights for football competitions.

18 Decision of AGCM of February 6, 2013, A418 - Procedure selettive Lega Nazionale Professionisti Campionati 2010/2011 E 2011/2012," nr. 20687, Bollettino 07/2013, concerning discounts offered for the acquisition of the second division football matches to acquirers of first division packages.

19 The Danish NCA in 2001 did not object to a duration of 8 years for the agreement between public broadcasters DR and TV2 and various sports rights holders (Danish Football Federation, First division football League, Danish Handball Federation) for the creation of a pay TV sports channel (Decision of October 31, 2001, Journal nr.3:1120-0388-171/mlp/Fødevarer og Finans); the Polish NCA accepted the point raised by Canal+ arguing that a 4-year agreement was necessary to provide the clubs with an appropriate amount of funding (decision of the Polish NCA on the sale of rights by the Polish Football League, Canal+/Polski Związek Piłki Nożnej, n° DOK-49/06 of May 29, 2006); the German NCA accepted in 2012 that the cycle for the sale of media rights for the first and second division football championships could be extended to 4 years (see Bundeskartellamt Commitment decision of January 12, 2012 in the Bundesliga case (Case B6-114/10)); in France, the *Code du Sport* was amended in 2007 so as to fix by law the maximum duration of agreements for the sale of media rights for sports events to 4 years (see Legislative Decree No 2007-1676 of November 28, 2007, amending Article R-333-3 of the *Code du Sport*); in Spain, although the law (Ley 7/2010 General de la Comunicación Audiovisual of March 31, 2010) also stipulates that agreements for the acquisition of football rights may not exceed 4 years, the NCA issued a decision in April 2010 informing that it would consider agreements for the acquisition of rights to the national football league exceeding 3 years as contrary to national and EU competition law; the NCA subsequently imposed a fine on broadcaster Mediapro and four football clubs (Real Madrid, Barcelona, Sevilla and Racing de Santander) for stipulating contracts for the sale of football rights that had a four-year duration (CNMC, MEDIAPRO Y CLUBS DE FÚTBOL II (Case SNC/0021/12) Decision of November 28, 2013); the Dutch NCA accepted a duration of 6 years for the sale of the rights to free-to-air highlights of the first division national football championship (Eredivisie), arguing that such duration was reasonable to ensure the launch of the relevant TV channel (ACM, Informele zienswijze Fox/Eredivisie, November 29, 2012, page 8). Concerning other sports, the Austrian NCA limited to 5 years the length of the agreement between the public broadcaster ORF and the national ski federation for the broadcast of the Austrian Ski World Cup events (Case 26 Kt 42/06, Österreichischer Rundfunk und Fernsehen − Österreichischer Schiverband, decision of February 18, 2008); the Danish NCA also accepted 5 years as duration for the exclusive broadcast of national handball matches (Aftale mellem DR, TV2, Team Danmark og Dansk Håndboldforbund om tv-, radio-, og internetrettighederne til dansk håndbold, Journal nr.3/1120-0301-0128/Industri/mvn, November 27, 2002); on the other hand, the French and Belgian NCAs adopted interim measures against, respectively, the French national rugby league and the organiser of cyclocross events Superprestige arguing that the 5 years agreements in place between these bodies and their broadcasters (Canal Plus for the French national rugby league and Telenet for Superprestige) were excessive (see decision 14-MC-01 of the French Autorité de la Concurrence of July 30, 2014 in relation to the request for interim measures lodged by BeIn France and the decision of the Belgian NCA of November 5, 2015 on cyclocross events organised by Superprestige).

The Commission included the "no-single-buyer" rule only in the decision-making commitments offered by the Premier League binding. There have been differences between NCAs in this regard. Some authorities have concluded that this remedy does not bring benefits to the consumers, who are best served when a single broadcaster acquires all the rights to a given competitions.[20] In other cases, authorities imposed the "no-single-buyer" rule at the national level or included it in the law that regulates collective selling.[21] It is also possible to observe an evolution in the practice of certain NCAs which have at first considered the imposition of such rule not to be necessary in view of the market conditions and of the structure of the bidding process, to later come to the conclusion that the rule had to be imposed on the sports body selling the rights under certain circumstances.[22] To date, the "no-single-buyer" obligation has been implemented in the UK, Austria, Denmark, Italy, Romania, Spain, and Germany.

In the UK, the NCA investigated a possible output restriction, since the national football league did not offer in its tender for live retransmission all the season matches. The case was later closed when the league increased the number of matches made available for sale to broadcasters.[23]

NCAs have also examined the behaviour of and agreements between broadcasters when acquiring and sub-licensing football media rights. Some of these cases have been conducted under Article 102 TFEU to assess whether broadcasters detaining premium sports rights had abused their dominant position when sub-licensing those rights to their com-

---

20 See for instance (i) the decision of the Brussels court of Appeal upholding the decision No. 2005-I/0-40 of July 29, 2005 of the Belgian NCA in the case concerning the sale of the rights for the first division football league (Jupiler Pro League) (Court of Appeal of Brussels (Joined Cases 2005/MR/2 and 2005/MR/5) Telenet N.V. and BeTV N.V. v. Liga Beroepsvoetbal V.Z.W., June 28, 2006, paragraph 44) and (ii) the opinion of the French NCA on the draft decree for the exploitation by sports leagues of audiovisual rights (Avis du 28 mai 2004 04-A-09 relatif à un projet de décret sur la commercialisation par les ligues professionnelles des droits d'exploitation audiovisuelle des compétitions ou manifestations sportives, paragraph 95).

21 The "no-single-buyer" rule was part of the commitments offered by the Danish Football Association ("DBU") and the Danish League Association ("DIV") concerning the joint selling of the media rights to Danish Football, see decision of the Danish NCA at the Council meeting on October 31, 2007, Journal nr. 4/0120-0204-0052/TUK/MIK and Article 9 of the Italian law regulating collective selling of rights for football (Decreto Legislativo 9 gennaio 2008, n. 9)

22 The German NCA in its 2012 decision on the sale of the Bundesliga rights (Bundeskartellamt Commitment decision of January 12, 2012 in the Bundesliga case (Case B6-114/10)) argued that imposing a "no-single-buyer" rule was not appropriate in views of the market situation in Germany; in 2016 it expressed concerns that the lack of such rule would harm competition, especially from digital platforms, and accepted commitments from the Bundesliga including a "no-single-buyer" rule (Bundeskartellamt Commitment decision of April 11, 2016 (Case B6-32/15)).

23 See Ofcom's investigation into the Premier League football rights, https://www.ofcom.org.uk/about-ofcom/latest/media/media-releases/2016/premier-league-football-rights.

petitors by engaging in restrictive practices, namely discriminatory treatment, margin squeezes, or excessive pricing. In other cases, NCA have examined collusion between the bidders as a potential Article 101 TFEU restriction.[24]

V. NEW DEVELOPMENTS, NEW CHALLENGES

The emergence of new platforms for the distribution of content, notably via online transmission, is changing the way sports events reach consumers. Traditional broadcasters are expanding their offering, by showing live sports events on multiple platforms (TV, online streaming, mobile). At the same time, new online entrants, such as Amazon or an online platform DAZN have recently acquired the rights to distribute football matches from some of the major European national leagues.[25] Digital distribution of content allows for greater interactivity and for the development of ancillary services accompanying the live streaming of sports events. Finally, the growth of e-sports and ever more advanced forms of video games provides additional revenue streams for organizers of sports competitions.

Against this evolving and changing background, a number of questions (re-)emerge. The first question concerns the principle of so-called "platform neutrality," which has long represented a key principle for the sale of sports rights in Europe as a guarantee of transparent, objective, and fair tender procedures. In the last round of auctions, the German NCA has singled out online/digital as a specific distribution platform, which needed to be ring-fenced so as to ensure competition and innovation, by imposing a no-single-buyer rule for internet-based operators.[26] There may be a trend developing in this respect that could also extend to other territories.

---

24 See: (i) the Spanish NCA's order to Telefónica to compensate its rival for excessive charges for wholesale access to its football channels during the 2015/2016 season (CNMC, case R/AJ/165/16: TELEFONICA, order of July 21, 2016); (ii) the Spanish NCA's investigation on alleged discriminatory conditions offered by Mediapro to OTT operators, closed with commitments in February 2018 (CNMC, case S/DC/0604/17: MEDIAPRO FÚTBOL, order of February 7, 2018); (iii) the Portuguese NCA's imposition of fines on Sport TV for abusing its dominant position in the national market for supplying premium sports content by applying discriminatory treatment of pay-TV retailers (Decision of June 14, 2013 in case PRC/2010/02, later upheld by the Competition Tribunal); (iv) the Spanish NCA's imposition of fines on Telefónica and DTS for colluding in the acquisition, resale and exploitation of football media rights for the seasons 2012/2013 to 2014/2015 (CNMC, case S/0436/12: DTS DISTRIBUIDORA DE TV DIGITAL, decision of July 23, 2015); and (v) the Italian NCA's imposition of fines on Sky Italia, Mediaset, Lega Calcio and Infront for arranging a reallocation of rights for Italy's first division football championship following the organization of an auction by Lega Calcio in June 2014, later overturned by the relevant administrative court which contested notably the NCA's characterisation of the arrangement as a "by object" restriction of competition (Decision nr 25966 of April 19, 2016, Bollettino nr 13/2016). On June 26, 2017, the Swiss NCA rejected Swisscom's request for interim measures against UPC for its alleged abuse of dominance in the market for the broadcasting of ice-hockey games (see page 13 of the 2017 Annual Report of the Swiss NCA).

25 See the following press articles: on Amazon acquiring rights for the English Premier League: https://www.bbc.com/sport/football/44396151; on the sports events broadcast by DAZN: https://en.wikipedia.org/wiki/DAZN. On October 16, 2018, the Bundeskartellamt announced the opening of an investigation concerning the cooperation between Sky Deutschland and Perform (operator of the DAZN streaming service) for broadcasting the UEFA Champions League in Germany (see https://www.bundeskartellamt.de/SharedDocs/Meldung/EN/Pressemitteilungen/2018/16_10_2018_Sky_Dazn.html?nn=3591568).

26 Bundeskartellamt Commitment decision of April 11, 2016 (Case B6-32/15). These concerns are raised in the recent German investigation into the sale of the UEFA Champions League rights, referred to in the preceding footnote; similar concerns were brought up in the sector inquiry launched by the Commission in 2004 about the sale of sports rights to Internet and 3G mobile operators (see http://europa.eu/rapid/press-release_IP-04-134_en.htm?locale=en).

The second question concerns the exclusive sale of rights for the major football club competitions to pay-TV operators or digital platforms. The sale of rights on an exclusive basis has not been put into question by antitrust enforcers, since it represents an important tool to generate the benefits for consumers (in terms of quality, innovation, and choice), broadcasters, and sports stakeholders. As observed above, while national team competitions are in general included in the list of events of major importance for society, this is not the case for club competitions. However, if exclusive licensing to pure pay-TV operators, in particular those that only operate online, leads to attractive sports content being available to a reduced part of viewers (for reasons such as low broadband penetration in certain countries/regions), there may be backlash from consumers and calls for public authorities to intervene so that popular sports content is broadcast free-to-air or made accessible to a larger public.[27]

The third challenge concerns the duration of agreements between sports right owners and broadcasters/platforms. Taking into account the increased cost of rights acquisition in relation to the possibility to monetise this cost through increased subscription fees, there may be renewed calls by new entrants for allowing for longer contract durations to enable cost recoupment.[28]

VI. CONCLUSIONS

While technology has brought important changes in the broadcasting landscape, it has not affected the role that sports events, in particular premium content such as top-level football in Europe, play as a key factor in attracting viewers. Premium sports enjoy a specific selling point because they allow for both strong individual loyalty (such as for certain football clubs) and a unique community factor (e.g. the World Cup finals). The importance of sports as a part of the audio-visual industry is not likely to decrease in the near future.[29] While most of the challenges highlighted above can in principle be well addressed at national level, taking into account national specificities and circumstances, the Commission will closely follow market developments and ensure the uniform application of EU competition rules across the Union.

---

27 See for instance press reports about alleged plans by the Austrian government to include the first division football championship in the list of events of major importance: https://orf.at/stories/3031625/.

28 For instance, the cost of acquisition of rights for the English Premier League was multiplied by more than 4 from 2001 to present, or a 428 percent increase (see the available statistics at https://www.statista.com/statistics/385002/premier-league-tv-rights-revenue/); by contrast, the price of subscribing to the SKY Sports package only increased by 22 percent between 2001 and 2009 (see figures made available by SKY in its submission to Ofcom in 2010 https://www.ofcom.org.uk/__data/assets/pdf_file/0025/45565/trends.pdf, page 70) and, in general, the pricing of pay-TV services in the UK has remained relatively flat from 2012 to 2017 (see page 24 of the latest Ofcom report: https://www.ofcom.org.uk/__data/assets/pdf_file/0030/113898/pricing-report-2018.pdf).

29 As shown by FIFA's reported plans to create a new, USD 25 billion world club competition: see https://www.ft.com/content/fc29924e-5852-11e8-b8b2-d6ceb45fa9d0.

Editors' Bios

Antonio Bavasso is a partner at Allen & Overy, co-head of the Global Antitrust practice and advises on all aspects of antitrust law, practising primarily in London and Brussels. Over the years he has advised on a number of precedent-setting merger and behavioural investigations as well as regulatory and antitrust litigation.

He is also a visiting professor at UCL where he is the co-founder and co-director of the Jevons Institute for Competition Law and Economics. He has published widely in this area and is a co-editor of Competition Policy International and consultant editor of Butterworths Competition Law Handbook. He is a non-governmental adviser to the International Competition Network of competition authorities on unilateral practices and merger control.

David S Evans is Chairman of Global Economics Group, based in its Boston office, and is Co-Executive Director of the Jevons Institute for Competition Law and Economics and Visiting Professor at University College London. His academic work has focused on industrial organization, including antitrust economics, with a particular expertise in multisided platforms, digital economy, information technology, and payment systems. He has authored 6 major books and more than 100 articles in these areas. His most recent book, with Richard Schmalensee, is *Matchmakers: The New Economics of Multisided Platform*, which won the 2017 Gold Medal in Economics for the Axiom Business Book Awards. Dr. Evans has taught courses related to antitrust economics, primarily for graduate students, judges and officials, and practitioners, and has authored handbook chapters on various antitrust subjects. He has served as a testifying expert on many significant antitrust matters in the United States, European Union, and China. Several of his books and articles were cited the Supreme Court in its *State of Ohio v. American Express*. He has a Ph.D. degree in economics from the University of Chicago.

Senior Circuit Judge Douglas H. Ginsburg was appointed to the United States Court of Appeals for the District of Columbia in 1986; he served as Chief Judge from 2001 to 2008. Concurrent with his service on the federal bench, Judge Ginsburg has taught at the University of Chicago Law School and the New York University School of Law. Judge Ginsburg is currently a Professor of Law at the Antonin Scalia Law School, George Mason University, and a visiting professor at the University College London, Faculty of Laws.

Judge Ginsburg is the Chairman of the International Advisory Board of the Global Antitrust Institute at the Antonin Scalia Law School, George Mason University. He also serves on the Advisory Boards of: Competition Policy International; the Harvard Journal of Law and Public Policy; the Journal of Competition Law and Economics; the Journal of Law, Economics and Policy; the Supreme Court Economic Review; the University of Chicago Law Review; The New York University Journal of Law and Liberty; and, at University College London, both the Center for Law, Economics and Society and the Jevons Institute for Competition Law and Economics.

Contributors' Bios

Allan Fels AO is a professor at University of Melbourne. He was generally regarded as the nation's leading regulator, serving as inaugural Chair of the Australian Competition and Consumer Commission and its predecessors from 1989 until 2003. He has had numerous other regulatory roles (for example, in insurance, agriculture, telecommunications and aviation). Professor Fels remains a leading figure globally in competition policy. He co-chaired the OECD Trade and Competition Committee from 1996 to 2003 and continues regularly to be a keynote speaker at major global competition events including the world's two peak events, the International Competition Network Annual Conference and the OECD Global Competition Forum.

A major activity of Professor Fels in recent years has been the provision of programs for top public sector leaders in China and India. The China Advanced Leadership Program – conceived, negotiated and directed by Professor Fels – is undertaken in partnership with the Organization Department of the Community Party of China, the Department in charge of all important personnel decisions in China and generally regarded as the most powerful part of the Communist Party of China.

Damien Geradin is a partner in the Brussels office of Euclid Law. Before joining Euclid, Damien was a partner in the Brussels office of Covington & Burling LLP. Mr. Geradin has assisted clients in many high-stake European Commission investigations, including some of the most complex abuse of dominance cases with a focus on the tech, media and telecommunications sectors. Damien has also developed expertise on the application of competition rules to the licensing of standard-essential patents (SEPs), and he is a member of the Commission Expert Group on SEP licensing and valuation.

According to Chambers Global, Mr. Geradin "is well known for his writing," with commentators describing him as "one of the best antitrust theoreticians around." He was also recognized by Who's Who Legal 2018 as a Competition expert. Mr. Geradin is a Professor of competition law and economics at Tilburg University and a visiting Professor at University College London. Over the years, he has held visiting Professorships at leading U.S. law schools including Columbia, Harvard, Michigan and Yale. He was also a visiting Professor at the College of Europe, Bruges, for 15 years.

Thomas J. Horton is a Professor of Law and the Heidepriem Trial Advocacy Fellow at the University of South Dakota School of Law. Professor Horton transitioned to a full-time academic career at USD in 2009, following a 28-year career as an antitrust attorney and complex litigator. Professor Horton teaches Trial Advocacy & Techniques, Antitrust & Consumer Protection, Civil Procedure, Discovery Practice, and an undergraduate honors' seminar on "The History and Philosophy of America's Antitrust Laws." He is also is a leader in applying evolutionary models and theories to structural and behavioral competition and antitrust analysis.

Professor Horton spent 15 years in the private sector, including partnerships in the Washington, DC offices of major international law firms Howrey & Simon and Orrick, Herrington & Sutcliffe. His representations included a diverse array of corporations and states. In his 13 years of public service, Professor Horton served stints as a Trial Attorney at the Federal Trade Commission and the Antitrust Division of the Department of Justice. He has successfully represented the United States as a lead trial attorney in major antitrust cases and investigations. From 1981-83, he served as a law clerk for United States District Judge William K. Thomas (N.D. Ohio). From 1990-91, he was appointed by the Governor of Rhode Island as Assistant Special Counsel to investigate the collapse of major RISDIC-insured banks and S&Ls in the state. In 1996, he ran as the Democratic candidate for the U.S. House of Representatives in Virginia's 11th District.

Bruno Jullien is Senior Researcher at Centre national de la recherche scientifique (CNRS) and the Toulouse School of Economics (TSE), and a Fellow of Econometric Society, MaCCI, CEPR, CESIfo, and CMPO. He currently holds an Advanced ERC Grant. His interests cover industrial organization, in particular network economics, IT, competition policy and the economics of multi-sided platforms. He acted as Director of GREMAQ, Deputy and Scientific Director of TSE, he was a member of the Economic Advisory Group on Competition Policy of the European Commission and of the Steering Committee of Association of Competition Economics and of EARIE.

Krzysztof Kuik is currently a head of unit responsible for State aid control in telecoms, media and internet, where he scrutinises the rollout of broadband networks across Europe and its compliance with the EU's State aid rules. He joined the European Commission in 2009 and, as a head of unit responsible for antitrust enforcement in the areas of media and sport, oversaw several landmark investigations into the contracts between Hollywood studios and pay-TV broadcaster Sky, the International Skating Union's rules, Nike's practices for merchandising products and Amazon's contracts with e-book publishers.

Prior to joining the European Commission, Mr Kuik worked as a private practitioner in the Brussels, Warsaw and New York offices of White & Case. He obtained a law degree from the University of Warsaw, and LLM degrees from KU Leuven and NYU School of Law. Mr. Kuik is a frequent speaker on competition law and media, and a co-author of a chapter on Media in Faull & Nikpay's The EU Law of Competition (2014).

Johannes Laitenberger is the Director-General of the European Commission's Director-ate-General for Competition since 1 September 2015. Under the political guidance of Commissioner Vestager, he manages the Directorate-General within the framework set by its mission statement and work programme. He has been Deputy Director-General of the Commission's Legal Service (2014-15), Head of Cabinet of President Barroso (2009-14), Spokesperson of the European Commission (2005-09) and Head of Cabinet of Commissioner Reding (2003-04).

Johannes Laitenberger started his career in the European Institutions in 1996 as an adviser in the General Secretariat of the Council. In 1999, he joined the Commission as a case handler in the Directorate-General for Competition and soon became Member of Commissioner Reding's cabinet (1999-2003). Previously, he studied Philosophy at the Portuguese Catholic University in Lisbon, and law at the Rheinische Friedrich-Wilhelms-Universität, Bonn. He qualified as a German lawyer. He was born in Hamburg, Germany and grew up in Hamburg and Lisbon, Portugal.

Gianluca Monte currently works as policy coordinator for the US and Canada in the Di-rectorate-General for Trade. He was previously a case handler for the Directorate-General for Competition's Unit "Antitrust – Media," responsible for antitrust enforcement in the media sector. Before 2014, Mr. Monte worked as a policy officer within the European Commission's Sport Unit. Before joining the European Commission in 2008, Gianluca worked as a consultant for KEA, a Brussels-based company specialized in creative industries, media and copyright law.

Gabriella Muscolo is a Commissioner at the Italian Competition Authority since May 2014. Appointed as a Judge in 1985, she sat at the Specialist Section for Intellectual Property and Competition Law in the District Court of Rome and at the Court for Undertakings in Rome. From 2009 to 2014, she was appointed member of the Enlarged Board of Appeal of the European Patent Office. In 2018, she has become a Fellow of the Centre of European Law of King's College London. Since 2008, she has been lecturer of Company Law at the School of Specialization for Legal Professionals at the University of Rome – La Sapienza and she is a lecturer at several Italian and foreign Universities. She publishes in Italian as well as in English in the fields of Intellectual Property and Competition Law. She co-edited the volumes "Intellectual Property and Competition Law: a European perspective" (The Netherlands 2012), "The Pharmaceutical Sector Between Patent Law And Competition Law. An International Perspective" (The Netherlands 2016) and "The Interplay Between Competition Law and Intellectual Property: An International Perspective" (The Netherlands 2012).

Maureen K. Ohlhausen joined Baker Botts after leading the Federal Trade Commission as Acting Chairman and Commissioner. She directed all aspects of the FTC's antitrust work, including merger review and conduct enforcement, and steered all FTC consumer protection enforcement, with a particular emphasis on privacy and technology issues.

A thought leader, Ms. Ohlhausen has published dozens of articles on antitrust, privacy, IP, regulation, FTC litigation, telecommunications, and international law issues in prestigious publications and has testified over a dozen times before the U.S. Congress. Ms. Ohlhausen has relationships with officials in the U.S. and abroad, with a particular emphasis on Europe and China, and has led the U.S. delegation at international antitrust and data privacy meetings on many occasions. She has received numerous awards, including the FTC's Robert Pitofsky Lifetime Achievement Award.

Bruce M. Owen is an economist and the Morris M. Doyle Centennial Professor in Public Policy, Emeritus at Stanford University. His career has spanned academia, government service and the private sector; his research interests focus on economic analysis of law, economic regulation and antitrust economics, especially in the telecommunications and mass media sectors. Most recently he has focused on Madisonian solutions to the problem of political corruption.

He was chief economist of the White House Office of Telecommunications Policy and later chief economist of the Antitrust Division of the U.S. Department of Justice. He was a co-founder and CEO of Economists Incorporated, a Washington DC economic consulting firm, from 1980 to 2003. He then became director of the Stanford public policy program and initiated Stanford's MPP program. He is the author or co-author of eight academic books and a large number of articles, and has appeared as an expert witness in several antitrust cases and regulatory proceedings.

Giovanni Pitruzzella is Advocate General at the Court of Justice of the European Union, Before his appointment, he has been Chairman of the Italian Competition Authority from 2008 to 2011. Commissioner then Chairman of the Independent Authority that regulates strikes in essential public services (2006 – 2011) and legal consultant of the Ministry of Health from 2008 to 2011. On april 2013, he was appointed by the President of the Republic as one of the ten experts asked to provide a comprehensive economic and institutional reform program and, on june of the same year, he was nominated member of a group of experts asked to provide a broad set of constitutional reforms.

Full professor of Constitutional Law, he taught in the Universities of Palermo, Cagliari, Luiss. Until he was settled as Chairman of the Italian Competition Authority, he was an administrative law lawyer. Author of several books, scientific publications in the sector of public, constitutional, administrative and competition law, his "Diritto Costituzionale", written with Roberto Bin, is the most common handbook in the Italian universities.

Craig Pouncey is a former Managing Partner of Herbert Smith Freehills, LLP, Brussels office. Under Mr. Pouncey's stewardship, the office, which was established in 1989 by Jonathan Scott (currently Non-Executive Director of the Competition and Markets Authority), has grown into one of the most established competition practices in Brussels advising on the full range of competition law, EU litigation, State aid, and trade law.

Mr. Pouncey was one of the leading competition specialists in Brussels. He built a broad-based EC and UK competition practice encompassing market investigations, litigation (with appearances before the European courts and the UK Competition Appeal Tribunal), as well as complex merger clearances for clients in highly-concentrated markets. He also led the firm's WTO and trade law practice, acting on a number of WTO, anti-dumping and anti-subsidy cases for clients in the EU, US, India, and Asia. "User-friendly and forthcoming" Craig Pouncey has a direct and accessible style that goes down well with clients according to Chambers Global 2007.

Veronica Roberts is a partner at Herbert Smith Freehills, LLP. She works proactively with clients to help them secure merger clearances for acquisitions and joint ventures in the UK, EU, and worldwide. She helps clients to deal effectively with competition and regulatory investigations. Based in Herbert Smith's London office, Ms. Roberts' also has 8 years of competition experience in the Brussels office. Ms. Roberts advises clients in a wide range of sectors, with a focus currently on telecoms, media, leisure and manufacturing. She has extensive experience of working with the CMA (Competition & Markets Authority), Ofcom, Ofgem and the European Commission.

She has been commended for her pragmatic and commercial advice in what can be a complex area, as reflected in her shortlisting for the Legal Week Intelligence Client Partner of the Year award at the British Legal Awards 2015. Ms. Roberts' business-focused approach was also highlighted by *Chambers* in its Competition/European Law rankings for 2014: quotes included "She just gets the commercial context so well" and "has an excellent feel for the issues."

Jacques Steenbergen is President of the Belgian Competition Authority. From 2007 to 2008, he was director general of the directorate general for competition in the Belgian ministry of economic affairs. He has taught competition law at the University of Leuven since 1979. Before joining the competition authority, he was partner in the Brussels office of Allen & Overy, and he has been legal secretary to the President of the Court of Justice under the presidency of Prof. J. Mertens de Wilmars.

He is also member of the Bureau of the OECD Competition Committee, member of the board of editors of the Dutch-Belgian European law review SEW, member of the scientific committee of the law review Concurrences, member of the Board of the Stichting van het Koninklijk Conservatorium of Brussels (the foundation of the royal academy for music of Brussels), and honorary member of the Bar of Brussels (Nederlandse Orde van Advocaten bij de Balie te Brussel). He is a former member of the Brussels and Flemish Bar Councils.

Joshua D. Wright is the Executive Director of the Global Antitrust Institute at the Antonin Scalia Law School, George Mason University and holds a courtesy appointment in the Department of Economics. He was a Commissioner of the Federal Trade Commission from 2013 to 2015.

Professor Wright is a leading scholar in antitrust law, economics, intellectual property, and consumer protection, and has published more than 100 articles and book chapters, co-authored a leading antitrust casebook, and edited several book volumes focusing on these issues. Professor Wright also served on the editorial board of the Supreme Court Economic Review, the Antitrust Law Journal, and the International Review of Law and Economics.

Christopher S. Yoo is the John H. Chestnut Professor of Law, Communication, and Computer & Information Science; Director, Center for Technology, Innovation & Competition at the University of Pennsylvania.

Professor Yoo has emerged as one of the nation's leading authorities on law and technology. Recognized as one of the most cited scholars in administrative and regulatory law as well as intellectual property, his major research projects include studying innovative ways to connect more people to the Internet; using technological principles to inform how the law can promote optimal interoperability;protecting privacy and security for autonomous vehicles, medical devices, and the Internet's routing architecture; comparing antitrust enforcement practices in China, Europe, and the U.S.; copyright theory; and network neutrality. The author of more than 100 scholarly works, Yoo testifies frequently before Congress, the Federal Communications Commission, the Federal Trade Commission, the U.S. Department of Justice, and foreign governments.

John M. Yun is an Associate Professor of Law and the Director of Economic Education at the Global Antitrust Institute at the Antonin Scalia Law School, George Mason University. He was an Acting Deputy Assistant Director in the Bureau of Economics, Antitrust Division, at the U.S. Federal Trade Commission. Also at the FTC, he has served as the Economic Advisor to Commissioner Joshua D. Wright, as well as a staff economist.

His experience includes the analysis of horizontal mergers, vertical restraints, and exclusionary conduct. Over an eighteen year career at the FTC, he has presided over a number of high-profile matters and investigations in various industries including consumer products, retail, intermediate goods, and technology. His research interests include law and economics, antitrust, regulatory policy, and industrial organization, and he has published in academic journals including the International Journal of Industrial Organization, Economic Inquiry, *International Review of Law and Economics*, and *Review of Industrial Organization*. He has also taught economics at Georgetown University, Emory University, and Georgia Tech. He received his BA in economics at UCLA and his PhD in economics at Emory University.